The Boiler Room and
Other Telephone Sales Scams

The Boiler Room and Other Telephone Sales Scams

Robert J. Stevenson

UNIVERSITY OF ILLINOIS PRESS

URBANA AND CHICAGO

First Illinois paperback, 2000
© 1998 by the Board of Trustees of the University of Illinois
Manufactured in the United States of America
1 2 3 4 5 C P 6 5 4 3 2

This book is printed on acid-free paper.

Library of Congress Cataloging-in-Publication Data
Stevenson, Robert Joseph.
The boiler room and other telephone sales scams / Robert J. Stevenson.
    p.   cm.
Includes bibliographical references and index.
ISBN 0-252-02265-3 (acid-free paper)
1. Telephone selling—Moral and ethical aspects. I. Title.
HF5438.3.S74 1998
381'.142—dc21
97-21082
CIP

Paperback ISBN 978-0-252-06934-5

For the late "Bob Miller," who introduced me to the world of the boiler rooms while I was in graduate school, and for "Moe," a longtime friend and fellow boiler who helped sharpen my ability to get the story straight.

Contents

Acknowledgments

I incurred a substantial debt to many of the salesmen, owners, managers, and staff who worked at the roughly two dozen telephone rooms where I was employed during the process of writing this book. Through their tips I was able to support myself and my family in a number of different locales. Unfortunately, many boiler room personnel were less supportive. I learned a great deal from them, as well, in the process of being fired, cheated out of wages, insulted, intimidated, and overworked. None of this occurred because I was discovered to be a researcher, however, because my research design was entirely covert.[1] My experiences stem from the nature of the industry itself.

Two people, the late Bob Miller and Moe, were extremely useful. Without their help I never would have been afforded initial access to the boiler room scene. They were protective of the "new man"—as I was known—and that allowed me to learn the basics (sales techniques, operating norms, and procedures) of an industry that is universally hidden from public view. I was able to explore other telephone rooms—first by circumstance, later by design, then by both—only because my initial experience was a recognized apprenticeship in the telephone sales world.

Both men provided hundreds of hours of conversation—over lunch, as part of the training, during coffee breaks, and between sales calls—on nearly every imaginable subject. More important, they provided access to a status that is critical for an ethnographer, that of "the newcomer." This made it acceptable for me to ask what probably appeared to be the silliest of questions, and it assured me an answer, a joke, or the sharing of some lore. In a boiler room, once one is welcomed "on board" one becomes part of an occupational group engaged in the active pursuit of sales.

My academic debts stem from three sources, each related to the sociological adventure. First, early in my graduate studies Ned Polsky convinced me that the study of active, that is, uncaught, deviants in natural settings is an important thing for sociologists to do, and Gerald D. Suttles taught the essentials of fieldwork. When I was beginning, and well into, my doctoral dissertation (on a project that was neither ethnographic nor related to white-collar crime), Hanan C. Selvin and John H. Gagnon offered friendship, encouragement, and intellectual stimulation, while my "escapes" to the boiler rooms offered a shift in perspective and subject matter, a chance to gather materials to enliven my lectures, and a much needed respite from the rigors of dissertation writing.

I also owe a collective debt to the students in my deviance, crime, and delinquency courses at SUNY, Stony Brook, the University of Maryland, College Park, and George Washington University, Washington, D.C., who served as sounding boards for my ideas. The sociology departments in these academic settings provided office space, computer support, and intellectually exciting environments of which I was privileged to be part. The Department of Military Psychiatry at Walter Reed Army Institute of Research, Washington, D.C., provided colleagues while I was between boiler room gigs and working as a research sociologist in an applied setting on projects unrelated to boiler rooms. The change of milieu was needed refreshment.

I also wish to thank the anonymous reviewers at the *Journal of Contemporary Ethnography* for useful criticism. On an earlier version of a paper that was to become this book, one reviewer suggested, "Write the book . . . or write three articles. I strongly suggest that you write the book." I hope that he or she is pleased with the result. Thanks also to the anonymous selection committee for the 1989 Edward Sagarin Prize in Qualitative Criminology (sponsored by the Ohio State University Press) for judging an earlier version of this manuscript a semifinalist. That recognition restored my spirits during a trying period of job instability and convinced me that my line of inquiry was worthy of fuller development.

The University of Illinois Press has been especially helpful and supportive. My anonymous reviewers provided both welcome and useful criticism that allowed me to sharpen and shorten my presentation, and Richard Martin, executive editor, guided me through the refinement process. Mary Giles, associate editor, helped ensure that readers will be able to follow my arguments by hammering out my prose: kindly, patiently, and painstakingly. The final product is better, clearer, and more readable because of their collective efforts.

The Boiler Room and
Other Telephone Sales Scams

Introduction

This book is about widespread but little studied forms of deviance and occupational crime that take place in businesses called "boiler rooms." It is written for students of social deviance and occupational structure, as well as for those who may wish to learn more about the kinds of social organizations that lie behind the increasing number of annoying telephone sales calls they receive.

Boiler room operatives are telephone salesmen. (The few exceptions to the sex-typing of boilers occur in industries such as auto parts and janitorial chemicals, where women are increasingly employed. Although a few women do make it to sales floors, most do not remain there for any length of time.) The salesmen spend the bulk of their time placing unexpected and unrequested calls to potential customers who have not expressed a prior interest in making a purchase and, in most cases, have not previously had dealings with the company—or even known of its existence—before answering a ringing telephone. What is said over the telephone depends on both the type of market being exploited and the company's ability to hire those with the requisite skills.

These businesses are housed in settings that range from a kitchen table in a private residence to desirable pieces of commercial real estate. Some are firms on paper alone, whereas others are part of an elaborate corporate structure and design. They are all socially organized to make sales calls—the sole purpose of their being.

The premise undergirding these calls is unspoken: to engage in what Howard Becker has conceptualized as "secret deviance," that is, rule-breaking behavior (promoting questionable merchandise and services, overpricing, the use of fraud, and the promotion of confidence schemes that involve both workers and customers) not perceived as deviant by either of the parties participating in the conversation.[1] That is the only premise governing some operations, whereas in others it is one of many. A boiler room is thus a site from which products and services are vended as well as a manner of organizing the sales process.

The boiler room entered my life, as it does the lives of most who work there, in an adventitious manner. When the infamous "Carey cuts"—the reductions in support to higher education in the early 1980s due to the financial crisis in New York State—found their way to my graduate school, the teaching line that supported me vanished. To continue my research and studies, I needed a job that offered flexible hours and adequate wages, and I had the good fortune to make the acquaintance of Bob Miller, a salesman who worked for a telephone sales company.[2] He invited me to accompany him to work so that I might meet his boss, Moe. Miller would be working the night shift in the chemical sales field as soon the company "got on its feet."[3]

I met Moe and observed the operation of his company. He handed me the telephone and invited me, "Go ahead. See if you can talk yourself up a deal." I was both excited and nervous. After a number of failed attempts, however, it became clear that this was easier said than done. "He has a good voice," said Moe to Miller. "Maybe he'll do OK." I was offered the job and given a few weeks to learn the ropes. "You will do just fine once you get the knack," said Moe. "Don't worry, we'll teach you. Miller here has the best gab around. Just listen to him." I became a serious study.

Although I thought that it might be interesting to study telephone salesmen, that was not a primary consideration at the time. It did not occur to me that such a study could be properly done without benefit of the researcher's status that was so valued in my earlier fieldwork experiences. My immediate concern was whether I had both the skill and psychological stamina to adjust to the harsh reality that I would need to survive on the sales floor just like everyone else. Moe was, after all, running a business, and I had little sales background and was not especially fond of talking to strangers over the telephone.

The hours were both reasonable and flexible, however, and the promised pay seemed fair. I could imagine worse. Many of my colleagues were waiting tables or tending bar; joining the reserve army of the academically underemployed by teaching part-time in distant schools; driving taxis, buses, or trucks; tightening their belts; and being forced to leave their studies entirely for lack of financial support or due to the closing of their academic departments.

Working for a telephone sales company is similar, in many ways, to other types of indoor work. The environment is safe, usually moderately clean, and socially organized as an office. One sits at a desk, uses a telephone, becomes familiar with the product or service being vended, learns the required administrative routines and ways of customarily interacting with staff and customers, and proceeds to attempt to accomplish what is expected. As in all formal organizations, the managers oversee, as well as informally convey, the applicable corporate norms that are assigned to, and govern, one's position in the company.

"You have no past here," said my sales manager, a Mr. Daniels, with a broad smile, in what amounted to my first lesson on the sales floor. "We all sink or swim based on how well we master the telephone." To the room he said, "Let's dial for dollars" (which was greeted by laughter) and intoned in a singsong yet melodious and certain voice, "Light 'em up."

By taking the role of observer in this volume, I will allow the actors to speak for themselves and also provide some explanation about the different kinds of boiler rooms, how they change, and some consequences of their being. This will be done by placing readers in the context of a particular type of telephone sales operation and examining how the scene appears from the selective perspectives of those who are engaged in its animation: the salesmen (working the telephones), their managers (who direct the staging of their performances), and the owners (who interpret the activities of both).

In saying "you have no past here," for example, Mr. Daniels exhibited the typical good form expected of him. He was encouraging, direct, personable, and humorous, and he had a lesson to teach related to job performance. The context of his statement is supportive. Nothing appears out of place. Only after a few months on the scene does it become clear that he was using a pitch that has been used hundreds of times before. It is convincing because it is designed to be. Each element is sufficiently nebulous to permit a modicum of personal identification; some listeners have pasts they would rather conceal, whereas others think that he means "previous job experience." The stream of interaction leads precisely to where Mr. Daniels directs it: five men dutifully pick up their telephones and begin to dial.

Those who run boiler rooms are primarily concerned with the ability of a salesman to sell over the telephone and to fit in with the chemistry of the room. Any other interests or aptitudes a salesman may have (or fail to have) are irrelevant. A boiler room is typically much more tolerant of all sorts of behavior, styles of dress, beliefs, preferences for offbeat working hours, and personalities than are most businesses. The room contains many moonlighters. Most come from conventional society, but others do not. As one salesman put it, "As long as you earn your dime [make enough sales], you can put in your time [on the sales floor]."

As a result, some of the rooms can be colorful in the broad spectrum of articulate life they attract from all parts of the social order. Part of this is due to the lure of segmented work, especially for those who have alternate uses for their non-boiling hours so as to not need a company to offer them a prime identity. "Boiling" is a skill. Once the basic elements are learned, it is sales performance alone that will typically override office politics, seniority, corporate ideology, or external indicators of talent—tests, evaluation committee reports, supervisor's ratings, and the like—in most cases. In a given shop, both income and autonomy are based on the bottom line: profits generated for the firm.

The creative often opt for autonomy. I have worked with journalists, artists, a ballet master, writers, lawyers (of the disbarred variety), playwrights, businessmen down on their luck, a pharmacist, dozens of students (with all levels of formal education), a number of educators, mid-level government bureaucrats "rifed" (fired due to a "reduction-in-force") from their once-secure positions, fired air traffic controllers, and more than a handful of those whose careers as musicians and performers were awaiting the next gig that would permanently lift them from the world of temporary work.

Although few rooms contain many of these people, their sporadic presence can mean the difference between sharing intelligent conversation between sales calls, during breaks, or over lunch and a special kind of mindlessness that often accompanies repetitive, low-paying, competitive, transitory work. Each shop also has a least one pro (an experienced salesman), and these people are usually gregarious and typically have a number of varied interests. Some also have "other deals on the side," that is, other jobs or businesses to which they attend after work. If nothing else, pros typically have thousands of hours of experience in boiler rooms, and, when they were younger, some have had a wide range of other experiences as well.

Moreover, most boiler room managers and owners typically enjoy conversation, and many have sold or attempted to sell (or feel they could easily sell) virtually every conceivable manner of product, service, or business opportunity that is promotable over the telephone. Each shop has its teller of tales, and some owners take considerable pride in their previous exploits in the industry. The routine nature of the work makes for ample breaks to discuss strategies, markets, training exercises, and innovations that define the larger business culture of which the boiler room is a part. This permits the taking of fieldnotes to be interpreted as a sign of a conscientious employee who is willing to learn from the masters.

The less-articulate ranks of the boiler room are filled with all manner of transient folk drawn from virtually every category of labor looking for work. Lacking the gift of telephonic gab, most of these are soon purged from the organization. "Tolerance," however, in the words of one informant, "favors the color green" and is typically extended to all who take to the telephones. As a result, many boiler rooms contain a number of the formally stigmatized: criminals, hustlers of every stripe, active and retired confidence men, and some who hold these people in high esteem. Said one owner, "If they're talkers, they get their shot. They come on board."

Most shops also contain, at one time or another, men who have spent the better part of their lives in pursuit of instant gratifications: fast women, horses, cards and dice, the slot machines, or the quick profits associated with the milder aspects of the drug trade (usually as small-time dealers). Alcoholics are not rare, but "heavy dopers," the less than sober, and those who are unable to verbalize a script are because they cannot pass the screening tests. Thus, the boiler room is typically clean with regard to its not containing current users of hard drugs, and it usually contains some people who hold fond memories of better times. Some of these operatives enjoy finding an attentive ear.

This study began as a number of questions which, at first, seemed highly idiosyncratic. I had worked for a number of companies that seemed to be having a great deal of bad luck: in staying in business, in hiring people they thought enough of to keep, and in regularly meeting a payroll. It was only when a number of segmented conversations with a few co-workers, one-time owners, and two pros who had been in the industry for a number of years coincided with the folding of a company for which some of us had worked that patterns began to emerge. This book is my attempt to explicate these patterns.

After being in the employ of a telephone room for almost a year, the idea for a study came to me when one of the house pros, in a paternal moment, invited me for coffee to explain the significance of the company's recent wave of firings and the newly implemented system of bonuses.[4] Discussing the day's events, he intoned (in uncharacteristic seriousness):

> It's *The Wall*. It happens when all is lost. It's a last-ditch effort. Sales have been off for the past three months. You can look at it two ways [said with knowing laughter]: The handwriting is on the wall, or that there is a wall of bricks that is about to come crashing down on our heads. Either way, get ready to pack your bags, check the newspapers, and get another job. I've seen this before. Too, too many times. They [the company] are going to go under. Trust me. Look, I've got some feelers out. . . . Mark my words. I'm tellin' it to you straight. Once *The Wall* is built—ain't nothing going to keep the company solvent. It's a dying cry, you might say. Sort of like the last dial tone [smiles].

The pro's desk was empty by the middle of the following week. Months of loyal work, thousands of pitches, hundreds of hours of social interaction, and a trusted, experienced salesman—gone. The owner of the company said that he had to be let go. "You know, you have to have the right attitude for this type of work," he explained. "You have to have the right attitude for the company. He was a good salesman, but not that great. He wasn't right for us."

Although hiring, training, and firing are contingencies of corporate life, the firing of an experienced man for no apparent reason, especially one who was a productive, well-liked, ground-floor hire (one of the original employees in a new company), flies in the face of both economics and common sense and suggests that darker forces are operative.

In the world of telephone salesmen these occurrences are more structured, and common, than in other lines of work because the industry itself is always in a constant state of flux and accommodation. Added to this are the pressures of telephone work (a set of routines common to all who use the telephone), sales (a group of skills and abilities that involve certain kinds of exaggeration), and fraud (unethical at best and illegal at worst). In the telephone sales business, the precise mix of, and interrelations among, these factors, which may come to dominate a company, are never clearly known or revealed to most who work there. This adds to the invisibility of the boiler room and creates many gray areas and psychological problems for those who "work the phones."

Perhaps the most important is that becoming a "boiler" is neither obvious nor recognized as such, and that has implications for the way the industry is run and organized. Although the perils of the marketplace are commonly known and well documented, it never occurs to most on the scene that these perils can be orchestrated by design. In the words of one disillusioned salesman, "There ain't no 'G' [guarantee] here. What they tell you is words, that's all it is. They make more promises to us than we do to the customers. It's air. Four years of my life and I get blown out the door [fired] like a trainee."

The salesman was referring to the ubiquitous, manipulative, corporate ethos that makes the boiler room a predatory, secretive form of business organization. Workers displaced in the process of varied types of reorganizations (shutdowns and firings) never know, in most cases, whether their termination was due to personal inadequacy or corporate machinations or whether the company that had once employed them genuinely went out of business or had changed its name and moved, clandestinely, to a different locale. Those who remain on board can never be sure whether promises concerning pay, benefits, entitlements, and promotions will ultimately be honored.

Over time, it became clear that a social world that had been heretofore unknown to me was much more complex than I could have possibly imagined. Over the years, I came to approach boiler rooms with an admixture of awe (over the skill shown by some of the salesmen); confusion (over the sheer invisibility of much of the predation); dramaturgy (because of the amazing levels of showmanship that are often displayed); adventure (because each new scene brought new characters, scripts, and a chemistry that changed with the personalities in the room); and remorse (because as I got to know more people from the world of telephone sales it became clearer that the sheer level of energy needed to support the fictions promoted on the sales floor rarely produced the kind of rewards being touted—for either the pitchmen or their customers—and often resulted in severe disappointments at best or totally disrupted lives at worst).

As I began to accumulate experiences in different companies, in different industries, and in different parts of the East Coast, I became more attentive to the structure of the industry itself as being the source of many of the outcomes I observed.

The Plan of the Book

This book is organized around a social process (the quest for sales) that takes on a special meaning in telephone rooms by manifesting itself in the form of heat (the use of manipulative, interactive techniques to overcome the many objections to a sale), pressure (social norms that encourage ruthless competition for economic survival), and the triple meaning of "work" (effective task orientation, coercion, and deception).

For a telephone pitchman, it is the specific combination of heat, pressure, and work that dictates the degree to which he develops and perfects his line of telephone talk—that exclusive instrumentality through which he earns his livelihood. It is the art of presenting both the sales call, and the company behind it, as being something other than what they actually are that differentiates him from a "phoner." A phoner merely uses the telephone to make a large number of job-related telephone calls; phoners work for an agency (insurance, travel, modeling, or advertising), an investment house, a manufacturer, a distributor, a charity, a marketing organization, a bank, or a host of other businesses where telephoning is common.

Chapter 1 examines the boiler room as a work setting. Like any business, large or small, upon establishing itself in a locale favorable to plying its trade it must field overseers and recruit and train workers. These fill the sales floor. All telephone rooms name themselves (and the salespeople in their employ) in a characteristic manner, and they place similar kinds of advertisements in the newspapers. The social dynamic, however, which lends atmosphere (called "tone" and "chemistry") to a boiler room—and distinguishes it from, say, a site of equal size at the local telephone company—is called action: the quest for sales, which involves specialized, highly manipulative, interactive performances.

The tools of the boiler's trade include a craft-orientation toward the work and a pitch which, together, are used to vend products or services. The workday is spent using standardized procedures to overcome objections to sales. Like all salesmen, boiler room workers face an external commercial environment that is dominated by market forces. It is the social organization of telephone sales work, however, which makes it distinctive. Absent the requisite action, an office filled with telephones and salesmen does not a boiler room make, but a pitchman calling from his garage qualifies.

Chapter 2 examines the product houses: boiler rooms from which all manner of inferior and/or overpriced goods are vended with a flair that would likely charm the most creative in the world of advertising. Sales are accomplished by crafting a pitch that caters to psychological needs and certain economic desires and through the use of a set of techniques that are empirically proven to have value in a given market.

Product houses are the first tier in the hierarchy of boiler rooms. Newcomers learn to use the telephone properly, how to talk about the product being vended, how to control the conversation, how to write up a sale, how to conform to the expectations of the management, and how to be persistent in light of failure. Virtually everyone in the industry begins in a product shop, and it is here that the mundane public image of the boiler room is formed: Someone has interrupted your daily or nightly round with a ringing telephone. Sooner or later, you realize that the person on the other end of the line has something to sell you. (Sooner, if you are being called by a trainee; later, if you happen to be pitched by a pro.) The structure and cadence of the pitch signals to the trained ear precisely which type of remarkable offer will surely, and shortly, follow.

Chapter 3 explores some implications of the boiler room's marginality. Because it is a deviant scene, its fraudulent nature must be concealed from both customers and the sales force. Hiring, training, firing, and sales are accomplished by defining the context of business such that the resulting tensions (economic competition, secrecy, deception, or unfair treatment of workers) appear to flow naturally from, and thereby reflect, the kinds of risk and uncertainty that characterize markets. The result is typically self-destruction, mutation, or forms of ritualism that are accompanied by a degree of implicit socialization as sophisticated as it is invisible to most on the scene.

Most boilers see themselves as sharp businessmen (with varying degrees of skill) able to match their gift for the pitch against the reluctance of customers. This is encouraged by the fact that "the sale" is the ultimate unit by which salesmen are measured. The natural division of labor between skilled workers and trainees, the gamelike atmosphere of most telephone rooms, norms of secrecy, and the universal social isolation of the recently fired, in addition to high turnover rates, mitigate against the emergence of a subculture. Although a classic boiler room is an all-male preserve, the natural selection of the sales process creates hybrids that are typically flexible enough to accommodate to the changing nature of the markets they face.

Chapter 4 treats the service shops. These are scams—boiler rooms where the illusion of expertise is artfully linked, and carefully crafted, to a client's revealed need for advantageous offerings, coverages (insurance and credit), or business opportunities. They vend real claims to fictional assets. All offer a program of some kind that involves a single, or sequential, cash outlay (via check, bank wire, or credit card) entitling customers access to a wide range of intangibles: purportedly insider's information such as favorable buying opportunities and investment tips, betting advice, personal betterment strategies (diets, dating, or training), travel arrangements, employment possibilities, or franchises and heretofore unexploited business ventures that come to define the type of fraud involved.

All involve a generous notion about what, in fact, constitutes a reasonable investment or opportunity. Boiler rooms deal in statistical likelihoods and sales; a claim is true in direct proportion to the number of sales it generates. If too many potential customers disagree, the wording of the claim is modified until a consensus is reached that moves the program.

Service shops successfully promote an idea: that the means to achieving a desirable financial or personal goal are programmatically available. The "good news" is that The Plan is for sale to a select few, for a limited time only, *if* one qualifies. Service shops compose the second tier in the world of boiler rooms. At the top of this stratum, only the very skilled are permitted access to the sales floor.

Although most telephone rooms deal exclusively in goods or services, a small number trade—or evolve to trade—in some combination of both. Chapter 5 explores boiler room techniques that any business with a product and/or a service to sell can use. Having their origins in the boiler room, fraudulent techniques migrate to other business settings because boiler room personnel frequently find themselves looking for alternative work. But they can also enter boiler rooms from the new talent that may be displaced from other businesses and the larger society. The line between conventional telemarketing operations and boiler rooms is often vague.

I conclude the book with some speculation on the future of boiler rooms by examining the core characteristics (stated as postulates) of all telephone operations and the trade-offs and dilemmas facing owners. They must match their ambitions with the skills of promotion possessed by salesmen and traditional business concerns over profits, economies of scale, production, and management within the context of running a deviant enterprise that comes under attack from many quarters: from irate customers (for the crimes it commits against them); from within (due to the fraudulent treatment of telephone salesmen); from agents of social control (who seek to shut it down); from traditional businesses (for discrediting the sales process); and from competitors (who would like a piece of the action).

The possible fates awaiting all firms that have a telephone staff are influenced by the degree to which differing kinds of assumptions concerning labor, markups, markets, technological change, fraud, and entrepreneurial climate hold true. An epilogue outlines some of the ethical issues that must be addressed when conducting covert fieldwork in natural settings.

Observing Boiler Rooms

This study is based on roughly nine years of participant observation, over a twelve-year period, on the East Coast. I studied four chemical telephone rooms; a gas house (vendors of oil and gas leases); three coin rooms (numismatic advisory services); two transmission parts houses; two auto parts boiler rooms; an auto parts brokerage operation; a trip house (a travel agency, in name alone); a franchise water purification scam; a school house shop (a scam purporting to offer usable training); a badge operation (fund-raising for the police); and five telemarketing concerns: an art house (an arts marketing company), an air shop (a heating and air-conditioning room), a media-oriented sales floor, a green house (a lawn-care operation), and a home-sit operation (a home service–based company).

Working in part-time and full-time capacities, consistently or sporadically as circumstances and opportunities dictated, I have spent as little as two evenings to as long as $2^{3}/_{4}$ years "on the phones" for different companies. Only three of these are currently in business; none has the same top management that was in place when the field research was conducted.

My informant pool includes about a dozen managers, 30 pros (18 of whom were, or are presently, owners), roughly 120 telephone salespeople, 34 solicitors, about three dozen office staff, and fleeting contacts with roughly 180 trainees. The materials on the structure of the market and the nature of the sales process are based upon tens of thousands of telephone calls, on thousands of sales, and on hundreds of protracted conversations with salespeople and regular customers in a number of different industries.

A small number from the latter pool of willing conversationalists were extremely important in my gaining access to knowledge about the national structure of telephone rooms. They came to compose a small network totaling roughly four dozen people, who over the years regularly served as "telephone informants": salesmen, owners, and customers with whom I kept in touch as I changed boiler room employers.[5] At any time the network contained but a handful of people, and it expanded or contracted in accord with the economic fortunes of the industries and telephone rooms that employed them. For comparative purposes, I also cultivated a number of colleagues and informants who were engaged in other lines of work that had nothing to do with boiler rooms and thus was able to gather preliminary impressions of how different kinds of people, at different locations in the social order, thought about, or responded to, unwanted telephone calls—and those in the industries from which the calls originated.

1 The Boiler Room

Reach out and touch someone.
—*marketing slogan for a major telephone company*

Yeah. Right. I'm going to reach out right now, and touch *someone.*
And when I do, the mooch on the other end of this line is going to be
touched real good. He will be dizzy. Dizzy minus some cold cash, that is.
[laughs]. The phone company is no dummy. They got it right on the but-
ton. Just like me. Right on the button [gestures to the touch-tone
dialing pad]. Here I go. Watch it happen *[laughs] . . . [dial tone].*
—*a pro, getting ready for his pitch*

Boiler rooms are crammed with desks and telephones in offices often lined
with acoustical tiles to cut down the din of the pitchmen and the shouts and
ringing bells of the sales managers.[1] A telephone room is said to be running
"full burn" when each telephone station is actively manned by a salesman.

The coordinated production of men, telephones, scripted presentations, and
noise that appears at first glance to be confusion is called "heat." Statements
such as, "Can you feel the heat?" and "We are really cooking now" are taken
to mean a desirable state of affairs, which management actively promotes.

Heat in a boiler room is said to be related to the level of collective enthusiasm required of the sales force to close certain kinds of deals over the telephone. It is generated through socialization and the use of coercive techniques.
Because the means of production is the telephone itself—and telephone bills
are the largest single operating expense—the control exercised by management over what is said (and how it is said) over the telephone constitutes the
bulk of a room manager's work.

Telephone rooms are named by identification with the corporate sponsor:
a complex name whose short form is suitable for the lead-in phrase the receptionist uses when answering incoming calls and the salesmen use to introduce the firm to potential customers. Each element connotes expansive-
ness, implies an elaborate division of labor, and suggests business expertise.
Thus, a typical boiler room operation might be called "Southern Industries:
Chemical Research Group." The salesmen would say that they work for
"Southern Chemical," and the firm would be known in telephone room cir-

cles as such. The inherent flexibility is by design, because virtually any industry can be imitated by using combinations of the core elements. For example, "S.I. Research" could as easily be construed to represent a nonprofit charitable organization as it could a political think tank, and "Chemical Group" sounds credible enough to vend either investments or janitorial supplies. The possibility that such a company could sell both investments and janitorial supplies (to different kinds of customers) cannot be ruled out, however.

Somewhere buried in the corporate literature a small, unobtrusive statement, such as "a division of KJF Industries," will identify the legal ownership. This is the payee to whom all checks are typically drawn and credit card statements issued. It is also a subtle clue that things may be less aboveboard than they originally appeared when the customer formed an initial impression of the company based on a fleeting telephone conversation. There is a better than even chance that "KJF" are the initials of one individual doing business as (DBA) a number of corporate-sounding entities.

To borrow a term from classical economics, telephone talk constitutes the value added by boiler rooms: a premium over and above the cost of procurement and created through the process of social interaction. A sale over the telephone is a pure sale in that it is based on trust alone and stands without regard to either the physical characteristics or the derived market value of what is being vended. Transfers of ownership claims occur sight unseen, and revenue is generated in direct proportion to the qualities of a salesman's voice. Arthur Miller's "smile and a shoe shine," those characteristics thought to be essential to a salesman, are modified and embellished according to the perceived needs of listeners.[2]

Seeing Action on the Sales Floor

When a new worker visits a telephone room for the first time, a variation of the short con is enacted.[3] The novice gets to watch a house pro at work and witness a smooth-talking salesman pitch an established customer. A few minutes of jovial small talk is backed with a well-executed close, and a deal is written, pleasantries exchanged, and the telephone is hung up ceremoniously.

For those unskilled in instant computation, an overseer is quick to extrapolate the substantial hourly rate of pay that such performances are taken to represent. In larger operations this sequence is often repeated, thus assuring that the atypical (a salesman consistently writing business) is presented as being commonplace. This manipulative strategy of baiting a worker—or a customer—is called the "take-away ploy." A pro explains the principles involved: "You set up the fish. You bait the hook, take it away, then sink the hook. You get the customer to believe what you present. To accept it. Then you *take the idea away* from him. You make him tell you to continue your presentation."

While the new man is heady with the sight of a smooth presentation (the setup), the owner will ask, rhetorically, "Do you think you can do this? Is it for you?" By the time an unemployed man stumbles upon a telephone room he has typically exhausted those options with which he is most familiar. The possibility (the bait) of earning a living by merely engaging in telephone conversations and writing sizable orders in a manner that appears to be both autonomous and effortless is appealing. Like skillful magicians, boiler room operators have planted a seed for an unfolding illusion.

This is a critical piece of stagecraft. Absent the possibility of sales—and the excitement and reward associated with selling in a corporate culture—few would come to interpret a room full of men talking, sometimes shouting, enthusiastically into telephones as something other than a sideshow most would likely puzzle over but otherwise avoid.

If a candidate passes the initial screening, the new hire is cut a deal (his terms of employment are negotiated).[4] He will then be given a few days' perk (percolation) to think it over (the take-away) before reporting to work. Most who get a chance to see a pro in action report to work (the hook), as requested, brimming with enthusiasm. A salesman in auto parts explains the rationale that precedes a recruitment drive and explores some consequences: "We need some new blood around here. We are getting stale. Look at last month's sales figures. . . . It's time to put some ads in the paper. We need new troops. When the new men come in they will keep the sharp ones, and we are in deep shit. . . . We will all be under pressure to impress the new men and make lots of sales. Be prepared. Get your orders in. . . . Maybe they'll find a heavy-hitter [a productive salesman], and if they do, someone here will be fired. You can bet on it."

Undergirding the excitement of writing deals and learning pitches is an important source of tension in boiler rooms. A salesman's job is safe (stable) only so long as the company remains in business, he can out-produce those below him in the pecking order based on sales figures, and those above him in monthly sales figures have not recently experienced a drop in income due to market contractions. Salesmen must constantly struggle to maintain, in the short run, their current level of income and, over the long term, their jobs. Over time, it is difficult to accomplish both of these goals.

Salaries, wages, commissions, and bonuses promised to those who work the telephones inevitably fall short of those received. The industry promotes mythically high levels of pay as enticements to recruit new personnel. For example, some advertisements read, "The sky is the limit," or, "Earn $1,800 per week." Newspaper advertisements run by boiler rooms can be roughly

translated as follows: When the advertisement reads "last week our top salesman earned *n* dollars," *n* is probably a fairly accurate measure of what a typical worker will earn in two months or so.

These hypothetical incomes, the recruit soon learns, are soon scaled down
substantially through what is informally called a "realistic talk" once the new
man is on the sales floor—and before receiving his first paycheck. A boiler
room owner, in what he later recalls as a temporary lapse of common sense,
has described what happened when, during his company's slow period, he
answered an advertisement for a telephone salesman:

> I gave them a call, and I get this guy on the phone, a "Mr. Charles" or some
> other phone name. We talked a bit. He liked my phone voice. I told them that
> I would need a minimum of $500 per week draw. "No problem," he says,
> "Come on down." So I went down there [to a coin operation], and we had our
> realistic talk. It turns out that they pay every two weeks and they hold the
> first two weeks' pay until "adjustments" can be made. Then they have a pen-
> alty system for orders that fall [are returned]. . . . Then, he said, "It is not un-
> common for some of our men to work nights, and Saturdays, to make some
> extra money." He was pitchin' me. He went on and on . . . I said, "Hey, this is
> bullshit. What about my $500 a week draw?" The manager said, "Look, I'll
> give you $200 a week to start. Fair enough?" I walked out of the interview. I
> should have known better. I guess that I saw what I wanted to see when times
> were bad.

His experience is typical. Moreover, although a company can offer a new
man virtually any kind of deal, it delivers only on production. Because all ne-
gotiations are in the firm's favor, few men in boiler rooms earn what they have
come to expect will be the case. All of them earn much less than the promises
advertised in newspapers. An experienced chemical salesman discussed newspaper advertisements:

> Yeah. The ads are come-on bait. . . . Look at this one, here it says, "Earn
> $28 an hour selling chemicals on the telephone. No experience necessary."
> Right. Let's see: "Bill [yells across the room to a salesman], what did you make
> on your last order? Just the commission" [pause]. OK. He made $26.25. Let's
> say it took fifteen minutes. . . . That's $105 per hour. It's bullshit. Just the bait.
> It works though. It *does* bring people in. . . . Now, here's an ad for you. Lis-
> ten to this, "HEAVY-HITTERS. COMMODITIES. TELEPHONE. COMMISSION ONLY. CALL
> MR. GEORGE [telephone number given]." Most people wouldn't understand the
> ad. The pros, of course, would. That's who George is after. George doesn't waste
> time advertising for trainees.

By carefully managing fronts, boiler room owners and managers create
the illusion of secure, remunerative, regular employment. While this is be-

ing done for newcomers, a firing wave is set in motion, and salesmen who are
retained are given the best paper (accounts) in order to increase the likelihood
of company profits. Over time, however, even prime paper gets overworked,
ages, and will lie dormant. When this occurs, a salesman's income falls.

The Pitchman: Working the Telephones

The telephone pitchman, like the pool hustler, necessarily enters the interaction with most of his skills invisible to his mark.[5] Seasoned salesmen have a
lore that has evolved over the years to help sustain the level of activity required to make the numerous telephone calls needed to generate sales. Examples are phrases such as, "Keep 'em on the line, and you'll earn your dime,"
or, as is said in many telephone rooms, "It's a numbers game. Make enough
calls, and you will sooner or later get the deals." As one boiler told me, with
reference to his interest in gambling, "It's all in the percentages—you have
to keep working the odds."

More intrusive rationalizations are also available. These take the form of
demands made by room managers as they oversee the work of their charges.
Some common exhortations include "smile and dial"; "light 'em up" (which
refers to the fact that certain telephones have buttons that light when the
receiver is picked up, and when all lines are occupied the pattern of lights forms
an unbroken bar); "dial for dollars"; "let's have some heat"; "let's sing folks,
the children need shoes, right?"; "find the sucker and win a prize" (which
refers to premiums given to salesmen—including cash—when a daily, weekly,
or monthly quota has been exceeded); and "get on the phones, drones."

Learning to work the telephones is similar to learning one's native language as a child. Without knowledge of a general structure, it is still possible
to assemble chunks of words which, over time and with numerous repetitions,
resemble sentences. With practice, they become sentences. Lore and one-lin-
ers provide the motivation for, and the syntax of, the pitch, which begins as a
printed script. Other salesmen help the newcomer refine the finished product. With repeated use a pitch becomes airtight: resistant to objections,
smoothly delivered, confidently presented, personable, and effective.

Working rules evolve to save the boiler room time and money by not wasting a pitch on someone unlikely to make a purchase. To this end, a sales manager will often exaggerate regional dialect and incorporate it into efforts to
make a pitch more effective both to increase sales and to screen unlikely prospects. Some variety of this pattern is present on all boiler room sales floors
and thus signals an observer that there is more here than first meets the ear.
In some sophisticated telephone rooms, for example, pros probe for the past
purchasing habits of potential customers through the use of sounders (phrases
that take their meaning only within a particular social milieu) to exclude can-

didates who have historically proven to be a waste of telephone time. Thus, a potential investor who fails to understand, and positively respond to, the meaning of "being liquid for five thousand dollars" will have his telephone conversation promptly terminated.

Managers use pitches on salesmen as well as on potential customers. Phrases such as "y'all now git a'crackin' on dem telly fones, hear?" or "An' doot 'fore da damn cows come home, alrighty?" (taken from a farm chemical boiler room) add humor to an otherwise pressured environment. They also serve as "contrast conceptions."[6] The use of exaggerated forms of rural and Southern speech implies that the (non-Southern, non-rural) telephone salesmen are more sophisticated and conversant than the alleged mopes, dummies, or clods on the other end of the line.

This, in part, makes techniques of deception more credible than would be the case if equals were being pitched. A variation of the theme is the phenomena known as "talking black," "talking like a farmer," "talking like a mechanic," and so forth. In these scenarios, stereotypes of customers common to the industry a boiler room is working—who failed to make purchases—are bandied about the sales floor as a source of generalized ridicule. These are sometimes sharpened by being linked to the images of popular cartoon characters.

Working the telephones requires persistence, yet everyone enjoys a laugh and the chance to make fun of those who "don't have the smarts to work smart" (those who work for a wage, do physical work, or speak ethnic English). Humor—including its off-color varieties—has pragmatic as well as entertainment value, however. In investment scams, for example, it is common knowledge that women are less likely to entertain the idea of becoming clients than are men. A rule thus evolved to prevent the waste of costly telephone time: "never pitch a bitch." Experience—in the form of large telephone bills—has taught those who run telephone rooms that women, on average, do not have purchasing authority. Worse still, they are also more likely to subject the purchases of their husbands, boyfriends, lovers, bosses, or employers to higher levels of elementary (sometimes sophisticated) scrutiny. A manager explains:

> Women don't know the grift. You have to explain everything to them. They're just too cautious. They're too damn polite. They aren't *players.* They don't take risks. You pitch out your guts, and then they say, "I'll think about it." It costs almost $25 to full-pitch California [twenty to thirty minutes of telephone time]. It isn't worth it. They've got too many men protecting them. There's the accountant, the advisor, the lawyer, the consultant, the husband. There's a whole damn network of objections. Forget it. *This shop doesn't pitch women.* If you do, fine, OK, be a charmer, but *you* pay the damn phone bill.

Men, however, are commonly thought to have business sense, to take risks, to take charge, and to make decisions concerning ventures. Pitchmen use this aspect of the male psyche to their own advantage to "separate the fools from their money" quickly, in the words of one informant.

Although women are popularly thought to be compulsive buyers, that stereotype is decidedly fiction when it comes to purchasing products and services offered by a boiler room. Boiler rooms rarely sell to women. Few are pitched, and few telephone rooms have sizable numbers of female customers. This is even the case, I am told, for the dating service operations.[7]

Moreover, social interaction in telephone rooms is commonly colored with the use of typifications that facilitate the "us-them" distinction.[8] Much of this includes sexist fare common to settings where men form the dominant group. Socialization proceeds through the use of humor and, at times, by blowing off steam and directing anger and frustration at customers. One salesman, for example, shouted loudly and slammed down the telephone with such force that it was heard throughout the room. His co-worker sympathized and explained, "Oh, that was a cold card. You know how they are. It's hard to sell a cold call. He'd better forget it and go on to the next card. There are so many dummies out there it isn't worth it to get upset. But every once in a while it is good to blow off steam. We take enough abuse from the mopes. It is good to dish it out once in a while."

Like many areas of social life, the sales process is unique. A huge publishing market to the contrary—which specializes in self-help aids and manuals for salesmen and managers—the phenomenon stubbornly refuses to be reduced to a single set of essences, techniques, or formulas that can be mechanically applied to achieve the desired results (other than, perhaps, for vendors of such merchandise). After making a sale over the telephone, a pitchman has demonstrated his sales skill to others; persuaded the customer that needs, fears, or dreams are more relevant than the actual product or service vended; acquired concrete, irrefutable evidence that the customer is gullible; and, perhaps most important, validated his role—to himself. After thousands of attempts, and hundreds of repetitions, these impressions are instrumental in forming the working persona of a telephone salesman.

It is through the use of a pitchman's skill that boiler rooms bring certain time-honored confidence tricks into the electronic age. Although the structure of the pitch precludes the salesman from being both forthright and competent at the same time—and boiler room economies usually prohibit the company from being a reputable vendor—these constraints interact to require both duplicity on the part of the salesman and complicity on the part of the customer.

Although customers are as fleeting as the rapidity with which a salesman's fingers work the telephone keypad, those who remain on the sales floor must be socialized. They must come to understand that although most telephone rooms ultimately leave the social space that they temporarily occupy filled with large numbers of fired workers, frustrated managers, and failed petty entrepreneurs, that will not happen to them.

The Use of Telephone Names

I had a number of "phone names" by which I was known, although a few informants knew me by my real name as well. A telephone name is a business tool required to gain entré to a working conversation directed toward the sale of goods or services. Because the name of a salesman is one of the first pieces of information a potential customer hears, there have evolved a number of conventions governing its selection.

A telephone name must be easy for a potential customer to pronounce and remember. First names usually contain no more than two syllables, and surnames no more than three. Names must be as unobtrusive as possible and be stated in proper English. Names of sports figures, common names, and partial variations on those of television and screen personalities are typically used. Dialect is unacceptable except in special cases.

Some shops use the practice of assigning the names of recently fired salesmen to new trainees, thereby creating a pool of training names that signals managers to monitor a new salesman's paperwork carefully. The rapidity with which a trainee assimilates a telephone name is a partial aptitude measure for telephone sales. That this causes difficulty for some salesmen is attested to by the comments of one trainee: "Hey. What's this John stuff? My name is Fred. I'm not John. Why can't I use my real name? Are they doing this to hassle us? It's embarrassing. I mean, sometimes I forget my sales name. I'm not used to someone calling me 'John.' This is stupid."

Sales names permit a modicum of social distance to develop between a salesman's personal identity and his sales persona. This is illustrated by the case of a trainee who had spent three weeks on the telephone: "You know, at first I thought that the name 'Bud Smith' was rather silly. But I'll tell you what, when those farmers start screaming at 'Bud' [for interrupting their work with a telephone call or for trying to sell them something over the telephone] it gets a little easier to take. I mean I would probably take it personally if I used my real name and these people were pissed with me."

Sales names can become part of a salesman's telephone identity because personal monikers, resulting from a successful pitch or perhaps a pattern of voice intonation, will stick with him as long as he remains in the employ of the boiler room. Most of these are functional to increasing sales and are commonly seen as good-natured forms of solidarity among salesmen. An example from a manager's congratulatory exhortation: "Hey, lookee here! Tom SCORES another DYNAMITE DEAL with his *killer* close. He's done it again folks!

They [farmers in this instance] just can't run away to the grain bins [get on with their daily round of activities] without partin' with the plastic [using a credit card] over the telephone. Way ta go, Tom."

After such public recognition, Tom was thereafter called "Plastic Man" as a term of affection and respect. Salesmen with sufficient tenure on the sales floor sometimes self-adopt similar off-the-telephone nicknames that maintain their meaning only during working hours. Examples are "Bulkrate Bill" (from the repertoire of a salesman known for trying to increase the volume of his sales by emphasizing the lower prices available "at the low bulk rate"); "The Fisherman" (a salesman who developed a flair for promoting fishing rods and reels as premiums to jailers, who formed the majority of his accounts); and "The Snake" (a new salesman so reluctant to close his orders properly that the owner said he "snaked around the close" frequently).

One informant uses one telephone name when selling to farmers (replete with a mild Southern drawl) and another for selling to industrial accounts. He claims it makes it easier for him to get into the proper "head" that will enhance the likelihood of a sale. The capability of certain types of personalities to adjust readily to this type of staged performance is not ignored by many boiler room owners, who activity advertise to secure the services of college students who major in drama and the arts.

Setting Up Shop

Since the advent of two technical innovations in the early 1970s (direct, non-operator-assisted dialing and the touch-tone dialing pad), a national marketplace is virtually accessible to anyone with a telephone. Callers do not "sound long distance," because there is no intermediary requirement for a long-distance operator and no delay in connecting the call. The rate at which calls can be placed is also substantially increased.

This, combined with the ready availability of names, addresses, and telephone numbers for purchase through commercial list companies (list brokers), has lowered typical start-up costs for telephone operations and made them more cost-effective as well. A telephone room can be started at home for a few thousand dollars. Much of the initial expense is consumed by the cost of acquiring the requisite level of inventory; the frugal can use the telephone book or the newspapers for leads.

A fourth factor critical to the establishment of a boiler room is infrastructure: the ready availability of relatively inexpensive, reliable transportation and delivery systems for parcels and documents. The fees paid to courier and parcel delivery companies are competitively priced and have the added advantage of circumventing postal authorities.

The mails are used for billing purposes only. No boiler room uses them to ship product. With moderate sums spent on business letterhead and stationery, even a one-man operation has access to a large market and can construct a corporate image and identity by relying heavily on symbols (created by communications and transportation companies) that lend credibility in the eyes of the buying public. A pro describes the delivery of a "precious coin deal" through one of the national courier services:

> We sell to people who see themselves as investors. This is not a mere product we are trading here—it's dreams. Look, we spring for the ten spot [$10] and have the courier service make a personal delivery "from our vaults." You always send the parcel to a customer's business address. Never to his home. You know when a coin is mailed to the home the wife is going to ask questions. Plus, there is the possibility of theft in the mail. Now we can't have "valuable investment materials" in the plain old mailbox, can we? [chuckles]. . . . Let me tell you, when they hear that our courier service will *personally hand-deliver* their holdings [a line from the pitch], well, that assures them that this is a good deal.

An experienced telephone salesman, upon hearing this comment, explains its multiple meanings: "I agree. Packaging is the name of the game indeed. What he [the informant] didn't mention, however, is that if he used the mails they would have nabbed him for mail fraud. The coin rooms are presently under lots of heat from the postal authorities. . . . He is right about one thing: what the customer is buying is 'the package.' Most of that is the charm of the salesman. What's actually inside the box he's sent usually won't stand up to scrutiny."

A capable salesman who has experienced the grueling regimen of telephone work (and also the disillusionment that accompanies his take-home pay) often concludes, in the words of one informant, that "there must be a better way." Working conditions in boiler rooms thus generate potential competitors, because a small percentage of the high turnover in most rooms will ultimately go into business for themselves.

The distinctions made among the types of boiler rooms are made clear when managers, pros, and owners talk with one another. In fact, there is no standard occupational code or classification for a boiler room. Shops come to be known based on what they sell and common impressions of the level of skill it takes to cut various kinds of deals. As a gas man (a swindler who sells fictional gas and oil leases) observes of those who sell chemicals over the telephone, "Never hire a chemical man. They are foul people and are too gross to work with. You have got to have some finesse in the oil and gas game—you can't scream the customer into submission."

Sometimes a salesman will tell of unpleasant experiences in other telephone rooms, as did one pro in a discussion with another on the merits of the "sports phone" (betting advisory service): "The sports rooms have clearly got to be the bottom of the barrel. They are the pits. The people there are very, very *seedy*. It's worse than chemicals. I don't know how to correctly describe them. . . . Slime is a good word. They are just slimy kinds of people. Real flakes. It just made me uncomfortable to work there. They just had bad mouths and looked dirty. Real gutterballs."

Virtually all telephone salesmen have fond stories of the high times and easy money to be had at various times in the past, when things were "really hot" on the telephones. The regularity with which the old times are constantly recounted seems to serve more of a justification function concerning the line of work than to indicate a genuine golden age of the telephone.

Small talk (between active sales calls) in boiler rooms encourages morale-building. Due to the structure of the industry, however, few telephone men would want to return to their previous positions. Inevitably, each move from telephone room to telephone room comes to be defined as a step "up" in spite of the fact that there is little long-term upward income mobility in boiler rooms. To the degree that sales volume increases substantially, it often has the consequence of saturating a given market and may be a source of social change as competing boiler rooms are forced to search out new territories or adopt new strategies for moving their lines. Although it is possible for an operative to have a run or to be on a roll (a short period in which sales—and therefore income—increases), such bursts are, for the most part, few and far between. This is similar to the kind of variable reinforcement schedule logic that psychologists have used to explain the persistent behavior of gamblers, wherein an atypical event—winning (a contingent probability)—is thought to be a permanent, defining characteristic of the game.

When income rises on the sales floor it has an important emotional impact. This may, in part, explain the lore about the "big season" that is ubiquitous in telephone boiler rooms. In the "big season story," the exceptional sales of a distant sales year are highlighted in conversations with owners, managers, and pros. Upon closer inspection, the tales of the big season turn out to be indicative of perhaps a month or so of increased sales for the entire boiler room. For an individual salesman, this usually turns out to be a few large sales (or a string of smaller ones) spaced closely together. The big season involves selective inattention regarding failures.

There are, of course, seasonally adjusted highs and lows, but most of the sales floor is usually fired before an actual calendar year lapses. Moreover, the economic health of a boiler room is perceived differently by each category of labor toiling within. After working for months with salesmen, one is thus likely to become contagiously optimistic, cynical, or withdrawn, because the language of discourse used to communicate routinely is, at the same time, a selling tool necessary for earning one's livelihood. Differentiation is rarely possible.[9]

The general atmosphere of a telephone room is always affirmative, by design, and a company profits when turnover is high. Also, in larger houses there are always one or two salesmen who have exceptional sales for a given week. Their enhanced visibility creates the illusion of prosperity. Moreover, house pros make selling over the telephone appear easier than is the case, and they are granted considerable autonomy from the relentless demands that sales managers constantly make upon newcomers to "keep on the phones." In many cases, the simple fact that these men are more relaxed, under less psychological strain to write an order, and better paid makes them more effective.

Tacit understandings come with increased sales experience. In the words of a pro, one learns to "never show your hand" (reveal your true feelings) and to control the anxieties associated with the sales process. A manager commented about the sales anxiety of a newly hired salesman:

> FLOPSWEAT. It's FLOPSWEAT. He is too nervous. He is so anxious for a sale that the customer can tell. How you feel shows. It's written all over your sales presentation. You can't sell when you *have* to sell. You slip up. You are so worried about the sale that you forget that you must be *believable* to the customer. You can't be believable when you are worried about paying the rent, reading the pitch, thinking about your own financial problems, or worried about keeping your job [laughs]. He should take a break. Be more relaxed. A good salesman always pretends that he is talking to a friend. Believe me. *Always* smile *into* the phone. The customer can tell. It carries through the lines. Watch [points to the nervous salesman on the cold floor], he is going to lose the deal [about ten seconds pass]. See, he did. What did I tell you?

Without regard to the size of a boiler room, the pressure for economic survival is intense. That fact, combined with humorous folk rules for performing on the telephone, a hodgepodge of partially articulated mores concerning sales, and a dash of entrepreneurial spirit and ambition—common to all sales floors—constitutes the heat in boiler rooms: the language, style, and operational procedures that initially entice, but finally compel, most employees to "dial and deal."[10]

Crafting a Pitch

Telehone operations seek to locate markets where real or imagined shortages exist. They capitalize by offering substitutes—which are not presented as such—or by locating a common item and redesigning an embellished presentation of its properties, followed by relabeling and repackaging. That is also accomplished through the use of private-label sources of supply that vend a generic product, which is renamed and sold as the boiler room's version.

A boiler's pitch differs from other kinds of sales presentations in that it contains a hidden agenda designed to assess a potential customer's willingness to believe certain forms of exaggeration. It is this characteristic, perceivable to the trained ear, which signals that "a fish is on the line" (a customer is in the process of being created). The following example comes from a compilation of pitches used in chemical sales. In the hands of a skilled pitchman, as mundane a product as simple household bleach can be promoted, given the proper intonation, cadence, and delivery style, so as to transform it into

> a highly concentrated industrial germ-killer for use in *your* [application site specified]. It's EPA-approved, Mr. [customer]. It's *easy* to use, full instructions *are* provided on each container, and [product name] contains *no* phosphates and is *non-basic* in formulation. It's easily dilutable, with no special equipment requirements. That's right: No special solvents! Now we make it available *to you* at the *low bulk rate* of only [price] in the easy-to-use five-gallon kick-pail. We also include that [naming of premium] as *our* way of saying thank you for your order. Fair enough? Do you work with MasterCard, Visa, or American Express?

If a sales manager were listening in on this pitch, he need only count the number of emphasis points (the terms in italics) to get a feel for the likelihood of a sale being made. While orchestrating such a presentation, the salesman is trying to sense, and measure, gullibility. The telephone call is a screen; anyone who will listen to the entire presentation will likely make a purchase. In part, this is so because a successful pitch sounds more credible than can ever be the case, because it is the evolutionary product of thousands of cumulative hours spent perfecting its final form.

If a prospect is familiar but not too familiar (if a salesman detects expertise, he is trained to hang up immediately) with a class of products—for example, insecticides, cleaners, solvents, and degreasers—but is unaware of buying in industrial quantities, the boiler room provides a rationale and a sales presentation. Epoxy patching material, consisting of hardener and resin, is available to industrial users in bulk (roughly five-pound) canisters, for example. The typical availability of this product in retail stores is usually limited to small tubes.

Whenever there is a discrepancy between a prospect's perceived need for a product and its local availability, a boiler room moves in to promote the latest real or imagined breakthroughs (in the following case, in polymer chemistry). As a direct consequence, roughly $16 (the wholesale cost) worth of material is sold for upward of $160, with the embellishments added through the pitch and the deal solidified with the offering of a premium or a bribe. Note the cadence and style of how a pro closes an order for patching material.

> That's all there is to it [customer's name]! You trowel out some [name of product]: some from can A and an equal amount from can B. [Pause.] Now, it'll be the consistency of *peee-nut-butter* in the ready-to-set state. Work with it. It will set stronger than steel. It works as an anchor-bond grout. It will fix [the problem originally identified in the presentation part of the pitch; tone shifts to that of a carnival barker, a common style native to fairs and commercial advertisements on early-morning television programs that feature miraculous products for "only $19.95"]. Look: You can sand it, paint it, or *even* add some pigment to make it into any color that pleases the eye. [Pause.] Oh, by the way, we include *full* instructions so that *even the help* can do a professional job! They are easy to read and easy to follow. Our applications division does a good job. [Pause, then tone becomes firm and authoritative.] Remember, if you have any questions, just give me a call. My number is on the business card I will enclose with the order. We are as close as the phone. And there is *never a charge* for helping a customer. Let me just verify your address, Mr. [customer's name]. [Pause.] I've got you out there at [a slow, careful reading of the address], is that correct? [Tone becomes stronger and assertive.] And that will be one kit at ONE HUNDRED SIXTY-FOUR DOLLARS and FIFTY CENTS. Do you prefer COD or do you use plastic? [Tone becomes jovial.] Beautiful! [Consummates the details of payment.] Oh, I almost forgot. [Pause, then customer's first name.] Is it OK for me to call you by your first name? Great! [Customer's first name], how about the Mrs.? Does she like to cook? [If yes, steak knife promotion; if no, select another premium.] Beautiful, and I bet she makes delicious pies for the holidays. Am I right? [Pause.] Outstanding! [Pause.] In with my business card, [customer's first name], I am going to put our BEAUTIFUL steak knife set. This is the nicest thing we've had in a long time. It's a six-piece set [salesman becomes extremely excited]. It's got *stainless steel* blades and *rosewood* handles. The Mrs. will love it! It comes in its own box! When it gets out there with the patch, give it to the Mrs. She will give you a *big kiss!* Now be careful, [customer's name], those blades are *sharp!* Make sure you are on her good side when you go near the kitchen! [Laughter, tone shifts to businesslike.] When the patch arrives, Mr. [customer's last name], all I ask is two things: Is it unreasonable to ask for a favor? [Pause.] First, work with the patch. Give it its best test on that [application referred to earlier in the pitch]. When you see that it forms the *strongest* bond, and works *better* than anything you have used before, I have a second favor to ask. Is that reasonable? [Pause.] All I ask is that you take out that business card I will enclose with

this order and pass it on to a neighbor. We sure can use the referral business. FAIR ENOUGH? [Pause, cadence increases.] Are there any questions about this order, [customer's first name]? [Pause.][11] BEAUTIFUL! I want to thank you on behalf of [name of company] for giving us a try. You'll be glad you did. Let me process this order right now. Watch for it to get out to you in about ten days. Is that soon enough? [Pause.] Great. Have a nice day, [customer's first name; hangs up the telephone after the customer does].

The salesman offers a solution to the problem at hand. That is part of the qualification process. After a few hundred telephone calls, salesmen become increasingly comfortable with presenting their products to solve an array of problems that typical customers might encounter. When a pro works a new territory, the nature of the objections customers offer is critically important. They compose a bank of tacit knowledge from which a salesman can create applications-possibilities, using experience and creativity. It can be highly individuated work. One salesman, for example, upon finding a need for a nonslip alternative to grooving the concrete sections of the holding pens used during the mating season of hogs, discovered that sows often break their legs by slipping on wet, ungrooved concrete. He learned by listening to farmers that the grooving process is not only expensive but also results in a hard-to-clean surface under which manure (and germs) can accumulate. The salesman correspondingly modifies his pitch to ascertain whether his customers "run hogs" (maintain a stock of pigs). If they do, he presents the same patching material as a nonslip safety compound which, with the addition of sand to the mix, hog farmers will see as desirable. All ears on the sales floors of smaller companies are attentive to modifications in the pitch.

Each shop, however, has a characteristic way of dealing with such innovation. Once a strike (a sale to a new category of customer) is made, the task of working out a more suitable pitch may be delegated to other salesmen, assigned as an extra duty to one of the house pros, or performed by the boiler room owner himself. At larger houses with a more standardized product line, however, creativity may be punished; by definition, "not sticking to the pitch" is a weakness that must be eliminated by managers who routinely monitor telephone conversations.

Another way in which imperfect markets are exploited is through the use of a probe or feeler. As one salesman, a fan of the *Star Trek* television series who took great pleasure in "Trek trivia," explains, "Here goes a probe. Let's call it 'Farm One.' I am now going to launch Farm One. This babe is an information-seeker but can be armed for sales [laughs] if the need arises. What I'll do is call some hog farmers and see if they have other problems that we can solve with the stuff that we sell. I think I'll be 'market research.' [He entertains an animated conversation with his telephone receiver.] Yeah, how does that sound? OK, Farm One, you are *now* in the market research biz."

The salesman proceeds to outline a "market research" pitch to be directed at farmers—and to think out loud to those listening to him. When the crude outline is worked out, he "goes out" as "the director of research, [name of the boiler room], agricultural sales division" from "up here in [the name of the state that contains the boiler room]." While the person who answers the telephone summons the owner of the farm, the salesman covers the mouthpiece of his telephone and intones, "Farm One, Farm One [in a voice simulating the abrupt telecommunications style used by NASA], WE ARE IN RESEARCH MODE. WE HAVE CONTACT. WE HAVE CONTACT. NOW THAT'S A ROGER." He uncovers the mouthpiece of his telephone to begin the pitch after the potential customer responds with a characteristic, "Hello."

Such dramaturgical skill and humor not only breaks some of the monotony in telephone rooms but also has the more pragmatic function of acquiring information about the market. By saying that he is conducting a survey, for example, the salesman may unearth a deep resentment of survey researchers. The pitchman knows that a sale can never be made if his presentation contains elements that trigger fear, resentment, or animosity. On subsequent telephone calls he thus deletes all references to surveys and adds, "We are expanding our production facilities in your area." This is likely to be well received by farmers who are hard-pressed economically in certain parts of the country.

One of the cardinal rules in all boiler rooms is to get a customer to agree as many times as possible. There is a much greater likelihood that a farmer in a depressed area will continue to listen to a pitch if it is somehow linked to the idea of prosperity. Boiler rooms, however, contain no market researchers, conduct no surveys, and own no production facilities. The introduction to a sales pitch is pragmatically derived from whatever turn of phrase will attract a potential customer's attention. Salesmen also learn that there are inopportune times to call on certain customers.

For each objection the boiler develops a comeback (a short, one-line statement used to make the product sound credible) that is measured in terms of its contribution to sales rather than its veracity. Each telephone room develops a comeback routine adapted to the needs of its customers. All boilers are thus engaged in a continuing process of education. It is here where techniques developed in other telephone rooms can be incorporated into the daily round of selling, overcoming objections, and trying to earn a living. This also adds to the chemistry of a room. A telephone room's chemistry embodies the collective store of knowledge, experience, and the interactive styles of all its members.

Although few boilers have genuine expertise, when what they know is focused through the lens of a pitch—and pitted against the few seconds of reaction time that most people have to respond to a ringing telephone—it can be formidable. A salesman explains:

A lot of people ask me how it is possible to sell *anything* over the telephone. Most people just hang up, right? Wrong! It's not an even battle. We have an edge. You figure that it takes about thirty seconds for the average customer to figure out what's going on. After all, how much happens in thirty seconds? Dialing and the ring—maybe eight to ten seconds. Then, "Hello? Who is this? What do you want? Who do you want to speak to?" How much can *they* say in thirty seconds? But it may take a roomful of men a few weeks, maybe months, to figure out *our* thirty seconds. If this stuff didn't work we'd all be out of jobs. . . . Hell, most of the time these mopes don't know what hit 'em. . . . You know [laughs] sometimes I get this image in my head of a farmer speakin' to his wife after I've sold him a five-gallon bucket [of weed-killer]. He hangs up the phone. His wife asks him, "Jethro, what did you *buy* this time?" He says to his wife, "Martha, who *was* that masked man who came into the barn? His phone took 'way my hundred and fifty dollars!" [Uncontrollable, proud laughter.] I bet that happens! I can see it so clearly. It's *got* to happen.

To sell successfully over the telephone, knowledge must be transformed into usable information that conforms to the taken-for-granted expectations of customers. That is, it must be coded into a workable form that increases the likelihood of a sale. The immediate goal is to "keep 'em on the line," in the words of a sales manager. To accomplish that, a boiler room develops a working rhetoric and assumes the posture of a credible firm. If guarantees are commonly given, the boiler room offers them. If registration with the local Farm Bureau, Better Business Bureau, or another organization is required, it is feigned. In a strict sense, the pitchman delivers exactly what his customers want to hear. The trick is to discover what this may be and how to present it properly and with some credibility. As one manager put it, "Customers are not stupid. They have needs. All you have to do is resonate to their needs. Watch, I'll *show* you." He picks up the "listener," a device used to monitor ongoing sales calls, and we listen in on a trainee.

Trainee: "I don't know. I'm sorry." [Hangs up the telephone.]
Manager: "You lost the deal, didn't you?"
Trainee: "Yes, I think I did. I'm sorry."
Manager: "You are *never* sorry! This is *not* a sorry company! What did he [the customer] ask you? What don't you know?"

Trainee: "That stupid farmer. He asked if the germicide was USDA-approved. I don't know."

Manager: "What? That is *in the pitch!* You didn't read the pitch! Here it is on page three [points to the pitch]. You have got to stick to the pitch. Stick to the pitch. The customer is not stupid. *You* are stupid. Why can't you stick to the pitch?"

Trainee [deeply upset]: "OK. I'll stick to the pitch."

Manager [realizing he has been too harsh on the trainee] to the entire telephone room: "OK guys, off the phones.—Let's review the problem here. [He offers a five-minute sales briefing to review the proper procedures and coach the new trainee and then summarizes and concludes], Get the information you need to complete the sale. Put the customer on hold, if necessary, and I'll do a TO [take over, i.e., complete the sale] for you."

This exercise serves many functions. In addition to offering a training opportunity for the manager and allowing him to read the quality of the sales floor, it permits him to learn the nature of the objections in a given market. Once a class of objections has been identified, they can be countered with the proper comeback. In such a manner, initial reluctance on the part of the customer can be transformed into a selling point. The lesson can be as elementary as not hanging up on a customer, not cursing or shouting at him, and not becoming flustered or tongue-tied (perhaps the most fatal of flaws for a telephone salesman).

The manager shows that most objections can be overcome, at least a sufficient number of times, by mastering appropriate sales techniques. He concludes his lesson with a demonstration. "This is called 'buying back the heat,'" he announces and then proceeds to get the name of the customer who had flustered the trainee, to re-call that customer, to apologize profusely, and to make a sale. The sale is credited to the trainee's account amid cheers from the assembled sales force.

It is critical that the manager take control of the room. He must assert his superiority in sales skills as well as his authority to make decisions concerning the resolutions of sales. In the preceding example, the manager clearly demonstrates that, first, he will work for "his" room (all managers adopt a possessive stance toward "their" salesmen); second, that he is on the side of the salesmen (i.e., he will always work to give his men the "best breaks"); and, third, that he is fair. As one salesman aptly validated his manager's performance, "Yeah. That's my main man: Mr. Smith [the manager]. He gave me credit for a sale I didn't even make! I've never seen *that* before. He's a good guy."

These strategies are drawn directly from the larger business culture and inhere in the assertion that management and workers are part of a team whose members mutually benefit if each cooperates to enhance the well-being of the other.

Skill Requirements

Five types of personnel work in boiler rooms: trainees, regulars, pros, managers, and owners. Telephoning skills are functionally hierarchical, largely cumulative, and, except at experienced levels, industry-specific. One ascends the pecking order by gaining experience through longevity, by dint of personality, by acquiring knowledge that is only transmitted orally, and by amassing, or having access to, capital. My discussion, for the most part, ignores those who are ancillary to the actual operation of the sales floor. These people have value, but only as props or technicians.

Because boiler rooms conduct business with vendors of goods and services, they must, of necessity, contain people who can interact with the larger business community. Such personnel, although immaterial to the social control activities of the telephone operation, do play an important symbolic role in making boiler rooms appear respectable as well as in connecting the company to a network (which is sometimes extensive) of other businesses. That linkage permits a shared definition of work to correspond with a large number of tasks and positions common to all small and moderately sized firms.

For both the salaried full- and part-time (largely female) administrative staff (secretaries, bookkeepers, and receptionists) and the male service workers (the help), boiler rooms represent pleasant (although temporary) jobs, where the pay is competitive for the region. The main office and the shipping room, if there is one, are kept physically separate from the sales floor, where the commissioned sales force (largely male) works the telephones.

Part of this is no doubt due to the fact that many boiler rooms are simply inhospitable to women, or to those women who have thin skins, refined sensibilities that cannot be held in check, or weak egos.[12] Boiler rooms are smoke-filled and often contain ribald sorts. The language that salesmen use when they have failed to make a sale is not the kind that is printable, and tempers sometimes flare. Some salesmen are ruthless, and many are as willing to exploit women as they are to fleece customers. At the higher levels of a boiler room—where the environment is much more subdued and the potential rewards much greater—the virtual absence of saleswomen is because these shops can only select talent from those boiler rooms below them in the skill hierarchy.

All that is required to work in a telephone boiler room is the willingness to dismiss some of the shortcomings mentioned earlier, to learn sales techniques, and to possess what is called in the trade a "telephone voice," that is, the ability to speak clear, unaccented English. Apprentices follow a printed script and submit to the requirements of a training schedule. Training rooms have a high turnover rate. As one sales manager wryly put it, "Well, you might say that it is sort of like in the Bible: Many make *calls*, but few are chosen [laughs]."

The more sophisticated operations require a telephone personality, which implies some experience in the industry and the ability to regularly, artfully, and personably close sales by overcoming the many kinds of objections that are inevitable in this line of work. These men do not work from a script and are noted for developing personalized styles of presentation. They learn quickly, readily adapt to the tone of a room, and are soon permitted to work house paper (established accounts). Telephone personalities are sometimes promoted (less frequently than most will admit) to the ranks of management, but more typically they move on to other telephone rooms.[13]

Location

In almost any major urban area one can find telephone boiler rooms in operation. These are usually identifiable by examining the classified advertising pages of a newspaper under the categories "Part-Time, Telephone," "Telephone Sales," "Sales, Telephone," or "Telemarketing."

The tip-off that a boiler room is in operation can be deduced by the number of promises in the advertisement: higher-than-average pay, shorter-than-average hours, and higher-than-might-be-expected commissions, draws, overrides, and bonuses for outstanding performance. The more promises made, the greater the likelihood that they will be mythical, that the workplace will be compact (as opposed to expansive), and that the character of the office environment will change radically once the job applicant moves beyond the receptionist's desk.

Other clues include the fact that the name of the hiring company, and a street address, will be absent from advertisements. Only a telephone number and a "hiring name," that is, a telephone name used exclusively for this purpose, appear in print. After an initial voice-screening, a salesman will systematically drill selected callers. The more sophisticated the boiler room, the more intensive the procedures designed to identify those with prior telephone sales experience and exclude the press and curiosity-seekers.

Boiler rooms tend to locate in those areas where the local labor supply includes many workers displaced from normal career paths. The physical dispersion of telephone rooms in a region depends on the number and density of "parent houses."[14] Because these businesses are formed only by those with previous boiler room experience, they tend to locate between the residence of the principal owner and the parent house. That is the case because hiring new people off the parent sales floor (called "raiding a house") is difficult if salesmen must travel too great a distance to jump shop (change boiler room employers). As one owner commented on the drawing distance of his advertisements, "Hell, they are answering the ad from [a major urban area]. When I tell them that the job is in the suburbs, they hang up. It is too far to travel. I can't pay the kind of money they do in the city. I guess you'd say I have to use local talent [laughs]."

Boiler rooms are largely an urban-suburban phenomenon. The scams tend to be heavily concentrated in areas such as New York, Florida, California, and Chicago (because of the presence of the commodities exchange), where they can tap into a pool of articulate men who are conversant in the language of business culture. Smart shops (small boiler rooms with a few exceptional salesmen) are increasingly a suburban phenomenon and draw people with previous boiler room or sales experience who have been displaced by the operation of the business cycle.

Product houses tend to locate where some of the sales force can be recruited from the lower ranks of the industries served. The one exception to this holds for telephone vendors of agricultural supplies, which are not located in rural areas and employ no farmers. There are no rural boiler rooms in the United States except for the occasional one-man shop, largely because those who have the required skills reside elsewhere. Telemarketing rooms, where most of the employees are women (chapter 5), tend to locate within regions served by mass transportation.

The Structure of Boiling

Telephone salesmen necessarily make more calls than they do sales. The invariant work routine can be conceptualized as a set of stages called the "sales sequence." Each step is ordered hierarchically in terms of both the level of difficulty required to complete the sequence—which results in a sale—and in terms of the economic cost of so doing. Thus, the longer the duration of a telephone call, the more complex and detailed the pitch; the more objections that must be overcome; the more costly the call is to the ownership; and the greater the abilities required of those who perform the work.

With a dozen or so salesmen on active wires (telephone lines), the telephone bill for non-sales can mount quickly for misdials that connect to other than a customer, calls where a customer is unavailable (or unwilling) to come to the telephone, and calls that result in burn-offs (the customer hanging up). With enhanced technology, larger companies can partition telephone bills into unitary wholes for billing purposes and thereby achieve economies of scale. These can be substantial because a salesman who is burned off continues to dial the telephone, and his fraction-of-a-minute incomplete call results in a whole minute's fee to the telephone room.

Table 1 shows the sales sequence (introduction, qualification, presentation, and close) and obstacles (objections) that must be surmounted to achieve a sale. Some can be overcome with training, whereas others are an inevitable cost of doing business. Telephone salesmen face the same kinds of resistance on the part of buyers that all salesmen do.

Added to the natural differences in talent and aptitude, the effectiveness of a salesman in completing the sales sequence—and thereby cutting deals—is influenced by structural factors. Some of the more important ones are time of the day (when buyers may not be available to come to the telephone), the seasonal nature of the product or service, and the density of telephone communication in a particular region. In addition, the finances, temperament, personality, needs, and available inventory of prospective customers—and their willingness to respond to telephone solicitation—are critical.

There are more ways of losing a sale than of getting one. Any conceivable variable can stand in the way—and probably has. Salesmen quickly learn that the likelihood of a sale using an incomplete sequence is remote, and, in the words of a pro, "If you don't do it right, it will come back to haunt you." By that he meant that if a presentation/qualification mix is incomplete or poorly executed an objection that could have been routinely handled will typically reemerge at a point in the sequence when a salesman has the least control over its redefinition—near the end of the pitch. A pitchman's qualification differs from the standard business usage of the verb "to qualify," however.

In a boiler room, a telephone salesman assumes a sale and will continue to negotiate until the telephone call can be terminated profitably. This is not obvious to new salespeople (it must be taught) nor to many surprised cus-

Table 1. The Sales Sequence and Objections to a Sale

Sales Sequence	Objections
Dialing	Wrong number, disconnected, or number changed.
Introduction	Unknown company; buyer not interested or available; foreign-language speaker.
(The opening)	Person who answers the telephone is not authorized to make purchases.
Qualification	No perceived need for product or service; no interest in premium; no funds available for purchase.
Presentation	No time to listen; no use for product or service; technical objections.
(The pitch)	Applications difficulty; credibility problem.
The close	Price too high; quantity too large; terms unacceptable; delivery problematic.
Method of payment	Unacceptable.

tomers who discover that they, in fact, have made a purchase after giving their credit card number over the telephone. By qualifying a customer, the pitch-man is systematically eliminating all but the most likely candidates. This is a smooth but ruthless process that startles many potential customers who, af-ter being charmed for a few minutes by a pleasant voice, are suddenly (be-cause of their failure to qualify) left with dead air: a telephone receiver hanging from their hand because the pitchman has hung up on them. As one owner summarized succinctly, "The purpose of qualification is straightforward: If the customer doesn't *want* it [i.e., the product or service], has no *use* for it, and can't *pay* for it, get him *off* the phone. Do it quickly! The phone bill is eating me alive. Always be qualifying. Qualify. Qualify."

Once a boiler locates what is called the "buying window" (the customer's interest, needs, and ability to pay), the mechanics of a sale will proceed in spite of the fact that this may be peripheral to a buyer's concerns of the moment when he or she happens to answer a ringing telephone. That rare occasion when the needs of the buyer happen to coincide with the offerings of the seller is called a "laydown"—the salesman proceeds unencumbered through the sales sequence and completes a sale with few objections.

There are always some objections. The goal of a salesman is to narrow a customer's range of choices surrounding a specific need to those selected from, and limited to, those available to the pitchman. An effective salesman over-comes objections until only four remain: price, quantity, application, and method of payment. The issue here is one of procedural closure. Whatever may constitute the almost infinite number of combinations required to sat-isfy a buyer that a purchase is optimal, to satisfy a seller only one need be met—that the boiler room gets paid.

One of the functions of a telephone sales force is to employ techniques of manipulation to persuade potential customers to make purchases. Because the distance (spread) between the cost of a product and the highly inflated sell-ing price must pay the entire cost of the telephone operation and also earn a profit for the owners, this can only be cost-effective if misrepresentation of one kind or another is used. Thus, a telephone salesman is free to use a set of standards that vary with the perceived needs of his clients, not the attributes of his wares. Likewise, anything that is promoted must necessarily involve certain kinds of exaggeration and, to this degree, is thereby subject to the use of deceptive practices as well. The amount of trickery required in a tradition-al market is largely internalized, however.[15] In part, that is because what so-ciety has come to agree upon as being conventional involves more deception than most are willing to admit, as even a brief survey of most criminology texts will attest. To cite one common example, consider the technical specifi-cations for a prescription drug and compare that text to the advertising blurb that usually accompanies the drug. The latter never mentions possible complications.

The most difficult part of a sales call is always the close (asking for the money). Customers are usually closed a number of times. The first may be thought of as a rhetorical close (the warm-up talk), where it is implied in the introduction that a product or service may be for sale. The purpose of the rhetorical close is twofold: It builds interest, and it lays the groundwork for the pitch. The following examples differ in subtlety.

> From chemical sales: As part of our tremendous promotion, we are offering . . .
> From automobile replacement parts: We are calling new customers in your area today. . . .
> From coin investments: We are looking for investors who enjoy the tangible. . . .
> From telemarketing: We are contacting those in the [name of industry] this afternoon to try to expand our wholesale market. . . .

The second close (the real, or money, close) occurs when the actual pricing of the product or service is either requested by the customer or the presentation stage of the sales sequence is complete. There is also the contingency (buyer's reluctance) that occurs when a customer finds the initially quoted price, quantity, or terms of the service prohibitive or otherwise unacceptable— "ICA" [initial cardiac arrest] quipped one salesman. Under such circumstances, the customer will be dropped, that is, a drop close will be used. The customer will be offered a smaller quantity, or a more limited investment, offering, premium, or range of services, which reduces the total cost of the sale and thus mutes the psychological impact of having spent a large sum.

A close must be timed so customers feel that they are receiving an advantageous offer that is sealed by their willingness to act promptly. The inability to close a deal properly can occur for a number of reasons among even the most seasoned salesmen, but it is especially noted among the less experienced. This is commonly called "overselling." It occurs when a salesman is unable to disengage his personal identity from his sales identity. A salesman, for example, may enjoy hearing himself talk, he may wish to depict himself as a technical expert, or he may enjoy charming his customers. A manager explains, "Don't talk them out of the deal. Don't oversell. If they [the customers] are interested, have the money, and want the product: Close 'em. Don't get carried away. Stick to the pitch: KISS [keep it simple, stupid]. Do you understand? KISS. The more you give them to think about, the more reason they will have to object to the sale. It's as simple as ABC: always be closing.

We are not in the education business. Remember: The buyer is a liar. Ask for the money."

Although all salesmen follow the sales sequence, some are more proficient than others. Those who have developed personalized styles add "tone" to a telephone room by being more visible, personable, and productive than those who have not. They are more likely to enjoy their work, to be singled out by managers for testimonials of varied kinds, to embody the norms of craftsmanship in a given shop, and to write larger orders. One salesman quipped: "Absolutely! Right on! I agreeeeee! The max! You might call it a 'dialing tone' [laughs]."

The structure of boiling includes the tone of the room, the nature of the marketplace, and the efforts of the salespeople to complete the selling sequence successfully and cooperate in such efforts so as to withstand the odds against their eventual burnout, frustrated expectations, and the psychological impact that the termination of their jobs, or the boiler room itself, may have on their lives.

When No Amount of Heat Will Do

Some objections cannot be overcome, no matter how sophisticated the salesmen. An illustrative natural field experiment demonstrates this. A warehouse owner solicited a telephone room to attempt to move (sell) roughly a hundred thousand dollars' worth of stock in the form of "photo packages" acquired from a huge distributor who specializes in working malls, shopping centers, churches, bazaars, and state fairs. Before the boiler room accepted the project, a few dozen packets were acquired, and the house pros had a meeting to design a marketing strategy. All documentation (bills, returned checks, and telephone numbers) was provided.

House opinion regarding whether the new account should be accepted was mixed. A script was developed, and the best pitchmen were assigned to the accounts. The room was busy a good part of the afternoon. First, a feeler was sent out (a pro made the first call to assess the market). Then, a trial pitch was hammered out. Third, a pair of salesmen worked on the presentation, streamlined it, and perfected the close. A meeting was held to discuss the emerging consensus regarding the product, and then the pros did another dry run among themselves. Finally, one of the solicitors was called in for a mock presentation. The names and telephone numbers of the prospects were then divided among those salesmen who wanted in on the deal.

Twelve potential customers expressed an interest in the photographs and promised to send in their checks. When ten days had passed and no checks were forthcoming, the salesmen had all the evidence they needed to go no farther with this account. By that time, however, the project became somewhat of a house joke and a challenge—and therefore the focus of much attention.

A pro developed a holiday pitch for the product and followed it up with a mailing that (likely unprecedented in any boiler room) included the photographs and a request to "send whatever you can [to pay for them] in the spirit of the holiday season." Each customer was contacted again and pitched. Four additional telephone numbers were dredged up using the "community screen."[16] Thus far, the company was overinvesting in time, energy, talent, telephone calls, and postage, but the challenge generated sufficient good will on the sales floor, and all awaited the results. No money was ever received. The lack of funds is one of the few objections for which there is no remedy. One pro lamented, "These deals *cannot* be closed. There is no amount of heat that will do the job."

The episode is instructive in three regards. First, it clearly demonstrates the limits of even the most skilled boilers. Second, it suggests the level of cohesiveness achieved in a working boiler room. Even in failure, the morale of the room is high. Finally, the episode embodies a caricature—and the dark side—of what might be called "the American business dream" as it is profusely lauded and promoted in sales manuals and self-help books. An entrepreneur (the protagonist in most of these tales) has engaged a self-motivated, professional work force in a small business setting, actively pursuing profits for the sheer excitement of the hunt. The team works in good-spirited camaraderie until the end of the workday, ever-ready for the next business challenge. There are no labor-management issues here; it's one big, cooperative team effort, at least for the moment.

Forced Attrition: The Circulation of Men and Accounts

Boiler room owners skillfully manipulate each category of labor so as to maximize profits. That requires a delicate balancing act between the flow of rewards and the number of salesmen working the sales floor. The chief instrumentality for income determination and distribution is the acquisition of house accounts from which revenues are generated and commissions paid.

Managers implement the policies of the owners. Usually recruited from within, managers are also salesmen, and, except at the larger houses, they actively work their own accounts. In that managers have allocational control over all house accounts, they are the chief beneficiaries of the turnover they create. Anything that increases the efficiency with which accounts are serviced is in their economic interest. Managers also recruit and train new people, some of whom have the potential of being their replacements. There is thus an inherent conflict between recruiting the most capable trainees (one goal of the ownership) and keeping turnover as high as possible. Newly freed-up accounts acquired from fired salesmen can be worked more diligently and profitably by the pros. What follows are the comments of a salesman about a common dilemma in the industry. His firm has recently hired an exceptionally capable salesman who became available because a boiler room that previously employed him went out of business.

> He [the new man] doesn't have a snowball's chance in hell of being here more than a week, week and a half, tops. He's too good. The guy sounds great on the phone. He has his act together. This guy's got ambition and a phone voice to match. Hell, he wrote a sale in the first *hour* they turned him loose on the phones, and he wasn't even scheduled to go live [engage potential customers before completing the training sessions]! . . . He smooth-talked the whole deal. It went right through the verifier [a specialized salesman charged with confirming the sales made by trainees by recalling the customers] on the first shot. Marty [the verifier] told me so. "Who is this new guy? He did everything right," he said.

In a conventional business, extremely productive new hires are typically seen as assets to the company. Not so in a boiler room. A pro explains why:

> Look, John's been the manager three years last November. He's an airhead, but he runs a smooth shop. Besides, anyone who's been around here a few months knows more than a trainee. So, John looks good when you compare him with the trainees he hires. The new guy is a threat. Anyone can see that this man is more capable than John. Hell, all the pros have already noticed this and the guy's only been here three days. John just *turns over the floor* [emphasis added]. That's all he can do. John will make life unbearable for the new guy and then fire him. Where else can he get a job? He impresses truck drivers.[17] What the hell is a sharp guy doing here working for John in the first place? Well, you know what I mean, the guy will be *gone.* No doubt about it. . . . Now the owner, what should he do? Yeah, the new guy could make lots of money for the company if he is allowed to stay. But then the owner will have to deal with John. It isn't worth it. John makes the company more money by hiring and firing. The owner *never* gets involved. That's why he hired John. . . . The owner likes a smooth flow: no waves, no demands. A fast-burner working for John? Never happen. John likes 'em stupid and docile. This way he has control. [The new man was fired at the end of the week.]

Smaller boiler rooms also have many of these problems without the specialized personnel (managers, trainers, and verifiers) to serve as buffers between the pressures of the sales floor and company policies. They face a dilemma that can never be fully or satisfactorily resolved: For an owner, skilled telephone men are expensive, and although the unskilled are the least cost-effective, their turnover generates profit for the company. A boiler room follows the path of least resistance. A pro explains that "it's the bottom line. We have to turn volume. If we write enough business, some of it will be good. I can't afford the salesmen I need, so I've got to use the ones I have. But the returns are eating me alive. If I fire the salesmen who need to be fired then I cut my own throat."[18]

As is true in all sales organizations, the commission structure rewards the successful. In a boiler room, however, it has the psychological power and merit of concealing managerial decisions to hire and fire personnel. Thus, images communicated by management are typically seen as personal troubles experienced by salesmen who transfer their emotions toward other members of the sales force, to bad luck, to fate, to seasonality, or to the stupidity of customers. Thus, the predatory structure remains invisible, and most telephone-men stick out their jobs until fired or the boiler room folds. Consider the following cases of an established regular (age thirty) with five years' experience in an auto parts boiler room and a trainee (age twenty-four) with two months on the telephone.

> Look, last year I made near 30K. I'm a heavy-hitter here, and the owner knows it. They need me. I am looking out for number 1. I'm here at 7:30 in the morning, and, yeah, I go home at seven as well. Sometimes I am here on Saturdays. But I know my customers. No one in this room can *sell* like I can. I'm on commission. I am not on welfare [he doesn't receive a draw that is not covered by his weekly sales figures]. If I could get more accounts I could make even more money, but that bastard [the sales manager] gives all the good accounts to his friends. Boy, I could show him . . . I've worked my way up. I started in the auto repair shops. Now that is hard work. Here I have a desk and look at my really comfortable chair. That's a tax write-off, you know [with a smile]. And I have my *own* business cards, look here [shows card]. I had them made up myself [at his own expense]. And I make the coffee in the morning. This is *our* coffee pot. It belongs to the salesmen, not the sales manager. Look at [points to a trainee]. He's a twerp. He can't sell. He isn't even on commission yet. I am paying his salary. That's right. Those of us on commission have to carry guys like that. They are in for a free ride at our expense. They can't cover their draw. If I were sales manager I'd really run this operation. Just give me a shot. I'd show the manager how to run this show [gets visibly angry].

> Well look, he [the regular] bitches a lot. He has a sour grapes attitude. He is making damn good money, and he still is bitter most of the time. He is a good salesman, but he is always fighting with the sales manager and is really not friendly to the new men. Now, take me for example. I've been here two

months. I have a degree in business administration, a wife, and two kids. I was
working as a foreman in a factory, and this deal is a bit better because it is cleaner. I expect to go on commission in two months [it took six months] and then
things will be OK. I work hard and keep to myself. This job will be better in
about a year, when I get to build my accounts. I see that some people around
here are making pretty good money. If they can do it, so can I. It just takes
time. I am learning the ropes. I have to find more customers, that's all. I keep
to myself and work hard. I've just got to make more calls. You know how it
is. Some of these customers are real dummies. But I'll make out okay. You just
have to hang in there.

Both of these men see frustration as stemming from, or amplified by, the
personalities in boiler rooms or the structure of sales work. Both offer idiosyncratic solutions. One is pessimistic while the other is optimistic. Both were
fired, nonetheless, at the same time—roughly nine months after these conversations were recorded.

It is difficult for someone new to a boiler room to understand that the taken-for-granted assumptions most people usually make about businesses—that
they wish to grow, that they will economically reward loyal employees, and
that one's stake with the company increases with time—simply do not hold
true. As a seasoned informant who has spent more than eighteen years in
various kinds of boiler rooms as a worker, manager, and owner said, "These
are all cockamamie operations. They aren't real. You simply cannot expect to
stay in business for too long. Your bags have to be packed. Make it while you
can and then leave. Quit while you are ahead. Move on to other things." He
then explained why that must be the case.

There is simply no way you can pay a high commish, say, 30 percent, on a
real product. So we sell lots of air. You find the mooch and take him for all he
will play for. Let's face it. It takes a certain kind of man to be a heavy-hitter
on the phones. They are all flaky in certain ways. Not everyone can do this
successfully. You have to be very, very good or an owner. . . . Of course, the
vast majority of men who work the phones simply fall into this kind of work.
Am I right? No one says, "Gee, when I grow up I want to sell things on the
telephone."

The One-Man Shop

A one-man shop contains the essence of a boiler room: a man, his telephone,
a room, and a dream. Old scripts typically litter a desk filled with coffee cups
and ash trays. Most of the calls are to old friends (previous accounts) using a
pitch so well honed over thousands of hours of use that it has become one with
the personality of the pitchman. The owner performs all sales and adminis-

trative functions, although he may have a part-time secretary if his book (account base) is fairly large.

He is his own resident pro, and working alone subjects him to unique forms of occupational and emotional stress. These are present at both the beginning and the penultimate stages in the evolution of boiler rooms, which take their present form from an idea that grew from the mind of the entrepreneur as he labored for someone else long and hard on the cold floor (that part of a sales floor or defined task where people work exclusively to open new accounts by calling prospects for the first time). What follows is a composite from the impressions collected from six informants who run such operations.

A "lone phoner" (as he is called) is usually at, or approaching, middle age and has a dozen or so years in sales and at least a half-dozen years on the telephone. He goes it alone twice: first when he starts out as an independent owner, and then again after his attempt proves unsuccessful and his company goes out of business. He then works the house accounts that his sales force was able to generate when the business saw better days. By working out of his house, in his garage, or in a small office (under a new company name), he can keep his overhead expenses to a minimum. He faces four choices: to leave the telephones entirely, to try to expand, to change industries, or to live in poverty.

Lacking capital, the second option is not readily achievable, but he will do the best that he can. He "gives it a shot" in the hope that his accounts still have some value. He works his paper relentlessly until his deck becomes saturated (the number of telephone calls increases much faster than the rate at which income is generated). He then considers the first option, but more often than not he has few skills recognizable by conventional businesses. As an informant said, "Right. There is no need for snake oil vendors in legitimate business. That's what they told me when I went for a real job." The final option is unthinkable. He ponders a change in the nature of the business. He also faces a number of crises that press on his life situation. These are so common that generalizations are possible.

Although lone entrepreneurs feel these concerns most acutely, all who work the telephones experience them to some degree. They are the most telling indicators of the heat in a boiler room as it is experienced by the men most likely to innovate. These overriding concerns can be conceptualized as crises because, when confronted, they render a continued life on the telephones problematic.

Crises Common to Professional Boilers

1. *His marriage may dissolve.* Virtually all salesmen who spend a few years in boiler rooms (working full-time) come under increasing pressure from their spouses to "get a real job," "earn a real living," and provide security for their

families. The pressure is greatest when the spouse realizes that a telephone job is not a permanent position.

Invariably, the professional uses the same persuasive sales techniques on his spouse that he practices daily on the telephone. That works for a while, but spouses often have non-telephone-room frames of reference from which to evaluate their husbands' work. The pressure mounts. Of sixteen informants who owned, or own, a boiler room operation, eleven are divorced and two are separated from their wives. They attribute that statistic, in part, to an unwillingness to leave the telephones. The illusions learned in boiler rooms are potent.

2. *Disillusionment.* The owner comes to realize that his dream of being a captain of industry, his own boss, and the president of a small company begins to tarnish with the years. He recalls the recent past when some decent money was made on the telephones and perhaps a new automobile or a home was purchased. The monthly payments, however, last longer than the sense of accomplishment. He recalls his younger children saying with pride, "Daddy works on the telephone," or "Daddy is the president." This can be painful for even the strongest optimist. He is getting older, and his business has failed. That wears hard on a man. A salesman explains,

> You know, it's funny that when it all begins, *you* choose the phones. It just works that way. You get shit-canned [fired], or maybe you see an ad or have a friend who wants to help you out. Maybe you've got something really important that's going to happen in your life, and you need to do something in the meantime. Maybe you're down on your luck; the old lady puts the pressure on to find something. You're waitin' for the big time when only the small time shows its ugly face. There's not a lot of plannin' to it. I mean, whoever thinks that they will be unemployed? You know the way it goes. . . . After a certain point, however, *the phones* choose you.

3. *Market displacement.* The salesman assesses his skills. If he chooses to remain on the telephones, he must either go back to selling cold cards (calling potential customers cold, with no previous telephone interaction), a frightful thought, and thereby earn a newcomer's pay (even more dreadful), or perhaps he might work as a manager in his industry specialty. If he reveals his telephone experience, however, he will not be hired, because he presents too great a threat to ownership (he may steal paper, divert accounts, or be indifferent to company training techniques).

An owner has commented on his decision not to hire an informant in chemical sales, who, over four years, had become an unemployed drunkard after being a sales manager with a company-paid car and gasoline credit card, a 2 percent override on what his team sold for the week, and the difference between his weekly draw ($1,000) and his commissionable percentage of gross sales (given as a monthly bonus) given off the books in cash (several hundred dollars in a good month). With nine years of telephone experience, the man failed to get a part-time ($5 an hour) solicitor position in a telemarketing operation: "The man is a drinker. I can understand that. The pressure can get to you after being on the phones for a long time. I used to visit with the grape myself a number of years ago. But this guy is either a liar or a threat. I don't want him working here. With nine years of chemical sales experience he is simply too dangerous [he will learn the business and start his own] or too stupid [any boiler who would work for $5 an hour can't be a pro to begin with]. He may be down on his luck, but I can't risk it."

That is part of what it means to be burned out in the boiler room world. Aside from being unemployed, the man has no respectable job history to report, and his skills are not likely to be well received by either conventional businesses or by other boiler rooms.[19] When experienced telephone salesmen lose their jobs, they face economic oblivion.

Personality factors loom large at this point. Some are submissive, some readjust, and some are amazingly adaptive. One informant took a two-week vacation after his company folded. "Take the good with the bad. You can't let this line of work get to you," he rationalized. Some become violent. One informant reports that an owner was gunned down (injured with firearms) by an irate manager who was fired. Sometimes a man may have family contacts or a family business in which he can participate. In most cases, however, these options were explored—and rejected—long before he first took up a telephone to earn a living.

The lone pro must change his line if he wishes to remain on the telephones. Telephone work is what he knows. "It's the thrill of the deal," says one informant. "It gets into your blood." Experience tells him that if he remains on the telephones he must shoot for a high-commission deal and try to recoup lost earnings. Because quick income is his goal, he will refrain from product boiler rooms. He becomes bolder. He will consider, perhaps for the first time, either the advisories (betting and investment rooms) or the scams (high-risk, high-return, fly-by-night operations). He knows that he has the skill, but can he learn the line? Can he get the edge (a working knowledge that makes the operation profitable)? Denied middle-class status (regular employment at a salary he now needs to support his family), he will try for middle-class income, at least for a while.

Working the scams or the advisories, he will find fellow travelers (many men with experience similar to his); virtually no imposed controls (what one perceptive informant called "self-hypnosis"—sales hype, ringing bells, and so forth); and straight commission, usually starting at 15 to 25 percent and perhaps going as high as 35 percent. Here he will survive based on his ability alone. As he sees it, he has nothing to lose. If he is successful, he will earn sufficient money to keep his shop running after he learns the ropes. So, in most cases, the owner of a one-man shop begins moonlighting for a more sophisticated telephone room.

For most of these men the foreclosing of options for legitimate employment, the declining ability to meet the economic needs to which they and their families have become accustomed, and the salary they could earn in a conventional job are at least as important as the imagined lure of sole proprietorship. Few are idealists in this regard. One thing is certain: Boiler room owners are among the highest paid of all who work the telephones.

In spite of the observed pattern suggesting that most one-man shops have a difficult time staying in business, not all of these operations inevitably fail. It is more accurate to say that the form is unstable. "Lone phoners" ultimately transform their operations or go to work for someone else. There are some successes, but they are, unfortunately, invisible because those who run one-man shops typically withdraw from telephone room social circles. One respondent, for example, who sold both chemicals and oil and gas leases, got out of the oil and gas business before the federal busts in 1983 by taking his sucker list (a list of previous customers) and raising $15,000 in venture capital from three of these accounts to start his own coin operation (numismatic materials). He has broken off all social contact with the world of telephone salesmen, however. Said another informant who sold chemicals with him, "Hey, we used to be pretty tight. We worked at the same chemical house. We've lost touch. He just doesn't talk to me anymore. Funny, he is a nice guy. But he doesn't want to have anything to do with chemical salesmen."

One-man shops are the sites of pure individualistic entrepreneurial activity. Small companies thrive or perish based on the sole efforts of their owners. One thing is clear: The reality of being alone in a room with a card deck and a telephone for eight hours a day (sometimes more and sometimes weekends) does not correspond to the romantic image of being in business for yourself or being your own boss. One philosophically inclined informant saw the irony of his current position when he confided, "I've been pitchin' the self-sufficiency part of owning your own business for some time. You know, quoting from *INC* and *Money* and *The Wall Street Journal*. You've got to be careful here so that you don't get taken in by your own line! Nobody ever said anything about the walls, staring at the four walls in your bedroom as you wait for the [telephone] line to connect you to the next mooch [laughs]."

If the owner of a one-man shop is successful, he will acquire more salesmen. If this proves psychologically rewarding and/or economically cost-effective, administrative staff will then be hired. Once the sales force is in place, a boiler room is fully defined, and heat becomes a socially interactive phenomenon. The owner will face the same struggles and rewards as do those who run small businesses, but he will do so in the company of others.[20]

Larger Operations

A larger operation may have different kinds of managers: one in charge of trainees, one in charge of regulars, and a general manager who oversees both. If the shop is large enough, a highly specialized sales force will be instructed by a product manager whose job involves having substantial technical knowledge of the product being promoted, for example, how an electronic control module in an automobile operates and its manufacturer's specifications (specs).

A product manager tends to be the oldest man in a telephone room and is recruited from the industries being serviced. He also serves a legitimizing function because in most cases he is in, not of, a boiler room. Technical knowledge gives him status and a salary. Any sales as he may make bring in extra income for both himself and the company. Because product managers have many years experience "on the outside," they, unlike most telephone room workers but like the staff, are necessary employees and not part of the social control environment. As one pro explained, "He [the product manager] just *knows*. Go to him with any questions that you have. He knows all the specs on the products. He is a real nice guy and really knows what our line is all about. But don't ask him how to sell. He's not a salesman. Yeah, he has his accounts, but he doesn't know how to *sell* them. He just chats and takes orders. But he is not paid to sell. He is one of the few folks around here with a real job. He could find a job at any auto dealership tomorrow if he wanted to."

The division of labor on a sales floor also defines the character of the telephone operation. For example, the larger chemical houses may have a verifier, and a gas house will also have an experienced pro who serves as a close man or takeover man who stands ready to take over a telephone conversation started by a less-experienced salesman who is seen to be in need of another voice (the use of seasoned talent) to close the deal.

Coin rooms use a loader (a pro in charge of increasing the rate at which regular customers continue to purchase). This is done by creating the impression of urgency, as is the case with the "European estate purchase" pitch, for example, where common British coins are promoted as being both rare and heretofore unavailable for sale.

Some operations also use fronters (non-salesmen who make the initial cold call, qualify the prospect, mildly promote the value of the service being offered, and send out company literature). Fronters are highly specialized; although some do not have enough skill to close deals themselves, others have previous experience as salesmen and have discovered that specializing in making initial presentations (which are followed up by a regular or a pro) involves less stress, creates fewer problems, and takes less effort than working on the sales floor. If done properly, this can also be more lucrative.

A fronter at an expanding fast-track scam (a get-rich-quick scheme) can also earn substantially more than a legitimate business would likely pay for a talent that is useful only in a boiler room. Informants report a professional fronter earning more than $600 per week, plus bonuses, for roughly twenty-five hours of work. He is called "Earnie the Front" in his telephone room, is well liked, and is an older man with many years of telephone experience. He has, thus far, resisted the efforts of the pros to convert him into a salesman.

The larger houses, and the most profitable scams, can have absentee owners (money men) who finance the operation but leave its management to professionals. It is difficult to obtain data on money men. Coin houses, however, have a reputation for being financed by dentists, doctors, and those in real estate. I am led to believe that family contacts are important, however. This is especially true as well in the operation of finance house boiler rooms (sometimes called "bank houses" because they involve working with banks and other financial institutions).

These operations are family owned and raise money in $500,000 multiples by aggregating secured collateral loans for smaller sums from investors. They make money on the spread, perhaps as large as one net point (percent) between the lower interest rates offered to large investors and the higher rates required of small ones. They then loan the money out through banks—and by networking—to smaller customers. The "1 point" would be split, half for the boiler room and half for the pro. According to one informant, "On a $500,000 deal, that's five dimes [$5,000]. Yep. I think you would agree that that's big enough pop for the room to pursue."

Unlike the coin houses, where the money man remains invisible, in finance house operations the back room or inner circle of the boiler room is composed of family members and receives frequent visits from money men. No salesman, no matter how skilled, is admitted into this inner circle.

The division of labor in a boiler room is determined by whether products or services are for sale. The sale of products requires packaging, shipping, delivery, accounting, receiving raw materials, and the allocation of space for these procedures, operations, and work requirements, in addition to having a sales force. The sale of a service requires only salesmen, telephones, and a simple bookkeeping system. Because intangibles are sold, these operations, other things being equal, are both more lucrative and require more skill on the part of salesmen than is the case for product boiler rooms.

Finding a Niche

All boiler rooms thrive because of imperfections of one kind or another. Sometimes these lie in the marketplace, sometimes in customers' perceptions (amplified by the sales process), and sometimes they are due to the manner in which the boiler room itself is organized. Market irregularities are often the result of fluctuations in supply and demand.

In certain industries, for example, one common flaw involves the permeability of normal sources of supply through which products are vended through regional distributors to retail and independent repair outlets. New car dealerships are a typical case.[21] They acquire parts and inventory through authorized distributors who sell original equipment manufacture (OEM) parts in OEM boxes. Automotive repair shops purchase replacement items through aftermarket vendors. Under normal circumstances, both traditional sources of supply offer quality control guarantees and institutionalized methods of payment and crediting procedures—as required. If a customer receives defective merchandise, there is recourse. Recent increases in imported automobile sales and the growing market for related parts and components have given rise, however, to the gray market and the simulated market.

Gray-market inventories are the result of dumping (the practice of underwriting or amortizing for-export production costs so the product is priced higher in the home market than overseas) or the diversion of product from the normally designated export channel, that is, goods meant to be shipped overseas are diverted to the local market. Simulated items are copies of OEM parts and component assemblies manufactured by foreign and domestic producers without benefit of OEM research, development, and quality controls. This results in minimal production costs and an inexpensive (and, for the most part, inferior) replacement product to be sold in the aftermarket. Taking advantage of the gray and simulated markets permits boiler rooms to offer lower price as an incentive to move inventory. In both cases, what is lacking in legitimacy or quality can be made up through the use of sales skill and enticements.

The bulk of boiler rooms serve as unacknowledged middle-men for distributors. Larger houses drop-ship the product (using the boiler room's shipping labels) and are themselves invoiced using standard commercial terms, for example, net due in thirty days. Smaller rooms simply repackage bulk purchases. Boiler room operatives thus ultimately serve as a cost-free sales force, because there is sufficient markup to cover the cost of the product, and salesmen are not paid until the boiler room is. This arrangement is appealing to many suppliers, and the boiler room has at least thirty days to generate the sales from which the funds to cover its current inventory are then extracted.

All boiler rooms operate under the premise that if enough presentations are made, without regard to what is being sold, a certain portion will result in sales and a somewhat smaller fraction will result in reorders. These together define the active account base of the operation. Once this base is established, specialized talent (pros and owners) are set to secretly renegotiate the original terms of trade contingent upon future sales.

Thus, logistically, the bulk of those in a telephone room will be busy opening new accounts. By so doing they establish the initial business arrangement with customers where a sale comes to define a baseline relative to product expectations and price. Future sales—and any required adjustments—are made from back rooms, where the most experienced salesmen negotiate price, quality, and incentives such as premiums, rebates, and discounts. This assures that repeat customers will receive more favored treatment than first-time buyers. The greater the number of the latter, the larger the profit and the greater number of sweeter deals that can be offered to the former. At the extreme, products and gifts can be given away to a select few. Because the vast bulk of a boiler room's customers make purchases at the terms established for new accounts, there are always resources to redistribute.

A boiler room finds a niche not in the general marketplace (competing with other firms in a manner described by economics textbooks) but rather when a favorable internal relation is established between its different kinds of customers: first-time buyers and regular accounts. It takes the profits generated from the former and pays its overhead, ownership, and management. The house then passes out some rewards to the latter (lower prices and/or premiums) and awaits the inevitable contraction of the business brought about by the inevitable shrinkage of these two populations.

When products are involved, a boiler room has to cover current purchases and make a profit. When a service is involved, it only has to race against the clock—hence the general accuracy of the statement that such companies are ready to fly by night. As long as the rate of new account acquisitions grows faster than the rate at which established accounts drop off, however, boiler rooms stay in business.

The Product Houses

I'm a product man, I can't sell air. . . . But, look at this [shows newspaper article]. These guys were selling oil tanker docking rights, supposedly with a fuels broker. Funny thing, there was no dock; there were no rights; there was no fuel; there were no tankers. It was promoted as a speculative venture for new port construction sometime in the future. What minds these guys have! It's hard enough for me to sell what I do [chemicals]. These guys were selling nothing at all. How do you learn to do that? I wish I knew, I'd like to meet someone like that. I bet you could learn a lot.
    —a pro in a product house, musing over other telephone deals

Industries and Boiler Rooms

Absent the sales force that distinguishes a product house from other varieties of distributing companies, it shares with them the need to acquire product. Merchandise for resale is obtained from wholesalers, liquidators, manufacturers, brokers, and conventional suppliers. Although telephone pitchmen can, and do, make virtually every conceivable claim for their wares, they can only procure what the marketplace provides. The first contingency to which a boiler room must adjust is alignment with the mechanics of supply.

Product houses work industries that are known and named by the types of products they sell. By far, the most common are industrial chemicals and replacement parts for automobiles, trucks, and small engines. To a much smaller degree, some cater only to specialized fields such as office supplies, tools, and assemblers of kits of varied kinds. Some parts houses offer equipment such as testers, gauges, and hardware used by mechanics and tradesmen. Occasionally, a shop will offer electronic goods such as calculators, radios, portable televisions, and computer games as premiums. Once products and premiums are inventoried or ordered through companies that specialize in drop shipment (invoicing and delivery), customers must be sought—the prime objective of a sales force.

Potential customers are grouped into categories conceptualized using the system of Standard Industrial Classification (SIC) common to the Census Bureau, because that is the format used by list brokers who provide the names, addresses, telephone numbers, and sometimes demographic or financial data. Product houses avoid residential customers for reasons that will shortly become clear.

When delivered to a sales force on sheets or on index cards, the names and industry-identification data relevant to potential customers (prospects) are formally called "leads" but may be informally called "SICs," "cats," "hot cats," "bleeders" (because the print sometimes runs and readily mixes with other inks, hand perspiration, and colored underlining markers), and "wild cards." If a business can be identified using SIC codes or is listed in the Yellow Pages, more likely than not it is fair game for boiler rooms with products to sell and premiums to give away.

Newcomers to the sales floor are free to invent their own lore—and most do. One salesman, for example, thought that "503" referred to a hot category reserved only for the pros. Over time, the survivors of his hiring cohort were called "The 503s" by regulars. As in basic military training and other contexts where many perform their tasks anonymously, any piece of information that marks the terrain may take hold to provide a sense of meaning to the scene. In such a manner do boilers acquire the special languages that influence their work routines: languages describing the world of products, customers, and sales.

Telephone rooms are always seeking customers. Salesmen seek to identify those with purchasing authority (an important step in the qualification process) and attempt to make sales. A call from a product house is always a business call and, although not always presented as such, is always designed to locate a buyer. That is the single most important, and time-consuming, task a salesman must accomplish.

Absent the name of a buyer, a knowledge of telephone numbers, corporate titles, and locations is useless. Once a person with purchasing authority is linked accurately to a company and a telephone number, however, the lead acquires value: a form of equity. This is more important to the house than making an initial sale, for even if a salesman fails in his attempt to sell on first contact, or on subsequent attempts, there will be others with more skill or luck who may call at different times—perhaps, ultimately, from different boiler rooms—who will likely be successful.

At the bottom of the skill, prestige, and profit hierarchies that characterize the different types of product houses are the office supply operators, called "pencil-pushers." These firms award inexpensive premiums composed of obsolescent advertising fare (promotional pens or trinkets such as mugs and refrigerator magnets) and sell distressed merchandise and what is probably best described as office humor items: ceramic replicas of jackasses depicting "The Boss"; ashtrays that carry the slogan "Official U.S. Taxpayer"; carnival prizes (inexpensive dolls, toys, posters, and cartoons); and somewhat off-color items such as salt and pepper shakers shaped like a woman's breasts, many renditions of the word *asshole* (on T-shirts, pocket knives, and ceramic figurines), and ceramic or wooden wall plaques referring to outhouses.

A pencil-pusher's prime market is composed of small businesses located in rural areas and small cities geographically isolated from large office supply discounters. Popular types of accounts include gun dealers, bowling alleys, garages, taverns, small restaurants, seed and feed dealers, country stores, and barbershops—those settings where men tend to congregate, or briefly assemble, to pass the time or conduct business. Pencil-pusher operations involve a dying breed of wholesalers and small vendors who were successful during the 1970s marketing tourist fare to seasonal resort areas across the United States.

Before this line of work became dominated by a few large wholesalers, it was composed of thousands of small independent vendors called "jobbers," who maintained a small stock of items and made the rounds to local businesses in station wagons, vans, or with their automobile trunks filled with merchandise. Many moonlighted from their regular jobs to work flea markets during the weekends and on holidays, and some were once employed as salesmen who sold or rented office equipment to businesses. Nearing retirement or already in its earlier stages and displaced by social change that renders small distributors obsolescent in the wake of the growth of warehouse outlets, shopping malls, and the widespread use of automobiles, these businessmen turn to the telephones. Folksy conversation, regional humor (many farm-joke items and some racist fare are available), and odd-lot pricing move their wares. All have the salesman's skill of being able to engage a potential customer in a running conversation on essentially trivial matters, a talent also mastered by barbers, barmen, and many in the personal services industries. A pitchman describes the logic of the market and making sales:

> They've got product, some prizes, and the phones. Hey, that's all anybody ever needs, right? You use the odd-lot price. It's an old trick they use at auctions. You move a group of things instead of pricing each item separately. So, let's say pencils cost a nickel and sell for a dime apiece: ten to the blister pack [$1], six packs to the box [$6], six boxes to the carton [$36], and ten cartons to the crate [$360]. Hey, where are you going with that? It will take you all day to sell $360 worth of pencils. Nobody can use that much. So you tell the customer that there are *twelve* pencils to the pack, *five* packs to the box [sixty pencils]. Here, you've trimmed. You know, you still have sixty pencils [six blister packs of ten each], but you've presented only *five* items [five packs of twelve pencils]. Trims are easy because it's easier to sell five things over six: the customer thinks he's spending less money. Then you bump [increase the

size of the order] in the packaging and play it [conceal information] in the pitch. You tell the customer that they [the pencils] come in the twin-pack [two boxes: 120 pencils] at only $14^1/_2$ cents each. What a deal! So you've got an extra $4^1/_2$ cents on each pencil because most people can't easily multiply $14^1/_2 \times 120$ in their heads. Besides, you never tell the *total* price, however, just the first break-out: $14^1/_2$ cents; twelve to the pack [$1.74], about $1.75. But they've actually bought a *twin*-pack, which is not twice the pack price [$2 \times \$1.74$], but ten times as much [$120 \times 14^1/_2 = \$17.40$]. Then you go into the promotion for the premium. . . . After they laugh at the presentation, you load 'em with the pen deal, and the paper deal, and the staple promotion, or whatever, then close 'em with the the the gift of the week. . . . When they get burned [smiles], well, it's a *small* burn, and people need the stuff anyway, so there is practically no heat. . . . You never line-close these deals [price-out each component of the sale], you sell *the package*. And, what the hell, it's only office supplies, so the buyer, in most cases, will absorb the loss rather than bring his foolishness to anyone's attention. It works because pencils, pens, and paper are something that every business uses and that few people think seriously about. That's the in: you talk about it and get an order by manipulating the offer. After all, no one buys just *one* pencil, you buy a dozen. So, we *sell* eighteen; it throws them off. The pitch is very hard to learn at first, because you have to have all this stuff [price, quantity, packaging] worked out beforehand.

As an industry, chemical boiler rooms have the most extensive division of labor. Those that specialize in agricultural chemicals are called "farm houses" because they sell primarily to farmers. There are many varieties, however, and each type of farm operation (hog, horse, cattle, dairy, grain, fish, tobacco, or chicken) has a number of boiler rooms specializing exclusively in that sector of the agricultural market. Although the majority of farmers use chemicals of some kind, it may take thousands of collective telephone hours to develop a line to talk knowledgeably about which chemicals should be applied at what times of the season and in what quantities, which price ranges will be effective, and which premiums will be appealing. The plot thickens, naturally, as a direct result of discoveries made by the chemical industry itself.

Rooms that concentrate on selling chemicals to industries other than farming are called "industry shops" because they do not sell to farmers, and they purvey industrial maintenance and other chemicals. Manufacturers, distributors, park services, institutions, hotels and restaurants, jewelry shops, shopping centers, airports, property managers, and truck fleets are common clients. Within a specific subcategory—say, property managers—there is further specialization; for example, residential, commercial, industrial, or institutional. These may, in turn, be further subdivided. "Schools," for example, includes public, private, elementary, and secondary institutions as well as colleges and universities. "Research facilities," yet another category, may or may not include centers of higher education, and may or may not have identified grounds-keepers, machinists, welders, mechanics, and janitors.

Each category may yield handfuls of specialized users, and that is only discovered by actively working the telephones. Functional task assignments also vary within a specific category of buyer, and these may provide clues to product requirements. Within the hotel industry, for example, the food and beverage manager may, or may not, purchase disinfectant cleaners, but he or she might be interested in nonslip protective coatings for walkways and high-traffic areas. If a salesman discovers that insurance premiums, for example, are real concerns among a certain kind of buyer, he modifies the pitch to reach those customers who may share this interest. When a pitch interests a buyer, the lead becomes hot; if it taps a type of customer heretofore unencountered, the lead is called a "newbie."

Referrals within a company are called "insides," but occasionally a boiler's promotion lands a referral to someone (a friend, colleague, or associate) located outside the corporate sphere of the initial contact. These are called "outsides." The odd case where a referral is made to a person disliked by the initial contact is called a "bummer" because the referral was spitefully made to annoy, upset, or irritate the referred party to be called. There are inside and outside bummers.

A certain percentage of all buyers and referrals will be more interested in a free premium than in the actual product being sold, and a skilled salesman will accommodate. The very skilled derive some usable knowledge from every call. Thus, even a bummer can sometimes reveal information that transcends the personalities of the called. Insides, for example, can reveal the strengths of divisional tensions, that is, sales versus marketing or where different profit centers (which contain buyers of varied kinds) may be located. Outsides can reveal industry rivalries or economic conditions in a sector of an industry. A pro can sometimes turn around a bummer by working on his pitch so as to solicit a favorable response from an otherwise wasted call.[1]

At all of the sites probed by a boiler's initial call, there is a person who ultimately puts these products to use. This is the elusive buyer. He or she is likely bored and invisible to most on the scene because the nature of their work is typically accomplished during nonpeak hours after regular staff have left for the day, and it is accomplished in the back regions of a building, plant, office, or work site.

The invisible army of helpers, mechanics, cleaners, fine-tuners, calibrators, servicers, maintenance personnel, and their overseers have access to two things of great importance to a boiler room: an order pad and a telephone.

Some chemical houses run contests for the salesman who discovers the most exotic buyer and makes a sale. Winners have included a brothel manager in Nevada; a "tool-pusher" on an offshore oil rig in the Gulf of Mexico (contacted by mobile telephone); a station master for a railroad; a horse breeder who specializes in Arabian stock (contacted at an airport where he keeps his private airplane, it was a double hit because two lines of product could be offered); and a mobster who owns a bar in Chicago. The contact that got the most applause was a safety engineer at a very large aerospace company on the West Coast who was contacted in a real boiler room, of the steam pipes and gauges variety, at a metals fabrication facility.

The longer a product boiler room has been in business, the greater the likelihood that it will specialize in selling to a narrow band of customers within an industry. But there is always some experimentation. If sales are brisk in a heretofore untried category, there will be an effort to saturate that sector of the industry with calls as quickly as possible (finding a virgin) before word leaks out via the grapevine that profits can be made or lest the competition beats the room to sure deals, either because they get there first or because they hire those fired from a given shop and thus have a working knowledge of the category.

Such efforts permit salesmen to acquire trade secrets (sales techniques that are effective for a specific kind of buyer in a targeted industry), which are a form of social capital that boiler rooms must tap, or develop, in order to ensure economic survival. Periods of intense work probing for new customers crystalize a salesman's knowledge of both the target industry and the relevant sales techniques. Because of this, turnover within a product house helps increase the general level of skill in a region's telephone sales force; a boiler trained in working more than one industry commands a premium when he changes jobs.[2]

By selling product a company becomes a product house. Its sales force reads what literature as may be made available from manufacturers (or is produced internally at larger operations) and modifies it to fit the presentation. Sales managers become proficient in learning the language of the firm's potential customers: from the customers themselves (as part of developing a pitch), from salesmen who ask questions, and in the process of dealing with customers' problems and complaints. The decision about which particular product will come to define a shop stems from the owner's previous experience and inclinations.

All boilers are engaged in a continuing process of education. It is the routine of making calls that creates boredom and permits innovative techniques to be developed, honed, otherwise refined, and incorporated into the daily round of selling and overcoming objections. Because experienced boilers typically have work histories older than the companies that employ them, the experiences learned in other shops can be useful as rooms adopt to changing markets. In the words of one salesman, "I've got to spice up my pitch. You say the same tired thing, over and over, and *you* get tired. The customer gets tired. The tone of the room dies. Man, this becomes *one tired operation* [laughs]. I'm gonna use some intros and closes I worked out in the 'light bulb game' [boiler rooms that sell light bulbs to raise funds for nonprofit organizations]. I've got to put some spark into the old pitcharoo."

Upswings in enthusiasm resulting from the attempt of a boiler room to seek and expand its market usually produce short-term gains in the take-home pay of the sales force. Locating new types of customers breathes new life into a company and helps workers psychologically postpone facing the eventuality of a pay cut, the loss of a job, or both.[3] At such times the room is said to be "up": deals are being cut, new information is being incorporated into the pitch, and bonuses are common. The swirl of activity also permits the management to use the skills of a salesman at a fixed level of expenditure more fully. Although a salesman's creativity may transform a boiler room's inventory, he is only paid on orders written.

In some shops managers are specifically tasked with developing new territories. In others this occurs by trial and error, but it is also influenced by the differing degrees of skill and experience of the recently employed. In one chemical boiler room, for example, a newly hired salesman requested that he be allowed to "work airports" in lieu of the industries currently assigned. The owner, being sensitive to innovation, agreed. By so doing, a new line of customers was acquired. The owner comments, "Hey, this is working out fine. The new man is OK. I won this one. Some other room paid for his experience. Their loss; my gain. They should have never let a guy like Jack leave in the first place. I could use ten of him. It would make my life a lot easier."

All product houses vend a number of items which, together, constitute a product line. This may be available as a generic group of devices or components—that is, automobile brake, transmission parts, or liquids and powders—in the case of chemicals, which are made available in standard industrial drums, containers, or tubs. Here the similarity with conventional distributors ends, however. A boiler room can be as creative as its suppliers' catalogs are extensive. A product house sells to whomever it can convince that it can fulfill the role of supplier. That operationally defines the goal of the company and distinguishes it from other types of boiler room operations. In some shops this universe of customers changes regularly. As an owner, somewhat disquieted by my inability to understand this inherent flexibility (and who was asked at an inopportune time), observes,

Look. We sell chemicals. . . . Well, sort of. What a dumb question! [pause, rephrase]. . . . I mean, we have a line of solvents, degreasers, and additives that we sell to farmers. That's *this* month. It all depends on what the [sales] floor wants, and which leads we buy. I'm always open to suggestions, you know that [mood improves]. Hell, let me tell you, Kansas City Mike [a salesman] just opened up [made a first sale to] dairies last week off of the new leads. So now we are learning about dairy farms. I never saw a damn cow before, but K.C. over there [gestures to Kansas City Mike] likes to talk it up with anyone who will listen [K.C. smiles, acknowledging the recognition]. He's good. Damn good [gesture of a thumbs-up sign in Kansas City Mike's direction]. Way ta go, Kansas City![4]

More heavily capitalized boiler rooms have large warehouses that may be physically adjacent to the sales floor or many miles away. They also tend to use an extended billing procedure—net ten days or net twenty days—and have access to 800 numbers (toll-free) for incoming customer service calls, placing orders, and making contacts with suppliers. Being larger operations (employing more than sixty people), they also have routinized crediting procedures and a full-time staff to handle shipping, billing, receivables, inventory, and packaging.

They also vend multiple products as well as entire lines of product, in the conventional meaning of this term (i.e., a functionally grouped array organized around a common assembly such as battery cables—automotive and marine—with which the related lubricants, cleaners, housings, and hardware share a common relationship). In one product house the inventory was composed of dozens of lines that totaled more than five thousand items, all of which could be combined in numerous ways to make tens of thousands of possibilities that might constitute an order.

Rather than essentially reselling commercially produced fluids and powders (chemicals), parts operations redistribute (and, in some cases, contract for manufacture) assemblies, components, and accessories. The illusion structure is somewhat different in that the technical knowledge necessary for discussing a particular product line can be substantial. Formal training to enhance product knowledge and build sales technique is required and provided. By working the whole country, parts houses thrive on the fact that tens of thousands of economically marginal garages, repair shops, service outlets, and other small businesses are engaged in a vast turnover process due to illnesses, retirements, close-downs, changes in ownership, and market fluctuation. In addition, there are double, perhaps triple, this number of mom-and-pop companies with an eye to cutting costs or receiving free gifts.

Product houses serve these customers in a market created by geographic dispersion. Many small companies are tens (sometimes hundreds) of miles from established distribution networks for conventionally produced products and components. By offering "service to your doorstep" (a line from the pitch), which is accomplished through the parcel delivery services, competitive pricing compared to what local suppliers charge, and a "full-satisfaction guarantee" (quite narrowly defined), a ready market awaits. That fact runs counter to the views of classical economists who claim that it is concentration and population density that influence the location of suppliers.[5] What may be true for conventional suppliers is often irrelevant to boiler rooms.

Unlike conventional distributors, boiler rooms never issue a fixed price list for their products, because price is always negotiable. Customers are always separated by many miles—and therefore not part of any unified communications network—so the price charged for a given product can, and does, vary substantially. Moreover, the social division of labor in many large companies is so specialized that physical proximity—historically an aid in comparison pricing—becomes irrelevant because customers carry different job titles and work for different divisions. Thus, a kitchen manager, a building superintendent, and a machinist for the same firm may be sold the same product at different prices. Although housed in the same building or within walking distance of each other, these customers are usually unknown to each other. Boiler room management is fully aware that it may be months before customers can identify, trace, diagnose, and correctly attribute a failed product to a telephone purchase.

Most rooms do not intentionally vend defective merchandise, but the likelihood of defectives being mixed in with sound products depends on the cash-flow position of the boiler room. Some houses acquire very well made products through closeouts and liquidations, and, if such items are in short supply, customers will be delighted to have access to otherwise unobtainable goods. All the larger parts houses contain at least a few salesmen who specialize in locating hard-to-find items.

Sales of this nature can give a boiler room a comparative advantage. As is true in all businesses, any customer loyalty so earned has future value. For some shops, that possibility may permit a boiler room to transform into a more conventional business (chapter 5). In specialized product houses (electronics, automobile and transmission parts, marina supplies, and fleet specialties), premiums are abolished and specials take their place; selected products are either given away or sold at a very low price in lieu of touting gift merchandise. Routinized talk of volume discounts begins to make its way into the pitch.

The nature of work in these larger operations, over time, becomes more routine, standardized, and less demanding of sales creativity. As specialization makes a pitchman's skill less relevant, the market begins to require higher levels of specialty knowledge because manufacturers' specs change constantly. Catalogs containing industry standards and applications guidelines begin to appear on salesmen's desks, and customers are sold a wider range of specialized products.

The creative expansion of a boiler room's market is more likely in smaller shops because of the direct involvement of the owner or owners in the sales process. For example, one boiler room acquired new types of customers when the owner of the firm "scouted new territories." That resulted in selling germicidal disinfectants to horse breeders and hog farmers; selling diesel additives to tobacco farmers for use in their "bores" (diesel-fired dryers); and selling nonslip snow-melt pellets directly to apartment house managers. Moreover, after a few hours of intense telephoning "to get the numbers up" (make sales), the content of work breaks in small shops turns into generalized discussion of products, markets, and the kinds of responses the house pitch is receiving from potential customers.

Bursts of creativity and innovation increase the level of interest in the work, the camaraderie among the workers, and the firm's profits. More insightful owners encourage this when sales are brisk, because it is seen as a form of insurance against the inevitable downside of boiler room markets: seasonality, account saturation, and cash-flow problems. The less insightful, or those with poorly managed operations, may perish if they fail to innovate.

The social impact of innovation, however, has a hidden dimension: It legitimizes the perceptions of opportunities in the industry. Many salesmen incorrectly reason that because certain product houses are more innovative than others, higher wages or better working conditions may be generally available; that one sort of product line has a greater commission-income potential than do others; and that there is a substantial variation in the dollar value of premiums offered or bonuses received. That may, of course, be true in specific instances, but it is not a valid generalization across product boiler rooms. It is a classic example of the fallacy of composition. Premiums typically average about 5 percent or less of the value of an order, regardless of what is being sold; working conditions vary with the size of the operation; and commission income is determined by whether a salesman is a trainee, a regular, or a pro, not by the kind of product a boiler room sells. Thus, a pro with an active account list of regular customers will always earn more than any other regular salesman within his company and more than a trainee in any boiler room operation. His relative standing compared to other pros, however, depends on where he plies his trade rather than the industry being worked.

In spite of their training and skill in manipulating the perceptions of others, boilers are willing to believe unsubstantiated generalizations concerning their own line of work. This is so common that it is institutionalized in what one informant referred to as playing the "grass is greener number," as illustrated by the musings of a salesman in a farm chemical house: "Boy. You wait 'til we get to sell 'Industry.' They're making money hand over fist at East Coast Chemical—selling protective coatings. And the premiums. . . . Hell, they give out TV sets and fishing rods, not cheese packages. I heard that the top man there made three grand last week. Hell, all we get to do is sell these stupid farmers."

Contrast that view with the comments of a salesman in an industry shop: "You know, I wish we could get the room to sell farmers like I did at Nation House. Farmers have lots of money. Hell, with the government subsidies and the Russian grain deal they are rolling in money. One guy sold a fifty-five-gallon drum of diesel additive to one big farmer in Arkansas. He made a cool $300 in ten minutes! On one deal! They are too rigid at this company. We sell building managers and jails, that's it. Boy, let me at those farmers, boy-o-boy, and the kids will have shoes real quick. I can taste that bottle of Jack Daniels right now!"

A telemarketer who vends contracts in a service shop likewise fantasizes: "Give me industry! There ain't no mooch here. No prizes and premiums. You can't make a living if you are not selling a real product. You know, something a customer can feel in his hands or you can give a premium for—like a hunting knife. But, service contracts? Where's that going? They [customers] can't even *see* it. It's a piece of paper, that's all."

Rather than increasing the level of scrutiny a salesman might hypothetically apply to his position, owners and managers sometimes encourage such wistful thinking as the ideology of a "golden phone" (as one insightful informant called it), which glamorizes the entire industry. Typically, after letting salesmen vent their frustrations and fantasies in such a manner, a sharp manager will pick up the telephone and immediately cut a deal. Nothing works better to silence opposition and build morale than the fresh flow of commission dollars over problematic terrain. Less-skilled managers are forced to convene sales meetings because that is the only form of persuasion they know.

All product boiler rooms offer some combination of premiums, incentives, gray market merchandise, items of inferior quality, specials of one kind or another, and bribes to sell products.[6] The precise mix determines the style of the house and thereby the emergent chemistry of the room, which will dictate which divergent evolutionary path a product house will follow. It can become a small, lean, creative organization wherein the owners, a few pros, and the regulars aspire to sell virtually anything and everything to a widening band of customers only limited by the size of the warehouse, the budget, and the ways in which the salesmen can imagine how their line can be used.

In a small shop the corporate names used by the house, the array of products offered, and the kinds of customers sold are flexible. For example, a sales-

man may go out as (make a sales call as) an outside rep whose apparent physical location is limited only by his ability to mimic regional dialects and voice
inflections. He may sell different lines of product that are limited only by the
number of dedicated telephone lines the company wishes to purchase. In small
shops, products sold to a certain type of industry have a number of telephone
lines and salesmen so assigned; other products and salesmen use other lines.
The illusion of an extensive division of labor is created through the call-routing process common to larger, conventional companies.[7]

If customers are not particularly responsive to his role as the outside rep—
and the repository of tall tales related to being on the road that are worked
into the pitch (these come from the salesman's experiences and imagination
as well as from information other salesmen may care to share)—a boiler takes
a different role and adopts any number of personas. He becomes a "sales
manager," a "market researcher," a "staffer" (a person in, from, or affiliated
with a part of the country in a distant time zone, such as New York, California, or any imagined exotic place that can be portrayed in a believable manner), or an "operator" (one who appears to hold a fixed position that is part
of a commonly understood division of labor, such as marketing, advertising,
sales, promotions, product development, and research).

A salesman's skill defines much of the staging within the symbolic universe from which he works: how the product is perceived and the kind and
size of premiums offered. Technical product specifications, applications guidelines, and various compatibilities with machinery or techniques (i.e., lubric-
ities and dilution requirements) are secondary to what one salesman called
the "size of the prize"—the size of the premium, gift, or bribe.

For a pro, even a company's inventory is irrelevant; if he makes a sale, the
product will be acquired afterward. The relevant folk adage is a common one:
"If you *sell* it, we'll *get* it." Small shops have a seminar quality to them. For
a variable portion of the workday a handful of salesmen are almost as engaged
in interactions among each other (working on the pitch, listening for objections, discussing business strategies and product attributes, training each other,
and working on the close) as they are with potential customers.

A small shop, however, contains desks and telephones. All else is fictive.
There are no production facilities, no centers of administrative support, no
extensive communications networks, and no divisions, departments, research
activities, or work crews. Most of what is commonly thought of as being the
constituents of a bustling office and the language landscape surrounding images of industrial production (pallets, drums, forklifts, bays, machinery, workers) and distribution (loading docks, trucks, traffic, scheduling activities) are
merely props to be used as pitch lines. They are imagined contexts and backgrounds against, and within, which a presentation is delivered.

In larger product houses the division of labor is real. Salesmen spend a great deal of time "specing out" an order, and some have computer terminals to assist in the proper assignment of parts numbers and ordering requirements. Orders may take a few days to be processed by a specialized staff: while the front office checks a customer's credit, packers and shippers assemble the order. Premiums and specials require their own paperwork, and the proper annotation and computation of commission statements is done by a billing department and typically overseen by accountants. Warehouse tallies occur regularly, and buyers are hired to increase the level and quality of required acquisitions.

In these settings, the walls of the boilers' cubicles are filled with product announcements, pricing guidelines, shipping specifications, delivery rate charts, and lists of telephone numbers of the relevant company personnel corresponding to each of the administrative junctures required to process an order properly. In some shops salesmen have direct telephone lines to product, sales, and division managers. A large part of management activity in larger houses surrounds creating and enforcing the rules for telephoning.[8]

Because conventional suppliers are usually limited by a physical territory, available shipping arrangements, and the prohibitive cost of maintaining road salesmen, the telephone can uniquely be used to collect information useful for locating customers who, due to shipping delays, bad weather, or regional pulses in demand, find their normal supply channels inadequate. Pros are "fast on the phone"; they can cover a sizable geographic area, in real time, with a dozen or so strategic calls placed to regular customers. In an ironic sense that capability permits product houses to sometimes police as well as create a market for a product. Being sensitive to price and quality irregularities in their current product line, salesmen can often embellish its attributes because customers are responsive to small changes in the presentation of a pitch.

A salesman can also adjust much more quickly to changes in perceived customer needs than conventional industries can retool, modify their production facilities, or launch time-consuming research, advertising, and marketing campaigns. Boiler rooms were touting computer screen cleaner, for example, long before a conventional product appeared on the shelves. Common solvents and cleaners were promoted as being "CRT Approved" or given exotic nomenclature surrounding the terms *laser* and *turbo*. Although these claims are fictional, industrial glass-cleaner became one shop's hottest item after one salesman, enamored with the world of computers and their special language, began modifying his pitch. To meet the demand, the manager went to the supermarket, bought the largest quantity of glass-cleaner that he could stuff into his car trunk, and emptied the bottles into two-gallon industrial containers.

This case is illustrative of how certain kinds of cultural assumptions can be used to a boiler room's advantage. Because computer buyers become increasingly conditioned to the wonders of technology, they are sometimes uncritical of it. Moreover, all new users have already experienced the shock of the price structure in this market. A boiler room, as always, trades on a chain of commonly accepted assumptions that contain at least one weak link, one flaw. In the preceding example, the assumption that virtually every component of a computer system is orders of magnitude more costly than the pens, pencils, paper, typewriters, ribbons, and calculators that it replaces is true. It is also true, at least in the introductory stage for a new computer product, that this relation holds for accessories (software and peripherals). It seems reasonable, at first glance, that this might also be true for related items, specifically cleaners and solvents. That is decidedly not the case, however. Boiler rooms thrive when they can locate customers willing to make such unsubstantiated logical extrapolations on a moment's notice.

A boiler room's policing function occurs when an already overpriced market happens to be stumbled upon during the course of probing for new customers and happens to be congruent with a product in the available line. A boiler room will also slash prices on any single item as long as the total order remains profitable. That can sometimes drive local suppliers, who carry only a conventional line, out of business. For example, certain selective weed-killers—of the nationally recognized variety—can cost as much as $75 a gallon. With some sales skill, the boiler room version can appear to do the same job for $35 per gallon. Because these products are typically sold in five-gallon containers, the $200 difference in price is very appealing to certain hard-pressed users of weed-killer.

If a boiler room's product proves acceptable—or does not fail immediately—a reorder is likely. If it does not please the customer, heat is simply bought back. As often happens, however, the trade-name chemical is often highly priced because of patents, distribution rights, trade laws, and the necessary costs required for its development. If the cheaper substitute more or less works, customers will be less willing in the future to pay top dollar for a brand name. That possibility does not please conventional companies, for their profit margin must cover all of their expenses.

Moreover, in parts houses—and in some chemical operations—a genuine item (purchased in a closeout) can sometimes be sold more cheaply than an aftermarket replacement part, or chemical, purchased through conventional channels. In that case, it is not congruence but actual substitution that can drive down the regional price of the item. In both cases, the degree of general overpricing is reduced by the boiler room taking its slice of an overpriced market. Then, conventional companies are forced to reprice or, as is more likely, to bring political, industry, and legal pressure to bear to shut the boiler room down.

Conventional distributors make different assumptions than does a boiler room. First, they have to divert money and time to keeping their sales force abreast of recent developments. That may involve applications suggestions, conversion charts (to translate one manufacturer's specifications to another's product), and what marketing professionals call "technical upgrading" (providing information that allows a salesman to speak comparatively of a company's product with respect to what the competition is offering). Conventional sales meetings are often filled with such information, which is based on the unchallenged assumption that a customer will be making a rational purchase, that is, comparing price, quality, and the performance characteristics of competing products.

Second, in a conventional company, "recent developments," by definition, will include product modifications. Although the language, and images, of such presentations are critical to any sales effort, the substance is not. Unlike conventional distributors, a boiler room does not seek to sell to those with expertise but rather to locate a buyer far socially removed from those areas where technical information is relevant. A salesman explains:

> No, you don't understand. Guys who design and actually use computers, we pump them for *information*. You can't sell to them. Don't even try. You *talk* to them. If you get one on the line, tell him that you have a problem. All techies love to talk about how smart they are. Ask them any question that you can dream up. Maybe you'll learn something. If so, tell me! [Laughs.] Techies are too cautious to ever make a buy, though. Hell, they are the kind of guys who do research when they buy a toaster for the Mrs. You know, *Consumer Reports*, product evaluations, technical stuff . . . it never ends. But it's the guy who controls the office cleaning budget that we are after, not the techie. He's the buyer. His people clean the [computer] screens when the techies that use them go home. He's the mooch. You *always sell* to the mooch.

Often by chance, sometimes because an owner or salesman is technically competent, or more typically because the boiler can get a technically competent customer to discuss problems in an industry, usually by trial and error, a boiler room accommodates to what the market seems to demand. Once that is discerned, the pitch is modified to reflect current product expectations.

The Rise of Nebulous Markets

The creation of new, improved products in a modern economy, coupled with surges of growth in certain sectors, creates a nebulous market, a condition of surplus concerning the old, unimproved variety of wares and the "problem" of new wealth accruing to certain kinds of buyers. A product boiler room works these buyers.

Although warehouses, junkyards, and other repositories for outdated products have been around for some time, it is only recently that the means of communication (a boiler's telephone) has become relatively inexpensive and widespread enough for a number of operators, given the proper preconditions, to try their hand at the surplus distribution business.

Product houses work those sectors of the market that conventional companies find too bothersome to pursue, those in which it appears that sufficient profit cannot be made, and those in which there are no production channels that seem to warrant the assignment of either an additional or a special sales force. Because each industry already has conventional suppliers, producers, manufacturers, wholesalers, jobbers, and retailers (most of which are extremely competitive, and some of which are internationally so), and because boiler rooms rarely trade on the cutting edge of anything, except, perhaps, the law, that they can remain in business at all seems puzzling to those schooled in classical economics.

In accordance with Say's Law, which categorically asserts that "all products will clear," the tactics of overpricing, false promotion, and deception would seem to indicate that telephone rooms ought not to be economically viable ventures.[9] In the long run they are not. But most economists agree that the long run is a substantial period of time, by definition, and boiler rooms have learned to master the moment. They thrive in nebulous markets, the ether of classical economics, where supply and demand are never precisely defined. On the supply side, what is sold is typically an exaggerated version of everyday fare, but that is not knowable empirically until after the fact of purchase. Discrepancies are always negotiable, because the premise upon which they are delivered remains unchanged. A boiler room makes offers (the initial presentation); reconciliation, if required, merely results in another set of offers (buying back the heat) that are ordered in the boiler room's favor.

Likewise, on the demand side what is required is more than a boiler room can provide at a given price, but that is never revealed in a sales pitch. Professor Say's "law" thus requires qualification: It holds true absent an aggressive sales force. With a salesman controlling the very definition of all workable transactions, the relationship between acquisition costs and final prices changes substantially. Not only is it theoretically possible for markets to clear at levels well above the acquisition cost of products, plus overhead and normal profit, but they also do so regularly, thanks to a pitchman.

Nebulous markets are also somewhat time-sensitive because they are made just outside the window of vendibility, wherein shelf-life and current consumption patterns influence the conventional operation of supply and demand and thus define what is considered new and current. Beyond the vendibility window lies a zone influenced by technology. The inner ring of this zone contains somewhat dated goods, and the outer ring contains obsolescent product, the production of later-generation goods necessarily rendering those of an earlier generation outdated. Before the edge of this zone, current products trade in conventional markets.

A boiler room operates at the edge of the vendibility window—after most of the conventional market clears but before obsolescence occurs. If a boiler room moves too deeply into the vendibility window, it cannot acquire product; it will be forced to purchase standard merchandise at prevailing prices. If it waits too long, only old product remains. Even a pitchman's skill has limits. Not even a boiler can sell slide rules, for example, in a market dominated by electronic calculators.

Extracting money from an expanding economy is made easier because product consumption horizons are typically increasing under such circumstances. When businesses expand they consume more, and different, products. There is thus some room for the kinds of manipulation practiced in a pitch, and premiums can compensate for shortcomings in a product. There is also an element of timeliness, however, because no product house can thrive when its target industry is contracting. There must be a buyer for a pitchman to charm. Budgets become tight during economic contraction. Buyers purchase less and have less discretion, and gifts and premiums lose their appeal. Entire categories of potential customers can come to represent a waste of telephone time.

When an industry collapses or suffers economic decline—as did domestic oil in the Southwest or peanut farming and cattle ranching in other parts of the country—boiler rooms shift their product line. Most owners can rest comfortably in the knowledge that a few overpriced drums of degreaser, soil conditioner, or germicide in the hands of individual oilmen, farmers, and ranchers will likely not be noticed amid the general economic devastation.

Boiler rooms work those markets where the line between them and more conventional ventures is usually drawn by pressure from the business community itself in terms of violations of commonly accepted practices involving the presentation, packaging, preparation, distribution, and sale of products. It thrives in those regions of the marketplace characterized as gray areas—above the underworld and the black market but below those sales organizations whose power, assets, and public relations skill have helped promote their commonly accepted definition as being conventional. Stated otherwise, a boiler room overprices, overstates the value of its wares, does not deliver as promised, and masks all of the above through misrepresentation.

It can thus work those territories that conventional companies choose to avoid for fear of tarnishing their corporate images as a result of lawsuits, product liability claims, and claims of outright fraud.

This is so because it is difficult to substantiate claims by customers or employees based on fleeting impressions. Conventional legal controls are largely based on the written word, the tangible product, and the visible difference between the two. It is extremely difficult to hold a vendor legally liable for an impression, especially when taped telephone conversations are inadmissible as evidence in a court of law. And, in the case of disgruntled employees, no boiler room signs contracts. Moreover, conventional salesman cannot make virtually any claim, because their registered products all have suggested use guidelines and applications limitations. Part of the mass appeal of purchasing a recognized product is that if it fails to perform the company may be liable. Boiler rooms do not concern themselves with these fine points.

Most product-liability claims can be readily circumvented, because all products contain labels bearing instructions for proper use and disclaimers, a latent function of the consumer protection movement. Disclaimers buy back the heat. If something fails it must be because the disclaimer was ignored. All disclaimers, of course, are written in consultation with lawyers. Moreover, it is difficult to begin the litigation process. It takes a substantial amount of time for an undefined critical mass of geographically dispersed customers to coalesce around an alleged grievance, assemble a knowledge of an almost limitless number of rules and codes that vary by venue, and press for litigation. Physical distance also impedes legal redress, and lawyers' fees are typically much greater than the cost of the product originally purchased. That fact forces some lawyers to be partially complicitous out of self-interest; they benefit more than their clients do from protracted exchanges with a boiler room.

Although a call from a lawyer may chill the soul and stiffen the spine of a conventional businessman, a pro who takes such calls in a boiler room is typically knowledgeable of all the deceptions collections agencies use. "Collections" is a specialized type of boiler room role, and most salesmen take great pride in talking shop. Although pros love to talk the ear off of lawyers located in different states, the long-distance telephone call for this rather exotic form of entertainment is typically billed, along with the attorney's hourly rate, to the boiler room's displeased customer. Buying back the heat buys time, and most laws are written to protect sellers. In most cases, legal action can only be taken as a last resort after a company's attempt at reconciliation has failed.

The key, for a boiler room, lies in the word *attempt*. The longer the rectification process can be stalled, the weaker the ultimate case against the seller (if there is a case to be made). For a particularly persistent complainant, a boiler room adjusts as it typically does—by doing the totally unexpected. A house pro profusely apologizes, sends an explanation in writing, and exchanges the product. If news media are involved, the pro offers the option of writing a refund check. That establishes that rectification is possible. One highly symbolic refund covers a multitude of sins, and because the boiler room "charges back" contested product the salesman ultimately pays for these public relations episodes.

Remove the overpricing and a boiler room, armed only with a quick turn of phrase and a pitchman's wits, becomes merely a less than reputable vendor of wares. The criteria of reputability reside in the business, not the legal, community, and legal contests merely attest to the market power of a limited number of firms that dominate an industry and by so doing help establish industry norms. These distinctions are socially defined, not physically given. To cite a common example, drinking water is readily available in most households at little cost. If the water has been highly filtered it may be sold in supermarkets at a premium. In a boiler room, it becomes a solvent and perhaps the major ingredient in, say, a weed-killer. In all cases, however, it remains, chemically, water. What is typically disputed is not chemistry but marketing rights, territories, labeling, packaging norms, purity standards, and sales techniques.

The decisive resolution of these disputes is of marginal interest to those who run product houses, however, other than for the fact that the bickering among traditional business interests focuses limited public attention, and legal resources, away from other concerns and issues. In the words of one salesman:

> It buys back the heat for us. Remember all of the fuss over Alar? . . . What a joke! Remember what they actually found? When all was said and done, the stuff was basically harmless unless you drank a quart of it. . . . *Every kind* of scientist was on Capitol Hill speaking for his lobbyist or the government. It was in all the papers. Hell, we were selling weed-killer faster than we could order it—with all sorts of ingredients you wouldn't want anywhere near your food. You know how we sold it? "GUARANTEED ALAR FREE." That's true, there was no Alar in our weed-killer. We even had tests done. "Alar fear" did more to help us than anything we could have dreamed up. Nobody ever heard of us, but everyone knew about Alar. It was a laydown. We were actually pitchin' avoiding lawsuits [laughs] as part of the close.

In like manner, shifts in certain sectors of the economy can create new opportunities for boiler rooms. Some examples involve the Soviet grain deal, the near failure of the Chrysler Motors Corporation, and Japanese successes in automaking and marketing. All three have attracted tremendous public attention, involved the transfer of millions of dollars, and no doubt consumed lawyers and litigants in thousands of hours of adjudication and ceremony.

Public attention surrounding these events, and the lure of uncommonly high profits, indirectly spawned three boiler room industries in the Northeast that were the direct result of boilers looking for telephone action. Some of them found it merely by reading the newspapers with care.

Farm chemical rooms appeared in large numbers for the first time, in part, because wheat farmers became a category of buyer worth calling. The liquidation of Chrysler inventories for pennies on the dollar to raise cash for the struggling company gave rise, in part, to auto parts boiler rooms, which now had product to sell. The intense competition between foreign and domestic automobile manufacturers to capture market share raised U.S. automobile prices. Japanese quality was not met by price competition in the United States but by advertising expenditures. That meant that many would be keeping their automobiles for greater periods in lieu of trading them in every two years. This spawned transmission parts boiler rooms and, in part, sparked the growth of an automobile aftermarket, where, perhaps for the first time, price rather than a local dealer's good will or the best deal on a trade-in became a central concern for car buyers.

All of these are nebulous markets where certain innovation results in new possibilities for the vending of products and materials that would otherwise languish in warehouses. When driven by historical events that produce an uncritical urge on the part of certain types of commercial buyers, boiler rooms can service a perceived need that acquires a life of its own. After the Soviet grain deal became history, for example, farmers who grew corn rather than wheat began to find their telephones ringing at unexpected times of the day. In like manner, many garages and small automobile repair shops across the country found themselves in contact with fictive wholesale suppliers, calling from boiler rooms, for the first time.

Whenever a conventional market fails to clear, as per Say's Law, surplus must be liquidated, written off, or otherwise disposed of at a loss to make way for more lucrative lines. If for no other reason, that is the case because warehousing products involves storage expenses as well as the foregone opportunity cost of stocking items in greater demand. Overproduction is thus a necessary condition for, as well as the prime source of, inventory accumulation by product boiler rooms. Without it they would be forced to make competitive purchases at prevailing market rates, which would make their jobs more difficult but not impossible.

Common misperceptions can also render traditional markets somewhat nebulous to the degree that a truthful claim may be irrelevant regarding the product being sold. Nonetheless, affected markets can shift radically. In one product house, for example, there was customer concern over low-quality Japanese electrical parts making their way into the U.S. aftermarket. The boiler room's variety were made in Korea and cheaply available because that country has lower quality control standards—for that particular product—than Japan. Inventories were quickly moved when the pitchmen simply stated that "our product is not made in Japan."

Further nebulosity materialized roughly six months later. "Japan fear," originally stemming from a few products of low quality, intensified on the part of some major industry buyers because some of the bad press Japan was getting for displacing American workers was associated with the high visibility of inferior parts. That resulted in many high-quality Japanese electrical replacement parts going unsold. Buyers from many boiler rooms immediately rectified the situation by offering uncommonly low bids.

All products that can quickly become obsolete have a certain "move it or lose it" quality that makes accountants nervous. This is amplified in areas of international trade, where currency fluctuations can eat into profit margins. The inventory thus acquired by the low bids was far superior to anything available through domestic channels. Surplus can thus occur through overproduction, through rumor, or through some combination of the two.

The condition of surplus can also occur if a product is too advanced or specialized for typical users—and thus has no rational reason. Under these circumstances, a truly superior product can fail to sell because a user does not understand the meaning of a particular breakthrough, which often occurs when product development proceeds faster than marketing efforts. Two cases will illustrate this point. In the first instance, during the early 1980s, an extremely effective lubricant was put into aerosol cans for the first time. Because it had never before been available in aerosol form it languished on shelves. Thus, a $9 retail item—which could not compete with a vastly inferior $5 substitute—hit boiler rooms through liquidators at $1.50 per can. In the second case, a few years later, when a car polish that contained acrylic resins—heretofore expensive and only used on aircraft—was introduced to the automobile market, it failed dramatically because typical users were only familiar with wax-based products.

Being in surplus, by definition, drives down a product's asking price. A boiler room thrives by using salesmen to conceal that fact artfully. By applying a pure sales process to surplus products, a product boiler room can theoretically function in any industry. Whether it gains inroads into new categories of customers or fails to do so depends on the skill and experience of the boiler room operator.

Promotion as Social Exchange

Boilers are promotion masters. Whatever they are selling is done enthusiastically. With a smoothly delivered pitch, a presentation sounds like a musical score; there is tension, drama, pauses, and a smooth transition to the close. A professional survives in a setting where ruthless competition eliminates all challengers. To be a pro in a boiler room is to be, as one salesman put it, "the best of what is left." Some of these individuals are extremely creative. They tend to be strong-willed, and they like to take risks. They genuinely enjoy conversation as much as the "thrill of the hunt [for sales]," as another salesman put it. In a sense, they are frontiersmen at heart.

According to Marx, "The criminal breaks the monotony and everyday security of bourgeois life. In this way he keeps it from stagnation, and gives rise to that uneasy tension and agility without which even the spur of competition would get blunted. Thus he gives a stimulus to the productive forces."[10] Although that is decidedly true for a pitchman, it is also true of the "consumptive forces" that are tapped in customers. It is the customers of a boiler room who must be sufficiently engaged such that they get something out of their boiler room purchases that is less than apparent to a casual observer.

Part of what is sold over the telephone is an illusion that taps a customer's desire for instant economic or psychological gain. That may take the form of a gift (bribe or premium), apparently remarkable products, or, in a surprising number of cases, social recognition: the acknowledgment of the possibility that one's opinions are valued and that one is the "kind of person who counts." In many cases, products are sold on the simple assertion that the customer is worthy of the cost of a long-distance telephone call.

Most newspapers totally ignore these critical factors in their accounts of the operation of telephone boiler rooms. A customer must be willing to accept the premises of a pitch, and all telephone pitches are grounded in the notions of both urgency and gain.[11] They are also all based on a false ascriptive assumption imposed by salesmen and believed by many customers: that customers have especially high levels of competence.

People liked to be charmed. Although that concept is, admittedly, analytically weak, a boiler room's customers, nonetheless, regularly make purchases to entertain a few minutes of flattery. That can be readily seen by examining a number of common elements in the typical close lines used: "After all [the salesman is taught to say, and many customers willingly assent], a man of *your* [ability, business skill, or experience] *can plainly see* that [this spectacular opportunity, remarkable product, or limited offer] is *exactly what you are looking for.* Am I right?"

When subjected to scrutiny, these lines are remarkably vaporous. An understanding of their power is clearly not revealed by a study of the text, however. Product houses only sell to businesses. That exclusionary fact eliminates the vast numbers of employees in any given company, along with virtually all of the explanatory power of character traits or personalities. A certain kind of person does not make telephone purchases, but a certain kind of status incumbent does. Product houses sell only to buyers—those who occupy a certain position within a company. It is his, or her, consent alone that is both a necessary and a defining condition for a sale.

Product houses operate only where any of three conditions is present: There is some imperfection in the target marketplace; a product can be sold using techniques of active promotion; and the customer has varying degrees of "larceny sense" and thus will succumb to exaggerated claims if they are presented properly.[12] Stated in terms of exclusionary characteristics (pitches are organized to exclude those who are not likely to make purchases), customers will not be pitched if they are not in the market, if they know exactly what they want and will not consider an alternative, if that is available locally or if they will only use conventional sources of supply, if they are not interested in free gifts, if they communicate genuine product knowledge, and if they are only interested in conventional products. Boilers are trained to promote, not educate.

An old pro who had spent more than thirty years of his life on the telephones and is credited with having originated a number of scams on the East Coast in his heyday has described the essentials of telephone promotion:[13]

> Look, it doesn't matter what you are actually selling. Watch me. Use your ear. We sell the sizzle, the hope, the flash, not the steak. It's the same for chemicals, futures, time-shares, and art ["investment lithographs"]. Read the script. Pay attention to nothing else. Concentrate. Ignore all the noise around you. Now *work it*. Read it carefully. Try it out on a cold call. But do something special on that first call. Listen, just listen. Work on your intro. Forget everything else. You don't want to sell the guy on the other end. Just listen [points to his ear]. You need *the ear* to control the conversation. The customer will tell you what he wants, what he fears, what he *needs* to know before he can be sold. When the ear tells you, go for the close. Always go for the close. Ask for the money. You can't get the deal unless you ask for it. Look, all that talk [the manager's one-liners], the constant drill on knowing the product, is just that: *talk*. You know half of these guys [in the boiler room] will be outta here in a few weeks. They won't make it. It's all in the ear. Watch. Let me show you that it doesn't make a difference what you are selling. Here is a pitch we used on time-shares [shows script], I'll show you. . . .

He then dials the telephone number from a lead provided to the new salesmen. After about thirty seconds of small talk—to "warm them up"—the pro launches into the pitch and acknowledges same with a thumbs up sign. A rare curtain of silence descends on the room. There is, but for the pitchman, total quiet. It is clear to all that a gifted salesman is at work. A pro hangs up on a customer to listen to The Master, as the pitchman is affectionately called. "Hey, you can't *pay* to hear this," the pro comments. "Watch him go. Damn, he's good." The owner confides that "he has built those skills over his entire life. Listen well. You won't see many like him around these days. He is part of a vanishing breed."

The Social Cost

A boiler room is a social form that over time generates a number of outcomes that are both discordant and consistent with conventional norms governing business relationships in contemporary society.[14] In that a boiler room is a business vehicle, it is socially organized to produce a profit for its owners. The social cost of using this form, however, has many latent outcomes that influence those who labor within these operations, as well as their immediate benefactors and customers.

Pencil-pushers employ marginal salesmen and typically create no physical harm in selling their line. As urbanization proceeds, many of these small operations close as owners retire and conventional office supply firms (their competitors) expand territories by producing slicker catalogs, lowering their shipping charges and initial order requirements, and making 800 numbers available.

Odd-lot pricing and folksy conversation appear to be relics of an earlier era when the nature of work in rural areas featured large blocks of time where men had little to do. That is still the case in certain parts of the country. After the crops have been harvested, many agricultural workers spend time at truck stops and other eating and drinking establishments. Pencil-pushing boilers are entertaining, especially to those who like to hear fast-talking salesmen (apparently an oddity in their everyday round of activities) and to certain members of an older generation, some of whom enjoy reliving parts of their childhood and are willing to pay a premium for the privilege of such conversations by way of an inflated price for office supplies.

A few of these operations can become more actively fraudulent if they choose to double-bill in hope of payment, a practice common to some pencil-pushing operations. One owner, for example, latently facilitated a scam when he sold his customer list on the black market to an operator who was vending fake service contracts (chapter 4) on office equipment. Informants report that he was thrilled that his house-list could fetch what it did, because he was sure the accounts were worthless. He was wrong, however. One boiler room's dead list can become another's bread and butter.

Office supply rooms share a number of social characteristics that distinguish them from other boiler rooms and thus place them in what may soon be an obsolete category. Most are small operations, employing fewer than ten employees; there is little heat, active chemistry, or action on the floor (one room that I visited in late August, for example, still had Christmas decorations in place); there is a notable absence of young people on the scene; and turnover appears to occur through natural attrition. Many salesmen's desks, for example, that I observed in two of these operations were covered with dust, and yellowing charts and artwork were affixed to the walls of cubicles. One informant, returning from an a job interview (where I met him), captured the tone of the industry:

> It's a burial ground for elephant-phoners. Those people were *old*, man. Did you see the desks? My garage has nicer furniture. I can understand it, I guess, but nobody there was making any kind of money. I mean, where are you going with a $28 sale? The biggest pop [sale] last week was for $104. Did you see that on the [sales] board? Hey, the [newspaper] ad was for a *salesman*. Hell, there ain't nobody in that shop who can sell anything. I didn't even stay to talk my deal [negotiate terms of employment]. I figured that since I've never done office supplies before, well, what the hey, I'd give it a shot. Well, now I know. This is the place where you go to die when you can't pitch anymore. Kinda scary: pens and pencils, weird prizes, no action.

There is, however, a great deal of action and real physical danger associated with some product boiler rooms. That is especially so in the case of chemical houses that cater to those who purchase these products without benefit of quality controls (farmers, industrial consumers, and institutions) or without complying with industry-accepted norms governing application, concentration, and storage.[15]

I have seen dangerous industrial solvents sold as general-purpose cleaners, all-purpose (total) weed- and vegetation-killers marketed as a topical (limited application) product, and powders and fluids diluted to the point where they are useless for their originally intended purpose. Some of these substances are toxic.[16] All of them are sold under circumstances where a telephone call to break the monotony of the workday, a free hunting or fishing knife, or a package of cheese are sufficient enticements to close the deal.

The building trades are a specialty of chemical houses, where boilers tout paints, adhesives, coatings, solvents, caulking, resins, sealants, and roofing materials. Much of this material is of low quality but typically features attractive premiums and gifts as incentives to entice contractors to become customers. Many do. Although these small businesses are typically licensed in and by their respective states to do business in the home repair or remodeling fields, the materials they select for their inventories is not subject to regulation. This market is also somewhat nebulous because many small companies routinely go out of business for a number of reasons but typically before their boiler-room-vended wares attract public attention. Modern economics has no term for inferior products with a half-life greater than the business life of the companies that sell them.

Except for the building trades, where a boiler room's product line is typically concealed by wood, brick, siding, finished surfaces, the insides of a wall, or a number of pipes and fittings, when overpriced chemicals fail it is usually apparent. Additives, lubricants, solvents, and weed-killers, moreover, are not normally used by people who lack the requisite training, and it is doubtful whether physical harm could occur as the result of purchasing shoddy materials, although the economic cost of such a purchase is substantial.

It is the consumer who is adversely affected when whatever is supposed to be treated (i.e., preserved, cooled, killed, lubricated, cleaned, or dissolved) is done so ineffectively. Parts houses pose the greatest threat to the general public because their wares are always totally invisible to consumers. That is because component parts are vended to commercial buyers who use them as replacement items that are installed away from customers and in the back regions of a store, facility, or service department. Parts operations also sell to those who rebuild, restore, or remanufacture components, assemblies, and accessories. Builders, in turn, provide outlets to the conventional repair marketplace, and most people are unaware of them because suppliers to the repair trade are not typically publicized.

One of the reasons for this is that concealing the source of one's materials and supplies is trade information and thus merits secrecy because it offers an apparent advantage over the competition. Thus, many replacement parts in automobiles, small appliances, power tools, and electronic devices may originate in some unknown boiler room, even though such items are typically installed under the corporate emblems of well-established firms, chains, and distribution centers.

Once a boiler room–vended part is incorporated into the rebuilding process it is visually indistinguishable from the conventional item, component, or subassembly. Moreover, even if it were visually distinctive, an expert would be hard-pressed to look inside a functioning transmission, brake assembly, carburetor, appliance, computer, power mower, or home appliance and be able to assign distributor origin to a component of a complex mechanical system. The economic cost of such substitutions is large, because thousands of boiler rooms are actively selling industry.

The social cost is even more substantial but equally invisible. Because virtually all mechanical components (even the shoddy ones) have an extant working life, it may be weeks, months, or even years before failures, disintegration, and mechanical malfunctions become noticeable. When a failure does occur, however, people may be injured, maimed, or killed. Long after the deal is cut, the premium enjoyed, the commission paid, and the initial transaction forgotten (and the original salesman likely fired), a goodly number of accidents will be waiting to happen.

It is impossible to discern what percent of all accidents attributable to the mechanical failure of components and assemblies were hawked by product boiler rooms to buyers looking out for something other than their companies' long-term interests. What additional percent may be due to shoddy maintenance performed with substandard products is also unknown.[17] It is, however, reasonable to assume that both numbers would be smaller if manufacturers' specifications and recommendations were adhered to rigorously. At least one reason why they are not likely to be, in part, stems from the collective success of boilers, who are adept at finding the buyer.

Following a mechanical analogue to Gresham's Law, boiler rooms that can obtain high-quality, reasonably priced parts have a comparative market advantage over those that cannot. Such items quickly displace the shoddier versions, which over time appear as surplus to be absorbed into another boiler room's inventory. The same general principle applies to marine, aviation, and sometimes military vehicle hardware, paints and lacquers, maintenance supplies, and virtually any item that can be procured for a drastically reduced price via closeout, distressed merchandise sale, through a private label house, or through liquidation.[18] There are active boiler rooms working all of these industries.

A structural problem must also be considered: the distribution of banned goods. Three classes of products are banned from the legitimate marketplace: hot loads (stolen goods); rejects (products that have failed manufacturers' quality control standards); and salvage (junked products). Boiler room owners are salesmen who have come to own their own companies. Like their customers, few meet suppliers in person, but they trust them to provide usable goods. The extent to which this trust is violated is unknown. Because the nature of the business precludes visual inspection of much of what is sold—and visual inspection cannot reveal the origin of product—there is always the possibility that an unknown percentage of banned goods will find its way into a boiler room's inventory from suppliers seeking to "move a load."

Physical danger does not come from stolen goods, because anything valuable enough to be stolen is likely to be operative. It comes from defectives (rejects and salvage). It is anybody's guess regarding the point at which a given supplier gets greedy. Because the acquisition cost of defectives is near the salvage value of a product, and much lower than even a volume wholesale price, the potential for substantial windfall profits cannot be lightly dismissed.[19]

I have never worked in a boiler room that did not sell something to someone in the vast social networks tied to the Fortune 500 list of companies—the companies themselves as well as their suppliers, retailers, jobbers, wholesalers, and distributors. Although product houses target maintenance and service personnel, service boiler rooms (chapter 4) also eye the discretionary incomes of higher-placed personnel. Few of us, however, are totally exempt from some aspect of the repair market. Although most people will never hear a pitch from a product room boiler, the same cannot be said for their repairman of choice. As one salesman put it, "If you live in it, rent it, use it, drive it, borrow it, work with it, or steal it, I can't help you. When it breaks, though, it has to be fixed. The guy who fixes it is a *businessman*. He's in the Yellow Pages. That levels the field a bit. If I don't call him, someone else will."

The Boiler Room as a Deviant Scene

Only the posters were real. I thought I had a job in the travel industry.
Who would ever believe that a company would just skip town? They owe
me pay and bonuses. I thought it was a real company. . . . Mary [the sec-
retary] first caught my eye when I was hired. She had a real office. It
turns out that all of the rest was just for show, just props.
  —*an unemployed salesman who sold vacation travel packages over*
  the telephone

Social Deviance and the Boiler Room

When asked, jokingly, "What are you doing on the telephone?" one salesman
retorted, "Boiling." Another chimed in, "We're boiling away." The term *boil-*
er room, however, is only recognized by experienced telephone salesmen. Like
other members of deviant groups whose style of deviance is attributed by
outsiders but rarely self-acknowledged (hippies, pool sharks, and white-collar criminals), boilers are not, except in jest, referred to as such but rather in
terms borrowed from the conventional sales world: telephone sales agents,
telemarketing reps, brokers, or inside salesmen.

When the term is occasionally used in sales talks given by management,
a form of deviance disavowal is practiced.[1] The working definition of a boiler
room becomes all the negative characteristics of the industry mapped onto
the competition. There are many negative characteristics. These are the result of the difficulties involved in negotiating sales over the telephone. Boiler rooms offer a range of disreputabilities, any of which clearly establishes
telephone salesmen as members of a deviant occupation, each of which may
be more or less dominant in a particular setting, and few of which are experienced in pure form. The disreputabilities are:

1. Some rooms engage in outright fraud (the scams), thus breaking numerous local, state, and federal ordinances.

2. No boiler room delivers all of what is promised to customers. Although
this is sometimes a matter of degree (i.e., product claims exceeding capabilities), it is often a difference in kind—a nondelivery or nonusable, sometimes
dangerous, product or fictitious services.

3. Marginal employment in a boiler room violates most contemporary mores concerning employment. Jobs are unstable, promotions and rewards are erratic and often nonexistent, and wages are unpredictable.

4. The deception used on the sales force is for the purpose of diverting revenue. Employees are fired so that their accounts can be redirected to back rooms, redistributed to other salesmen, or confiscated by the ownership, and the manipulation of sales figures and fraudulent charges ensures that salesmen will not receive previously earned commissions, bonuses, or salary.

5. The deception used by the sales force is an organizational requirement. The industry is strongly influenced by both external market constraints and internal financial arrangements that effectively prohibit a reasonable correspondence between promises made and products delivered.

6. Because a boiler room is a pure sales organization, virtually any effective instrumentality will be used. In most instances, boiler rooms avoid both contemporary corporate responsibilities for delivery of products or services as promoted and concerns such as intermediate- to long-range planning, product liability, conformity to local and regional ordinances governing product use, and customer relations.

7. None of the preceding rationales for being, however, are made clear to workers. Employees typically work amid a sea of uncertainty and secrecy and are sometimes bemused by how all of this is possible.

Because all boiler rooms are organized as businesses, most of the routine behavior therein is no different from that in other kinds of sales or administrative work. In performing their jobs, telephone salesmen learn a great deal about the formal and imagined attributes of the products they sell, but they rarely have a chance to see what is vended or shipped. Such matters are categorically defined as "not their concern," and information control networks are extremely active. Boiler rooms do not serve organized illegal markets such as drugs, contraband, or weapons. Social controls in the underworld are effective and do not tolerate deception, and the requisite social skills applicable to black market operations do not lie in the construction of illusions.

Whether social deviance is defined as a process that can result in the breaking of a norm, a rule, a law, or a set of expectations, or as an outcome that results from social reaction to perceived violations of one of these, the activities of a boiler room qualify for inclusion.[2] Some (the scams) meet all four criteria, but most meet only three; most do not break the enforceable letter of the law. It is not illegal to sell overpriced products, to fail to pay employees as promised, to fire them routinely, to subject them to ruthless competition, or to maximize profits; nor is it illegal to be silent while so doing.

It is technically illegal to steal from workers; to cheat customers; to fire an employee for other than due cause; to sell distressed merchandise as new; to use bribes, gifts, and/or premiums when vending to federal or municipal employees; to sell services that meet only the dictionary's broad definition of the term; to hire people as independent contractors to beat local, state, and federal taxes applicable to employees; to misrepresent products; to sell banned agricultural poisons and inferior replacement parts that can cause accidents; and to discriminate on the basis of age, race, color, creed, or sex. Yet all of these activities fall into gray areas that require interpretation, documentation, clarification, and conformity with rules of evidence overseen by lawyers.

Boiler rooms avoid the company of lawyers unless they are hired to protect the firm's interests. In this area, there seems to be no shortage of willing candidates. An informant explains:

Whataya mean? [Adopts a "Mafioso" style, with considerable humor.] Where do we get our lawyers? Where does anybody get a lawyer? We *hire* them—and, damn, they cost us. Where do you think the bottom of the graduating class find jobs? Eh, Guido? IBM? AT&T? Ford? Don't you know that the business of America is business? Ya gotta be in business. They gotta be in business. I'm in business. . . . Why? Do you need a lawyer? Dem creditors gettin' to ya? Are you in trouble? [Laughs.] Hey, our guy is pretty good. He has lots of connections.

Much of the sustained enthusiasm in a boiler room obtains from the fact that telephone work attracts people who are looking for a growing income in a white-collar occupation and lack the social credentials for such employment, or, for those possessing such backgrounds, who are looking for supplemental earnings or a fast buck—a fact managers and owners do not ignore. Recruits in all cases are only selected if they are willing to believe that an opportunity is being offered them.

The flow of people to a boiler room involves self-selection and is greatly facilitated by disruption and dislocation in the occupational order due to layoffs, plant closings, firings (as occurred with some air traffic controllers), failures in business, industrial stagnation, having a criminal record, and numerous other contingencies that encourage workers to seek additional income, change jobs, or think about entering a new line of work. Or perhaps one's prime occupation does not generate sufficient income to meet everyday needs, as is the case with homemakers, students, moonlighters, part-timers, and the underemployed. The appeal of "inside, sit-down work" also attracts road salesmen, routemen, and those with low levels of sales skill but some sales experience, who may turn to the telephones in an effort to try something different.

Occasionally, there are disbarments (lawyers) and the loss of licenses, as is the case for commodities traders who are unable to work legally in the financial district due to previous fraudulent conduct. Those who have gained some telephone experience may turn to a boiler room to increase their earnings over and above what telephone solicitors are paid, and those in different boiler room industries may decide (or be forced) to change employment sites. Partial occupational displacements also occur when employers move job sites and employees must search for ways to avoid a long commute.

The proximate cause of boiler room employment is the response to newspaper advertisements. These are often artfully worded to attract a diverse audience and, in a few cases, to ensure that management will be entertained by a wide range of applicant talent, with no actual hiring being done. Thus, even the simple assertion that want ads are placed to hire people may prove suspect. One manager in a chemical house, for example, runs occasional advertisements as a ruse to meet larger numbers of women than would normally be present in his social circle. After an afternoon spent reading through a stack of, in most cases, dutifully completed job applications, he compiles a list of names, addresses, and telephone numbers. These are then used for whatever purposes he—or his salesmen—may divine.[3]

Job screening is, nonetheless, arduous work. The bulk of those who apply usually lack the requisite verbal skills and will be rejected. An informant explains, "There's no one way to fill a room. The bottom line is that few people have an aptitude for this line of work. I run a number of different ads to pull in as many different kinds of people as I can. Believe me, I'll listen to *anyone* who can convince me that I should hire them. If they can do that, they can 'talk a line' and have what it takes in this business. . . . One company I was with ran ads just to shake up the sales floor. They didn't hire anyone, but it sure kept the salesmen on their toes."

When a parent boiler room, where initial training and experience is provided, works a growing sector of the economy, spin-off shops, which spring up to feed off the turnover on the parent's sales floor, become increasingly common. That increases the level of boiler room activity in a region and provides training for the next generation of boilers. This was most notable in chemicals during the early 1970s, auto parts in the late 1970s, commodities in the early 1980s, and in the growth of the telemarketing and service operations.

A boiler room's expansion cycle corresponds with downturns in the white-collar sector of the economy, which can attract categories of labor with above-average levels of interpersonal skills (teachers, furloughed government workers, retail sales personnel, social workers, keepers of small shops, and realtors are common) as well as college students seeking part-time jobs.

General economic growth can also force the breakup of boiler rooms because of policing activities directed at the more successful (and therefore visible) operations. That creates more opportunities in the industry. Unlike shakeouts in conventional industries, crackdowns prolong the life of some rooms that might otherwise go under were it not for the infusion of new men and ideas from the sales floors of strong but prematurely defunct competitors.

When authorities shut down a boiler room, its workers need only consult the newspapers or their friends in other shops for knowledge of the availability of telephone action. As an owner anticipated a "new lease on life" that resulted from the shutdown of a chemical boiler room, "Did you hear the news? They just busted Delta Chemical last week. Delta is *gone*. They're out of business. They had to 'cease and desist.' There is a run on pros. It's unbelievable. When the pros are forced to walk they might turn up here, knocking on my door! Hell, even if we don't get a pro, a regular at Delta is probably as good as our best man here. Maybe better, even. It's a new lease on life."

Although deception in the telephone sales industry is widespread, many specific practices are unique to boiler rooms. These include dropping (selling fictional merchandise COD, wherein purchasers receive bricks or paper and a note of delayed shipment); burning (shipping goods that were not ordered, in hope of payment); and writing wood (writing a fictitious order and earning a commission for it). The case of "wood" is one of the more common examples of deceptive techniques learned on the sales floor and used against management. A salesman expecting to quit will often write wood to increase the size of what he expects will be his last paycheck. Managers may also use fraudulent techniques against the owners of a boiler room. In addition to writing wood, they may engage in what is called a "paper run," wherein they make copies of all house accounts and sell these to competitor boiler rooms.

There is a black market in active boiler room accounts (the paper market in product rooms), and the vending of "sucker lists" among those rooms that specialize in services is common. When a pro leaves a boiler room, he often takes his account list with him, thus ensuring that the competition will benefit from his knowledge. He can sell his list outright, use it as a negotiating tool in determining his terms of employment with a new company, or both. Depending on the tenure of the pro, this can present a serious threat to the economic fortunes of a boiler room. A "top writer" typically amasses a substantial percentage of the firm's best—that is, most frequent and largest— accounts, which by definition and custom are only given to the most skilled salesmen.

Managers and owners must also be alert to the "long dial," when employees dial long distance for the express purpose of running up a company's monthly telephone bill. That sometimes requires additional controls on a sales force, such as call-monitoring, telephone logs, and back room counseling (wherein a sales manager threatens a worker with job loss). Such controls add to the level of frustration, anxiety, and paranoia in most telephone rooms.

There are also deceptions derived from the world of business that a boiler room adapts for its own purposes. These include credit phoning (using a fictional company name for the sole purpose of obtaining credit reports on potential customers); double billing (billing a customer twice for the same order); double shipping (shipping the same order twice); "switchabouts" (shipping a more inexpensive product than the one ordered by the customer); "premi-swaps" (shipping a less valuable premium than the one agreed to at the point of sale); padding (inflating the size of an order by falsely increasing the number of items ordered); and the technique of recording a customer's credit card number by using a ruse and then entering an order after the customer refuses to make a purchase ("fast plasticking the deal," or FPD).

A boiler room differs from the standard confidence racket, however, in one important regard: Con men, for the most part, are part of a criminal subculture. They do not try to deceive themselves. There is no criminal subculture in a boiler room, and its salesmen pay a novel price for lack of subcultural support. They are surprisingly more vulnerable than one would expect to exaggerated claims. As one pro explained, "Look, in a way, salesmen are an easy mark. Hey, we all like to take a gamble once in a while. This is because of the kind of work that we do. Hell, you work hard pumpin' out your guts in a pitch, and you do it over and over again. You know, you want to be a player yourself once in a while. To take a shot."

By working the telephones, pros, regulars, and trainees produce different levels of company profit. When demand is brisk, a boiler room must replenish its inventory. Weakness in the flow of capital to the room, the ability to find and service a market, and the profitability of the enterprise drives a boiler room to constantly adjust the size and scale of its operations. Owners of smaller companies must be capitalists, managers, salesmen, agents of social control, businessmen, and also personable bosses to their non-sales employees. At worst, because all of these attributes are fairly rare—in one individual—many telephone rooms fail because the requirements of the division of labor accumulate faster than the management capabilities of the owner. Owners face other problems, however, that concern trust, the sharing of knowledge, and the delegation of responsibilities that are more pressing than those of their conventional counterparts.

Successful salesmen can pose a threat to the stability—and even the continued existence—of a boiler room. In part, this occurs because a seasoned boiler has enough knowledge to be dangerous to a company. He is one of the few who fully understands the techniques of deception and how to use them to his personal advantage. Such personnel are usually isolated from "fresh blood" (trainees). In larger houses the pros circulate between the back rooms (which contain their peers) and the sales floor. If knowledge and power are shared with a salesman, the more ambitious among them may strike out on their own, as did, in all cases of which I am aware, the owner himself. Thus, secrecy is the norm in most boiler rooms, and in larger shops managers are purged as regularly as salesmen.

No organization can provide career security if it routinely purges or loses its most capable people. Nor can a boiler room afford the luxury of warehousing the inept, the complacent, or the incapable. As the successful come to understand the techniques of deception, those who remain on the sales floor become demoralized, because such knowledge highlights the basic instability of the operation. To avoid that, an owner will sometimes bring in a new manager to run training rooms and generate the necessary levels of enthusiasm. By so doing, he keeps his back room in line by implicitly threatening them with the loss of their jobs. "Look," an owner explains, "I have to manage my chips the right way. Everyone here works for me. So I play a chip and bring in a new manager. If the pros in the back room get pissed, that's good. It keeps them in line. They work for me. The minute that they forget that, they are on the street. I can't watch these guys all the time. So I bring in a new manager for the cold floor. If the back-roomers start diverting accounts, I fire one of them. Then, I've got the new guy, right? If he doesn't work out, I fire him. I can always promote from the sales floor."

Marginality

The realities of a boiler room, in part, are brought about because it lacks respectability. Not offering middle-class status, boiler rooms seek to attract those with middle-class skills. A boiler room recruits (at best) temporary middle-class visitors (students, unemployed white-collar workers, homemakers, and moonlighters) who have been dislocated from their normal career paths. For these people, a boiler room is a half-way house, to be left as soon as better job options materialize, school is out, their spouses fare better economically, or the economy improves.

Boiler rooms are, for the most part, what economists call marginal enterprises in that these companies are usually initially financed using family savings; launched as a venture that must redeem the owners from being wage workers and afford them a chance to become economically independent; and unlikely to survive for more than a few years. At worst, telephone rooms face at least as many obstacles to their success as do other small businesses.

Although a desire to sell is largely self-imposed, the pressure to sell is imposed by the boiler room. Salesmen must work increasingly harder to maintain a given level of income in a market characterized as erratic at best. It is common for even the better salesmen to have days when they must make a hundred or so telephone calls without making a sale. Moreover, even the best salesman can have a blank day when no sales are made. Some folk wisdom from a pro:

> One blank [day]: *You* blew it. Two blanks: *It* blew you [lighten up, you're taking this stuff too seriously]. Three blanks: Blow *the company* [they're getting ready to crash, pull out before you get thrown out]. When blanks happen, that's a rough road. When you draw three blanks in a row, however, there ain't no road left. The same is true for paychecks. Hell, we all have a bad week once in a while. Two down checks [each smaller than the one that preceded it]: be careful. Three downers: pack your bags. If you don't do it yourself [look for another job], they [the company] will do it for you [you'll be fired].

For most, the knowledge that a salesman gains with regard to useful techniques and strategies for selling over the telephone does not accumulate as rapidly as do the psychological disabilities associated with failing to make sales. Only a few survivors remain long enough in the employ of a boiler room to acquire a self-image of being successful in this line of work. From these limited numbers, a tiny fraction will emerge as owners of their own shops when they make the decision to strike out on their own.

The rest become house pros when they outlast everyone else in their hiring cohort. Based on the size of the boiler room operation, most trainees last a few weeks; salesmen last a few months; regulars, a year or so; and pros or managers, a few years before they are either fired or the company goes out of business. It is only a matter of time before such turnover becomes public knowledge. That this occurs segmentally in the larger rooms, where the division of labor produces notable skill differences, where a salesman works a larger portion of his own accounts, where workers are segregated by skill, and where the average tenure of a worker may be directly influenced by the operation of the business cycle, creates the illusion of external causation.

Staffing a telephone room is always problematic. Those in the working class, on average, do not have the necessary telephone personalities and are not particularly verbal. Fearing the pros and unable to attract workers from conventional industries because it can neither pay competitively nor offer permanent employment, a boiler room settles for marginal people—the luck of the draw with regard to the patterns of displacement in the regional economy.

As a general rule, an economic recession brings those of higher social standing to the door, whereas an expansion brings the more entrepreneurially inclined, some of whom may have had previous run-ins with the law. Inflationary times bring changes in the number of boiler rooms vending services (promoting various scams), but that typically does not alter the social origins of salespeople.

To adapt to these contingencies, owners draw upon the one skill that they all possess by virtue of being telephone salesmen: their skill as pitchmen. Manpower shortages, social isolation from legitimate business opportunities, fear of salesmen and managers, distrust of success, and the pressures of the market all force owners of telephone boiler rooms to construct an increasingly imaginary world. They adapt by incorporating sales techniques and language into a working philosophical system, a usable shorthand for adapting to a chaotic environment. That puts a great deal of psychological pressure on the permanent staff, who must now spend increasing parts of their business day listening to the troubled owner as well as the concerns of salespeople. This causes attrition from the ranks of the non-sales personnel, who often share gossip, and adds to the instability of a company because it further increases turnover. A secretary, age forty-two, in an auto parts boiler room said:

> I came here a year ago. I work part-time. I took this job for a little extra money, and it looked like something different and interesting. I can't stay here much longer, however. There is no future here, and what really frustrates me is that I have to listen to his [the owner's] troubles all day. I'm not a psychologist. Believe me, he tells me things that I'd rather not hear. I don't get paid for that, and I don't like it either. I've got to get out of this place . . . I'll tell you one thing, though, he [the owner] is really a good salesman [laughter]. When I first came here, he really had me convinced that this was a real business. I mean, a real company. What a joke. In a way I feel sorry for the salesmen. They are trying to make a living here, and they get fired quite regularly. For me, well, my husband has a good job. I don't have to work here, and I won't. [She quit seven weeks later.]

Although pressure for increased output is common in the conventional sales field, traditionally available economic rewards are usually assigned throughout employees' careers: distribution of territories, mobility via transfer or promotion, an increased share of administrative activities with tenure, supervisorial arrangements, retirement perks, pensions, and overrides on previous sales. Few of these are available in boiler rooms, primarily because capital is never built up, and profits are constantly siphoned off to the ownership and redistributed to managers and pros before their eventual termination. The exception to this general rule occurs in larger parts houses, which do acquire inventory of substantial value.

Because boiler rooms are run within the context of a small-group setting, the types of controls and deceptive practices used are necessarily bound up with the personalities of the overseers. A salesman works, ultimately, for a small handful of people and, if his socialization is effective, imagines himself in business for himself. Secrecy and competitive norms usually preclude concerns that are not centered on the sales process from any kind of effective hearing, especially on company time. Thus, many deceptive practices remain invisible because they are incorporated into the taken-for-granted round of seeking sales.

Because there is substantial variability in a given house regarding skills, longevity, tenure practices, income possibilities, reasons for being on the scene, and the kinds of personalities selected for management positions, a shop, to some degree, develops its own character. This is not usually articulated and becomes part of the chemistry of the room. Part of the chemistry involves the socialization process. Learning to become a salesman requires that all collectively engage in common activities and share certain values. Because boilers are salesmen, much of the passing of daily events is experienced in terms of the operation of the business cycle, which has a special language found in the financial pages of any newspaper.

Boilers, like most salespeople, spend substantial amounts of time talking about their deals: sales made, anticipated, or being actively sought. They do so, however, in a context where this constitutes most of the content of the formal training they receive, and that influences their informal conversations as well. In some shops, sales are the only topic of shared discussion.

One seasoned informant (an owner) made the following insightful comment during a power outage, when all telephone lines and lights were temporarily off and the room had a morguelike quality: "This is a strange business. You have the telephones and you have your accounts. That's it. You can't borrow on it [there is no recognizable equity]. With the telephones out there is nothing much to say, or do. When power comes back on, we will all dial and then go home. There is no company, no staff, no nothing. It's a joke. What I simply do is try to make a living. All the rest is hype. In fact, much of what we do is hype [fumbles for a different word]."

While most salesmen welcome making telephone calls, many often leave work at the end of the day "talked out," not so much tired from either conversation or routine as from the psychological pressures of experiencing a series of segmented social relationships. The cycle (dialing, pitching, and closing) repeats anew with each telephone call. Many salesmen refuse to answer the telephone in the privacy of their own homes. "When I blow outa here at the end of the day. That's it. Forget it, babe," says one who is experienced. "My wife answers the phone in our house. I can't deal with it. I either feel sorry for the guy on the other end 'cause I know what he is going through, or I get mad. I can't take the phone calls. No. No. No. Not at home. I have enough dealing with the phone right here." Others have taken to writing down telephone numbers important in their personal lives because, in the words of one salesman, "The numbers are all the same. I went to call my sister the other day, and I forgot her number. I had to look it up! I felt stupid. Look, you do thousands of numbers a month. Now I know how a telephone operator must feel."

A boiler room begins because the combination of market forces, profits, predatory working arrangements, and frustration initially forces entrepreneurial owners (who were once salesmen) to strike out on their own. Once they do, they are free to organize their own companies in any manner they wish. Although many are adverse to recreating the conditions from which they have recently fled, they also know that keeping people on the sales floor requires deception, secrecy, incentives, and considerable control. The primacy of the commission structure in this regard warrants special attention.

The Economics of Control: The Commission Structure

Commissions are the grail of all sales organizations. They represent an important, readily measurable, goal for each salesman, provide the firm with a unit of account for measuring productivity, and are central to the system of incentives and sanctions used for the social control of workers and managers (called "motivation" in business circles). The quest for commission income has an elusive, almost spiritual, quality that becomes internalized as part of a salesman's socialization.

At root, commission is what drives the culture of sales, although it is easily mistaken for those latest techniques, aids, schemes, manuals, and managerial ideologies promoted by other salesmen at heart, of the wordsmith variety, who trade in the bustling market for quick fixes to the problem of providing all manner of uplift to workers, short of decent pay, meaningful work, task autonomy, and job stability. Absent the commission structure, a boiler room would lose its heat, chemistry, tone, style, and reason for being. Working the telephones without commission would come to be precisely that state of affairs all telephone salesmen deeply fear when they are down on their luck, awaiting termination, or are losing their edge: using the telephone to service some organizational requirement. The commission structure in a boiler room has four elements, each controlled by the firm.

1. *Payment rates.* Commissionable rates are the overall percentage of total sales paid to a salesman, whereas commission rates are variable line-item rates, per product sold.

2. *Terms of payment.* These concern adjustments to sales figures. In a charge-back, the company deducts fees, penalties, returns, freight on returns, and handling charges from the money due a salesman. The boiler room thus deceptively retains the difference between the true cost of the loss, if any, and the inflated charge.

3. *Order of payment.* Each type of account receivable has its own payout schedule, for example, credit card orders, new account sales, reorder business, bank wires (for those promoting services), promotions of new products, and other types of promotions. Order of payment is important as a vehicle for fraudulently retaining commissions due a salesman. It is a source of interest-free loans while the salesman is employed and profits after he is fired. For example, if house policy is to pay out commissions on all reorder business on the tenth of the month following the collection date, it has use of this money from the date of collection. If a salesman is no longer in the employ of the boiler room, however, on the payout date for the receivable, he loses his claim to commission.

4. *The draw schedule.* An adjustable, guaranteed weekly income charged against commissionable sales, the draw schedule is a negotiable salary that is typically not presented as such in four regards. First, most salesmen assume that a draw is an industry standard and therefore not negotiable. Second, most salesmen are not told that once a draw is lowered it will rarely be increased. Third, they are also not told that their draw is their float (break-even) point. When it falls below the initially quoted figure they will likely be fired. And, finally, most salesmen are not told that they may be required to repay the draw from future comissionable sales. A draw schedule is the prime source of much unexpected debt in a boiler room, because salesmen soon find that they come to owe the company money based on the manipulation of sales figures.

When a salesman earns more for the company than it, in turn, pays him, he has passed his float point. Float is the amount of net profit a salesman generates. The float of an entire sales force determines the overall profitability of the boiler room. Boiler rooms are perpetually, and accurately, seen as "short on float." Because it takes time—usually a minimum of a hundred telephone hours (time spent on the telephone)—for a salesman to learn the administrative routines common to his shop as well as master sufficient technical knowledge so as to sound knowledgeable and build a usable core of sales skills, the larger or more profitable operations (except for the scams) pay a base salary while a salesman is training.

While the new man "floats on the float" (is paid a token starting salary), arrangements are made to ensure that "dead wood" (those deficient in sales skill) is removed from the company and managers are promoted and fired in an orderly manner. Although the most important lure to assure a regular flow of men to the cold floor is the initial presentation, what ensures a flow of personnel through a boiler room is the constant circulation of accounts—which ensures that maximum cost-effectiveness (i.e., each worker's contribution to float) is optimized by generating turnover of personnel.

Because a salesman is paid a percentage of the selling price of a product rather than on net revenue, which is determined by the markup typical to an industry, a company necessarily accumulates income much faster than a salesman does. An owner explains, "'Training salary,' 'up-front money,' 'guaranteed base'—call it what you will. It doesn't matter. It's all the same. It's a *tool*. The bottom line is that I make money off of the cold floor. . . . Hell, there are many ways to make it to the door. The managers dream them up all the time. That's their job. . . . But the trainees, hell, I don't have no crystal ball. We run 'em, lose 'em, keep 'em. They must earn their keep. When all is said and done, they do. There's no other way."

An employee is typically kept at his training salary long enough for the firm to recoup its loss on paper. When that occurs, the salesman is either fired or given a salary increase, for which he must now work, proportionately, much harder. A boiler room typically marks up its products 200 to 1,200 percent. Assuming the lower figure (200 percent), if an item costs $10, it is sold for $30. From the $20 gross profit, a salesman is paid, perhaps, 10 percent of $30 (the selling price), or $3. The gross return (payout) on the sale is $17 of gross profit for the firm and $3 for the salesman. The relevant computation for the firm would be: Assuming a 100 percent operating or overhead expense, $10 (overhead cost) is subtracted from $20 (gross profit). That leaves $10 (adjusted gross profit), from which $3 (the salesman's commission) is subtracted. $7 is the net profit. Thus, the company's return (net) based on the commission structure is $7. For each dollar a salesman is paid in commission, the company earns $7/3$ dollars—a $2.33 net return.

The computations that the salesman must make are different, however, because they are based on a percentage of sales, not net profits. Thus, a salesman who writes $3,000 worth of sales is entitled to 10 percent ($300). If doing so takes, for example, two weeks, and he is hired at a $200 per week draw, he is seen as having earned $300 and having been paid $400. He is, in the eyes of the company, given the commission structure, "in the hole" for $100 (his take-home salary was $100 larger than his sales figures justified). The company has netted $600 from the salesman's efforts. From gross profits ($2,000),

it paid out $400 (a $300 draw and a $100 advance). Assuming $1,000 in operating expenses, the boiler room is ahead $600.

The commission structure is a powerful social control technique in two
regards. It makes it appear as if the firm is being overly generous, that is, paying out more than the salesman is generating. It also permits management
to know precisely what the float point is for each salesman. The net contribution of each salesman continues to accumulate as long as the level of sales
remains above the float point. What varies is the length of time before a salesman will be fired. Once the basic premise behind the draw schedule is accepted—that it is rightfully based on sales figures—a draw can be lowered with
"pencil-in-hand" managerial justification. Management, having established
that a salesman is in its debt through the use of commission figures, can also
create the illusion of largess by canceling out all the self-same debt that the
salesman believes he has acquired.

The commission structure of a boiler room and markup, realized together, are the two central forces ensuring that the boiler room will remain disreputable, its sales floor will turn over, and there will always be a shortage of
sales talent. As a practical matter, as long as promises can be made that will
never have to be honored, recruits—innocent of what goes on behind closed
doors and in back rooms—will always find the company line appealing. An
unobtrusive measure of this occurs when boiler rooms place job advertisements in local newspapers. In most cases, the telephones ring continuously,
and most houses must assign a salesman or two to assist receptionists with
keeping up with the volume of incoming calls.

Nascent Ideology

That most boiler room operators take themselves to be legitimate businessmen and that most telephone salesmen self-refer to the "salesman" part of
their job description rather than to the "telephone" part accurately captures
both their aspirations and socialization. This is facilitated, in part, by the lay-
out and design of the shop and the forms of interior decorating used.

The selection and arrangement of office decorations is influenced by the
amount of capital available to the firm, the scale of the operation, and whether the company saw its corporate origins as a telephone operation (in which
case eclecticism is the norm) or was attached to a company that manufactured
or distributed physical products (in which case the telephone room will look
like a service department).

Seeking the illusion of a long corporate history, longevity artifacts must
be acquired, for example, old photographs of a founding corporate family or

the first plant, shipping dock, and original office staff of a defunct company. Items that have sentimental value are called "discards" in the office furniture business and are inexpensive. They serve as props as well as decorative items.

In the scams, a failed business will often be purchased for a small sum just for the right to use its original incorporation date in the new owner's literature. "I.T.T. Wholesalers," for example, which may have been a long-defunct plumbing supply house, can have new life as a boiler room vending products or services totally unrelated to its original line. If a few people remember the original company or if the name sounds similar to a widely recognized concern, so much the better.

Closeouts are the major source of the posters that adorn salesrooms, and they communicate values drawn from the larger business culture. Themes range from the mundane (smiley faces) to the avant-garde (posters advertising art exhibitions) but center on "business schlock," in the words of one informant, a theater student. The posters feature pastoral or urban scenes and have bits of folk wisdom inscribed in a corner of the view. Examples are, "Happiness is found along the way, not at the end of the road"; "Nothing is ours but time"; and, "You can do it if you try." The universal favorite is the photograph of a kitten struggling to maintain its grip on an extended broom handle. The message "hang in there, baby" is printed on the bottom of the poster.

Any particular item, viewed by itself, seems to reflect the individual personality, beliefs, and preferences of its owner. A content analysis of four dozen images, however, reveals a pattern in the selections made and, perhaps more important, in the omissions. The decorations in a telephone boiler room highlight the almost unlimited potential of an individual to achieve success. Teamwork themes are popular. Examples include "Working Together for a Common Goal" (a scene from a NASA space event); "Go the Course" (a white-water river rafting photograph); "Take Charge" (a football scene); and "We Work Together for Success" (a shot of a racing team changing tires in the pit).

In product boiler rooms the poster I observed most featured an expensive European automobile with an attractive woman posed seductively in front of it. "Poverty Sucks" was the caption. Among posters where text was more predominant than illustration were the ubiquitous "sales rules": "Always Listen to the Customer," "Help the Customer and You Help Yourself," and assorted sayings often accompanied by cartoon characters. A picture of a frog with a telephone in its hand carried the following advice: "If you can't beat 'em with your brains . . . Baffle 'em with your bullshit." The most commonly occurring line of text is, "Today is the first day of the rest of your life."

Boiler room wall adornment is selected to facilitate the social control of a sales force as it is commonly incorporated into sales presentations made by managers. The collective image revealed by all these depictions is clear: You are the captain of your own fate, you can recover from any hardship, and you must aim toward the future and forget the past. The most commonly occurring theme in the posters, examined as a group, is wealth, which takes the form of the dollar sign, photographs of cash, and stacks of gold coins, or as a handwritten overlay on the letter S appearing in poster text.

Absent from the walls of a boiler room are items not amenable to manipulation for business purposes: photographs of rock groups, religious depictions, pornography, automobiles (except in auto parts boiler rooms), motorcycles, sports and recreation scenes, and artifacts suggestive of youthfulness, rebelliousness, or social awareness. Youth-culture items featuring allusions to drugs, sex, or defiance of adult authority are common in shipping rooms of most boiler rooms, where occupants are socially and physically isolated from those who work the telephones. A sales manager's comments are typical of the industry's views: "We are a sales force. . . . When you work here you are a salesman. If you don't like it, you can stare at the walls in the shipping department or go work somewhere else. Here, you adopt a sales attitude, and you learn to close the deals. That's what we do. I'll help. That's what I'm here for. That's what the posters are here for: to help you get a sales attitude."

Sustaining Illusions

Boiler room operators are in the business of manipulating images and symbols that sustain a set of illusions, and several illusions surround boiler room work. The first is that a boiler room is a stable, secure company that subscribes to the central norms of business culture. These are not limited to, but would certainly include, the corporate expectation of remaining in business for the immediate future, expanding if possible, and rewarding workers with job security on the basis of merit, seniority, or the demonstration of economic productivity. The second illusion is that what is sold is worth the asking price. The third is that the sales force will be highly paid at some day in the distant future. A final illusion is particularly compelling, so powerful that it is readily self-consumed by virtually all parties who remain on the telephones: full middle-class occupational rewards (a career, an increasing income, retirement provisions, and social recognition for being an accomplished worker, manager or owner) are available to those who have only partial middle-class skills but are willing to work long and hard at the tasks at hand.

If status is defined as a positional location within some hierarchy of valued goals, and respectable white-collar work is defined as one such goal, a boiler room cannot provide it. Middle-class skills, however, are an entirely different matter. These are commonly understood to be related to education, verbal ability, ambition, tastes, persona, persistence, and self-image. They are interchangeable with the kinds of learning and self-management techniques taught in schools: interpersonal competence, certain values, attitudes toward the symbolic world, skill in manipulating abstractions, and social skills acquired in addition to the content of curricula. Perhaps the most important of these are patience and willing acquiescence to the demands of authority.

A boiler room is a sales organization involved in the communications business. The division of labor in modern industrial societies, as this relates to the media and communications industries, differentiates and highlights certain aspects of personality and rewards them highly. Boilers share this commonality with celebrities, technicians, athletes, and record-setters of all kinds who have only one part of their being, as it were, come to meet the market.[4] In like manner (in the deviant world), prostitutes, professional criminals, con men, and gamblers have a certain limited set of skills that command a short-term premium in the marketplace.

Learning to be a telephone pitchman requires partial middle-class skills: learning presentations and how to open a pitch, mastering the close and comeback techniques, practicing voice control, and taking charge of a telephone conversation. Moreover, boiling requires the discipline to stick out an eight-hour day in an office, to submit to managerial authority, and to have the ability to absorb the training offered. Although none of these attributes alone would qualify a typical candidate for all but the lowest-paid varieties of white-collar work, a new dynamic appears to be possible when a telephone pitchman provides the instructions.

Those who are fully members of the middle class in terms of cultural skills desired by the business world (students, unemployed office workers, certain homemakers by virtue of education, the underemployed, air traffic controllers, and displaced businessmen) do not leave boiler rooms because they cannot handle the telephone but rather, at worst, because the work is disreputable and neither pays well nor offers the option of permanent employment. At best, it is a temporary job. It takes considerable time, however, for many to discover that.

A telephone boiler room cultivates certain verbal skills required and taken for granted in the middle class and develops them through torturous repetition. After hundreds of hours and thousands of dials, a trainee becomes a regular and sounds as a salesman would be expected to. Other than for this glaring overdevelopment and over-reliance on a narrow band of verbal skills, the use of telephone talk in a boiler room appears similar to that in other sales occupations. A textual analysis of sales scripts would reveal as much.

When doing his job, a telephone salesman is an office worker in a middle-class world.

Being a telephone pitchman is having a temporary master status, a pivotal, identity-bestowing, occupational position (that of a salesman) with all auxiliary status characteristics—those other qualities that typically surround a conventional position—residing comfortably in the realm of illusion.[5] All middle-class semblances quickly vanish with the click of a telephone receiver. One pro described the experience of hanging up the telephone after a pitch as similar to "waking up after a dream." "It is sorta like a dream," said another. "Yes," added a third informant sardonically, "one illusion is over and the bad dream remains." Hanging up the telephone in a boiler room creates an existential tension between the "world that was, and the world that is."[6]

A boiler may routinely face a windowless office, his garage, his bedroom, a dirty shipping room, an exhausted group of fellow workers, or a table of greasy auto parts and drums of industrial chemicals. The dreamlike quality comes from the repetitive and partial social interaction in a world composed of symbols alone, which, reinforced by the commission structure, creates a sense of adventure in the best salesmen. Hunting down the deals becomes a game. In the words of one informant, "It's sort of like an electronic safari. I've got the pitch. I've got the phone. It's time for the hunt to begin."

Like all well-played games, the required procedures absorb full attention in a focused performance sustained until the round is complete. Over a cigarette, some coffee, and while writing up the paperwork for a recent order, one elated salesman described his victory: "Hot damn! Look at *this* [his order form]. It's amazing. I just sold a ten-gallon pail [drum of weed-killer] to a farmer I've never seen on the strength of my line alone. Now that's a power pitch! Believe it. I just *talked him out* of almost $500. Goddamn! This is wonderful. Way to go, Ralph! Can you imagine this kind of bread for a few minutes of bullshit? I love this job. Really, it's dialing for dollars. I should be on television."

For those who fail to make sales, the termination of a sales call brings other thoughts. More likely than not, a salesman will hear the din of other salesmen and the blare of rock and roll music. The carefully orchestrated interaction that could have resulted in a sale has been shattered by a dial tone, which many swear becomes louder when a customer hangs up. That can be disorientating for some and disillusioning for others. As time in the boiler room increases, however, all salesmen face a receding horizon of legitimate opportunities available elsewhere. By the time a seasoned boiler's disillusionment is complete, he has two choices: to quit or wait and be fired. That even experienced members of a boiler room sales floor are all ultimately fired signifies yet another way that such employment varies from the conventional variety. Although few escape this fate, it can be postponed with some luck and a thick skin. At any given time a few in the boiler room will always be writing deals, and success is always contagious.

Disillusionment, however, must be routinely neutralized. That requires considerable amounts of emotional work on the part of owners and managers, who themselves may be marginal to the middle class.[7] Sooner or later, illusions fail to be sustained, most of the sales floor turns over, and the shop folds, to reopen in another location and with a trimmed-down, more aggressive staff.

In large measure a boiler room operates successfully because it offers employment and is structured as a business, replete with a corporate charter in the majority of cases and with the requisite tax privileges in all. The ideology of a sales organization provides the rationale for taking the kinds of risks commonly associated with promoting products and services, and the rewards associated with such performances are granted legitimacy through the operation of the market system.

As a pure sales operation, a boiler room is subject to fewer constraints on the pursuit of profit than are conventional companies. One critical constraint is the generally accepted cultural understanding that there be some positive relationship between the value of a product or service and its asking price. Although few industries show a perfect association between the two—perhaps supermarket chains come closest in this regard—a boiler room affords the weakest, and possibly the most negative, association. Not only are the products and services overpriced, but some are also dangerous; many can result in the loss of income or in damage or costly restoration expense if they are used as promoted.

Although a boiler room represents a marginal manner of conducting business, its rootedness in the social order is deep and pervasive. There are substantial social impacts that are more difficult to quantify than those simply measured by the number of telephone rooms and the small armies of people who are run through them. These include the total societal contribution of boiler rooms to vending products and services that would otherwise fail to trade in the marketplace and the incomes thereby produced; the taxes paid on such income; and the impact of telephone rooms on American marketing practices. Other indirect effects include attitudes generated regarding the sales process, the unemployment entitlements not drawn by fired workers because most are hired as independent contractors, and the psychological costs that are held to no accounting standard.

The devastation unleashed on telephone salesmen, however, is likely to remain invisible, because their calls are perceived to be merely annoying—and thus readily dismissable. That is the case because the economic risk of failure (being unemployed) when working as a salesman generates little sympathy, creates no cognitive dissonance, and may not even attract much attention. Being unable to sell is both understandable and logically consistent with the dictates of a market process that requires no special explanatory apparatus. Moreover, the marketplace provides irony. When a salesman is marginally employed in a nebulously legitimate sales organization and is then victimized by such an alliance, the event can be readily attributable to bad luck, personal shortcomings, misfortune, greed, or the lack of appropriate insight, acumen, skill, willingness to learn, or common sense. This line of reasoning is familiar to all who work the telephones because it is commonly used—by them—to explain the behavior of boiler room customers.

The Control of Illusions: Confronting Customers and Salesmen

Although all boiler rooms create a notable percentage of disappointed customers, only very skilled boilers get to interact with them after the initial sale has been made. When they respond to customer complaints, pitchmen are carefully trained to offer solutions that ensure the illusion of redress upon completion of what appear to be routine and legitimate business practices.

The redefinition of events requires procedures and techniques called "buying back the heat," all of which involve deceptive practices.[8] Boilers, however, are marginal to both conventional and organized deviant worlds. They enjoy only the rewards of salesmanship and receive no subcultural support common to certain types of criminals; nor do they achieve the recognition and prestige associated with success in the business world. Although they use the symbols and language of the conventional world, they are often treated like a deviant group.

Unlike other deviant groups where conflict can engage redefinitional processes that enhance the bondedness of social life available to the membership, boilers are involved in a business operation. The only working identity available is that of a salesman. The use of sales skill and related techniques to buy back the heat in telephone rooms is a segmental role performance. After the telephone call is complete, the slate of interpersonal skills and interactive styles so critical to participation in subcultural forms of social interaction (dating and courtship, drug use, black markets, homosexuality, religious cults and worship, and upper-world and lower-world crime) is erased, only to be created anew with the next call.

Resolving conflict over the telephone represents a unique kind of social interaction that does not require the physical presence of others: The mark neither appears nor remains on the scene. An interaction membrane (those rules, roles, strategies, and goals that are part of a personally interactive social scene) fails to develop.[9] The other, so critical to the social definition of a group as a group, is a disembodied electronic impulse that reproduces the human voice.[10] Boilers thus do not constitute a class, nor a unified group, nor a subculture. There are, in the words of one informant, only "deals and dials. You get a deal, or you don't. Then you dial again. Then you go home."

Lacking the relatively permanent sense of continued social participation that characterizes most deviant groups, the boiler buys back the heat and returns to the interactive world of the telephone room rather than to the company of his peer group, fellow users, criminals, companions, believers, or other birds of a feather who can participate in interactive worlds and rituals that contain values not shared by "them," the generalized other.[11] Buying back the heat does not integrate a salesman into any particular kind of social world, it merely permits him to salvage orders.

Each boiler room overcomes criticism of its products or services in a manner consistent with the available skills of the sales force. As the level of skill increases, so does the sophistication of the retort selected. These retorts are called "comebacks": procedures used to rectify, redefine, clarify, neutralize, or dismiss customer dissatisfaction. The following discussion presents a general description of procedures that can be used by any business and those typically selected by boiler rooms.

The hierarchy of comebacks in Table 2 is grouped by the required trade-offs between the salesman's energy and the company's cost. The less energy it takes to resolve a dispute in a customer's favor, the more it will cost the company.

All the choices in Group A require varying degrees of salesmanship but little or no cost to the firm. The first comeback requires a great deal of smooth talk from the pitchman. If that does not work, the second option—requiring more skill and telephone time—will be used. If the first two options fail to placate a customer, the salesman must make a choice: Should he simply discredit the customer (comeback 3), or is he skilled enough to redefine the situation (comeback 4)? If his choice has not successfully terminated the call in the firm's favor, the salesman will use his last option (5): the fictitious credit.

Group B represents two choices that will cost the firm product and additional premium (steak knives, cheese, fishing gear, small appliances, and gift certificates). These comebacks are only used by the very skilled: pros and managers. In addition to the telephone time of a salesman, negotiation must take place. Comeback 6 requires an additional sale and/or a premium adjustment, and 7 requires an exchange. These options are time-consuming and require additional paperwork and a great deal of quick thinking so as to minimize the company's cost and maximize the dollar value of the transaction to the firm.

Table 2. Comebacks Ranked in Terms of Cost[a] to the Firm

When a customer is dissatisfied with the product or service, the management can select options from:

Group A: Low Dollar Cost (High Emotional Energy)
  1. Ignore the complaint but feign remediation.
  2. Transform the complaint into a customer error (failure to follow approved procedures).
  3. Discredit the customer (personality attack).
  4. Acknowledge the complaint and transform it into a selling point. Provide partial redress (premium adjustment) conditional upon an additional purchase.
  5. Offer a fictitious credit.

Group B: Moderate Dollar Cost (Moderate Emotional Energy)
  6. Offer a conditional partial credit and premium adjustment based on an additional sale or contingent upon continuation in the program.
  7. Receive the product back at the customer's expense. Offer something (which may or may not be the original product) in exchange. Charge inflated shipping and handling fees.

Group C: High Dollar Cost (Low Emotional Energy)
  8. Receive the product back at the company's expense and exchange the original for a substitute. Charge inflated handling and service fees.
  9. Upon receipt, refund part of the customer's money, prorated. Conform to industry norms regarding service and handling fees. Issue a credit.
 10. Refund all of the customer's money. No questions asked upon receipt of the unwanted merchandise or program.

a. "Cost" refers to the total dollar value of all transaction costs: administrative, telephone line charges, and expenditures of emotional energy. The latter represent the opportunity cost of sales lost due to the alternative tasks to which the skills of a pitchman could have been directed. The point at which comebacks become decreasingly cost-effective is reached when transaction costs begin to approach the level of profit resulting from the original sale.

Group C represents three options that cost the company time, product, and money. These are purely administrative and require no sales skill and little emotional investment. Comeback 8 involves substitutions, 9 involves partial refunds, and 10 involves full refunds. Only the owners of a boiler room get to routinely use these options, but some shops will permit a very skilled pro or manager to do so if the owner is preoccupied or unavailable.

In addition to illustrating the most common forms of retort in a boiler room, Table 2 can be read as a general frequency response grid. The ranked comebacks—during a customer-company interaction—can be tallied. Comeback 1 may be used a certain number of times, comeback 3 may not be used, comeback 8 may the most common, and so on. This procedure serves as a rough operational guide for differentiating boiler rooms from companies that merely use boiler room techniques and from conventional sales organizations that have nothing to do with either boiler rooms or their techniques but share only the common attribute of having a telephone number available for customer service. Table 2, in effect, becomes a disreputability table.

One can rank-order any business in terms of how it uses the comeback hierarchy. To identify empirically boiler rooms or companies with boiler room potential, one need only examine the actual dispositions of customer complaints for the firm in question. A boiler room will consistently, the vast majority of the time, rely almost exclusively on the first five comebacks (Group A, 1–5), occasionally on the next two (Group B, 6–7), and rarely on the last three (Group C, 8–10).

A company using boiler room techniques will typically use comebacks from Group B, occasionally from Group C, and rarely from Group A. A conventional firm conducts most of its business using comebacks from Group C, rarely from Group B, and never, intentionally, from Group A. The comeback techniques highlight the fluidity that characterizes conventional firms, somewhat disreputable companies, and boiler rooms. Using Table 2, it becomes clear that a boiler room can acquire legitimacy as its modal response to customer complaints achieves a higher numerical value by moving down the numbered scale. Conventional companies, in like manner, can become more disreputable as they come to rely heavily on the comebacks common to telephone rooms by moving up the numbered scale and achieving a lower modal value.

A boiler room operates on the principle that most customers will not pursue their grievances for protracted periods. Smaller companies have a very simple returns policy: none, ever, under any circumstances. In chemical rooms the freight charge on a five-gallon drum of chemicals can exceed the cost of the product contained therein. For this reason, COD terms are favored. As one owner said, "Once they sign for it, they own it. They've paid for it. End of discussion."

The greater the time-lag between payment for, and use of, a product, the greater the advantage to a boiler room, because the illusion of a customer's culpability is more easily sustained. Comebacks are forms of stalling designed to achieve this end. Some center around the nebulous routines and qualifications that must conform to a salesman's definition of a "correct application" (comebacks 2 and 4). Others are used in conjunction with the manager's judgment concerning the potential value of an account, as is the fictional credit (comeback 5). In this instance, an irate customer is finally told, "I understand. You are perfectly right. I'll arrange for your account to be credited. You will receive confirmation in ten working days. Fair enough?" The credit, of course, is never issued. If the customer follows up the request for a credit, the salesman apologizes for the possible administrative error and thus buys another two weeks.

In lieu of issuing a fictional credit, a salesman can stall by referring to an array of problems that can be purportedly prevented if the customer is more attentive to the proper use of the product (comeback 2). This involves educating the customer concerning the correct application of the product or imparting an accurate knowledge of the limitations of the service vended. A correct application (or proper qualifying condition for a service) is as varied as the salesman is creative. The salesman will extend the requirements indefinitely. The procedure used is to question the customer relentlessly until some violation of approved technique is discovered or invented.

A certain percentage of defrauded customers will insist on talking directly with their salesman after making an incoming call. These customers are told that their salesman is ill, out for lunch (at any hour of the day), or that he "no longer works here." Salesmen refuse incoming calls unless they have been trained to handle them and are psychologically prepared to buy back the heat. A sales manager in a chemical room explains how this is accomplished: "Well it's simple! It's like a puzzle. You find that part of the puzzle that the customer failed to do properly: that becomes the key. Once the customer admits that he failed to follow instructions, use the product properly, prepare the surfaces for application, properly store the material, or supervise its correct application, you are off the hook. It's *his* fault. It's that easy. Now we can't be responsible for someone who is stupid, can we? Of course not."

In the following demonstration, given during a sales meeting, a pro shows how virtually any objection can be redefined in the boiler room's favor. The session begins with a simulation of a commonly encountered complaint in the industry being worked by the telephone room: dissatisfaction with the quality of an overpriced protective coating and the customer's demand for a refund of the purchase price.

> No problem. I'm glad that you called. How are things on the farm? [Pause.] How's the Mrs.? [Pause.] How can I help? [Pause.] Let me fill out Customer Rectification Form 1905. Do you have a minute? Fine. Please provide the proper documentation. [The pro runs through a list, item by item, describing terms of the sale, the product, the premium, the date of sale, the method of payment. It takes a few minutes.][12] And now, the *purchase order authorization number,* what is it? [Pause.] Oh, you *don't* have it? [Laughter from salesmen in the room.] Gee, I am sorry, Mr. Andrews, we cannot honor a return without a purchase order authorization number. Please call us back when you get the appropriate documentation. Thanks. [Hangs up the simulated telephone and smiles.]

Such performances have didactic as well as confidence-building functions. The pro then solicits criticism from the assembled salesmen by challenging them to find flaws in the presentation. He categorically rejects, and artfully refutes, all attempts until one of the salesmen offers the correct response in terms of a question: "But aren't these orders paid for COD? How can the customer have a purchase order authorization number?" The pro and the owner then exchanged the following comments:

Owner: Exactly.
Pro: No problem!
Owner: Hey, they are catching on.

If the customer has placed a large initial order, or if it is a reorder customer, the pitchman will consider both the cost of the order and the cost of the premium, attempt to transform the grievance into a selling point, and try to place another order and make an adjustment for the original (comeback 4). For example, customers primarily concerned with cost may be given a sharper price on their next order, whereas the greedy may be given a larger premium.

The first step in buying back the heat is to establish that some error on the customer's part was committed. Perhaps the customer made some mistake in application, or perhaps the help failed to follow instructions or the product has been applied improperly (comeback 2). This time, however, rather than a prompt termination of the telephone call or a personal attack (comeback 3), the pro searches for plausible sources of error. Once those are identified, the salesman declares that the resultant problem, in part, was attributable to the customer's possible misuse of the product.[13] He is now free to demonstrate his good will by ascertaining the customer's need for another product, negotiating a price, and selling that product. Notice the subtle shift in the structure of the action: from an apologetic understanding of the circumstances surrounding a customer's complaint to the consummation of another sale. The shift is very practiced and happens quickly.

The customer will rarely get a refund.[14] Usually, however, a good salesman can turn the customer around. Most of the time they do. Sometimes they cannot. Not all heat can be successfully bought back. When that is the case, the customer faces the hard reality that his funds are lost forever. Even in the case of a persistent customer who continually complains (at his own telephone expense), the boiler room reaches its limit of being willing to entertain illusions. This is called a "burn-off." The customer is allowed to state his case, which is ridiculed; the customer is then insulted; and the telephone is hung up, as follows:

Manager: This is Rogers from Product Development. Let me get to the point. You purchased some of our degreaser some time ago, am I correct?
Customer: That's right. And it don't work worth a damn. I want my money back. You guys are a rip-off. I could buy the stuff you sold me at the local co-op for about 10 percent of what I paid you.
Manager: The exact same thing? You know that's not true. It's a lie. You may have been able to purchase *something,* but not our product. Ours isn't sold in stores. Am I right?
Customer: Well. But, that's not the issue. . . .

Manager: Look. We tried to *work* with you. How about the *cheese* package [the premium]? You *liked* that, didn't you? You *ate* that, didn't you? My friend, you [sing-song voice] are looking for something for nothing. You've got *our* product! You've got the cheese! Hey, this man's got *the cheese*. He's the big cheese! [Laughs so that listeners in the room can hear.] You want it all! Don't you? Now, you are now wasting my time because you think that you're a sharp cookie. Hey, eat some more cheese and have a good day.

Customer: You goddamn carpetbaggers. You are just air. Do you mean to tell me that I sent my money to a voice over the phone? That I am not going to get a refund?

Manager: You got it. You are absolutely right. I'm just air. Whoooooossh. Eat shit and die. Bye. [Hangs up the telephone.]

In some telephone rooms a special kind of comeback is used against salesmen, a refund ploy, which facilitates the termination of those who in the eyes of the sales manager have reached the point beyond which it is no longer profitable to continue to employ them. This deception is usually conducted in back rooms where the pros, normally changed with cooling-out disgruntled customers and creating fictional redress, get to use their talents internally.

In this scenario, an unsuspecting salesman working new accounts on the cold floor is told (wrongly) that the company has chosen to refund a customer's money due to a return, that is, the customer's return of defective or unwanted items. In such cases, the salesman is docked (charged-back) his commission on the sale in addition to the full value of the loss (the price of the order plus freight). In what follows, a salesman recounts his experience in a chemical shop of being called into the back room and given the bad news. Salesman [to his fellow workers]: "Damn. They gave a *refund*. It was a $350 sale. Now I am down my $70 commission [20 percent]. I owe the company $280 [80 percent], plus I got charged-back the freight [$21.65]. I am down $371.65. I'll never make it here."[15]

When he was later asked to leave the company—due to the feigned loss and his poor promise as a salesman—the owner agreed to "split the difference"; the company would also "forget about the freight." The salesman was docked $175. He reported that the owner had told him that "there are no hard feelings." "Look," said the owner, "not everyone is cut out for this line of work."[16]

One informant described the way actual returns were secretly handled at an auto parts house that previously employed him and how fictional charges were created:

Well, the garbage [defective parts] comes in and circulates. If it has not been destroyed, it goes back in the bin and is mixed in with the regular orders. When the customer complains, some do, most don't, it's a numbers game. Remember that the typical order has many items. Let's say that, for example, of a thousand items shipped, 2 percent [twenty] are junkers. OK. That's twenty pieces distributed over as many orders. Maybe, over a few months, five will come back again. No problem! Out they go again. Over a year it all disappears. The market can absorb lots of junk. It's like the service charge game they pulled two years ago. . . . They simply added on a dollar to the cost of each order and called it a service charge. A dollar is no big deal, right? Wrong. Those bucks add up.

Boiler rooms promptly create the illusion of rectification in response to customers' complaints, but that can be truly offered only for a tiny fraction of all accounts. Sales managers are alert to give such occasions the requisite publicity during sales meetings and morning announcements. Because replacements for unsatisfactory product are always shipped with an additional order—never separately—and the salesman controls all pricing, the price is easily marked up to more than cover the cost of the return.[17]

Psychologically, the ordering process begins with low-ball prices on items needed by the customer. Additional lines and items are then tacked on (added after the most essential items are vended). In most cases, after the customer is carefully quoted the items that will compose the first part of his order, price is hardly mentioned at all. The salesman punctuates quantities with terms such as "the wholesale price," the "yellow/green/blue sheet price," "our regular customer's price," and the like.[18] The salesman then writes up the order, filling in prices after the telephone conversation has ended.

Customers get a feel for the price structure based on prior experience with the boiler room as well as by comparing the prices charged in their local market for apparently similar parts.[19] Orders are also expanded with apparent loss leaders (underpriced items purchased in large quantities and stored in the boiler room's warehouse for just such occasions).[20] Most customers are pleased to hear, for example, that supplies in general shortage can be obtained. In their enthusiasm to receive wanted materials, most customers are willing to equate the boiler room's stock with the original item in shortage. In such instances, customers are also less likely to be attentive to the fictions in a salesman's pitch.[21] This is especially true for certain sectors of the automobile replacement market called the "highway trade" and composed of automobile service stations that deal with customers they will never see again. A salesman explains:

> The highway trade is located on highways where there are lots of transients and tourists. What the hell, they figure, the car that they fix will be in another state by the time any problems arise, if they arise. We get very few complaints. Besides, when a mechanic does a job, who is to say that it was our

part that caused a problem? . . . The guys who buy this stuff are trying to save some money. A guy whose car breaks down wants it fixed. Yesterday! Now you know that the garage is going to catch some heat in any event because they were called in on an emergency. No matter what they charge will be seen as a rip-off. So what can a garageman do? To charge reasonable prices to the customer, he buys cheap parts. We sell the parts. We all work together, you might say.

The better salesmen are aware of regional price discrepancies, and they overprice some of their line accordingly, earning the extra commission and relying on the fact that locals typically lack comparative information. The possible heat is diffused with a well-timed stream of compliments. The psychological impact of this on customers (based on the frequency of reorders) is that most feel that a good deal is being offered. The actual value of a salesman's accounts, however, is always problematic, because the salesman's relative status in a boiler room is always changing. A salesman in need of an extra order to meet a sales quota, a contest, or daily expenses is often tempted to pad orders. Some padding always happens, and because the boiler room benefits from the additional sales little is done to police the experienced sales force, who also bring home larger than normal commission checks as a direct result.

Excessive padding, however, requires strict control. Because a boiler room's management knows that discontented salesmen may excessively pad orders before leaving the employ of the firm, they usually terminate salesmen with no notice on Friday afternoons. The strategy of controlling both padding and the tenure of a salesman guarantees that the salesman will write the maximum number of "clean" sales and that padding will not become so extensive that customers refuse to place future orders. All managers know, however, that not only customers generate heat, which must be bought back, but also that part of their job involves the necessary termination of employees.

The Parting

Few people leave a boiler room voluntarily if they can survive the shakeout that constitutes the first few months of employment. There are a number of reasons for this apart from the time investment required to build accounts: There is considerable satisfaction in learning new skills and techniques; survivors are visibly recognized, as such, and most salesmen-to-be like to see themselves as being successful; and it takes at least two weeks to receive one's first paycheck and an equal or greater number of weeks for payroll adjustments to be made. Added to this is the psychological pressure to keep a recently acquired and much-needed job, a fact sales managers do not overlook.

After the training period, managers select a few who have potential and eliminate most who do not. Dismissal usually happens at or immediately after the hour at which the workday ends. Thus, the next workday sees a clean desk, to be left vacant until the next training cycle. Because few are paid weekly, the salary held in arrears affords management some leverage in minimizing the worker's disruption to the sales floor.

The fact that a soon-to-be-terminated man will likely have harsh feelings toward the firm is simply another kind of objection to be overcome. It is often used by management as a teaching tool to suggest the fate of those who have "bad attitudes" or communicate a sense of injustice ("sour grapes"). A manager giving a training session highlights the shortcomings of a salesman by commenting, "Stay away from Smith. He has a bad attitude. His life is out of control. His marriage is breaking up, and he has a sour grapes attitude. It's affecting his work. His sales have been down for the past six months. Don't listen to him. Now, I can't tell you what to do, but believe me I've been in this business a long time. His 'sour grapes' will only make it harder on him."

Smith is physically isolated from the trainees (sent to a work station remote from the training cubicles), and his lunch hour is rescheduled so he can only dine alone or with those who will now avoid him.[22] Those who dine alone are socially isolated from important networks that provide social support, pass on training tips, and provide product knowledge that can enhance sales skill and facilitate interaction with the group.

Management will sometimes select a man with failing sales for indoctrination, ritual display, and apparent rehabilitation. By giving the man a second chance, recruits are led to believe that the boiler room is basically a fair and reasonable place in which to work. A manager introduced a salesman who had "seen the light" (i.e., granted validity to the manager's criticism of his sales techniques):

> Now I want you to meet Mr. Jones. He has been with the company for three years. Three months ago he fell into a slump [describes]. So, we worked out a program. He came to me, and I taped his [telephone] presentation, and we both listened to the tape and made comments. I showed him a few pointers, and he worked to make his presentation better: to become a *volume* salesman, to ask for larger orders, to learn to overcome objections. I am always willing to help a man who wants to help himself. That's my job. That is why I'm here. Well, Mr. Jones, tell the trainees how it worked out.

Jones gives a testimonial to the effectiveness of the sales manager's techniques, his slow recovery on the road to becoming an effective salesman, and his gratitude to the sales manager. He also reports the size of his last paycheck.

An informant comments,

> In a pig's eye! What he didn't say was that Jones was fed [given choice accounts]. Jones is a laggard. The manager needs a guy like Jones who is too stupid to realize what is going on . . . Jones is a floater [a salesman who wanders from one boiler room to another]. He will never be a heavy-hitter. It's kind of sad. He is being kept here to use as an example to the new men. I predict that they will keep him hanging on until this next training class gets about two months' experience on the phones. Then there will be enough young sharks on the floor to drool over Jones's paper. They will can him and redistribute his accounts.[23]

Washing out newcomers is routine yet difficult work, because it must be accomplished swiftly, without emotion, and with no hint of personal bias. Failing to do this properly can be disruptive to the flow of production on the sales floor. One boiler room uses the common technique of having an affectionate authority figure—in the case to follow, the owner's wife—deliver the bad news to a trainee in the presence of its formulator: the sales manager. A pro has described the "quick-cut bitch pitch" in response to the question of what constitutes the surest, least-complicated way of effectively ridding a telephone room of unwanted personnel.

> Oh, that's *gotta be* the quick-cut bitch pitch. Hands down. It works every time. They use the owner's wife. Now she is a looker—know what I mean? . . . Well, they get this trainee that they don't want on board anymore. . . . So what do they do? I mean you don't want a scene, right? So her and the manager go to the back room. Two things happen: the regulars laugh and make bad [off-color] jokes, and then the newcomer is called into the office. The broad reads a statement that says that the employee is no longer needed by the company, and that she is sorry that this had to happen. Or something like that, I'm not sure of the exact words. Now the manager, he is a nodder: he nods his head as the owner's wife reads the pitch. . . . Now, I ask you, what do you do if that happens to you? Nothing much. You pack your bags, that's all. The men call her a quick-cut bitch. Her knives are into you before you know what's happening. From there on, well, you take your hat in your hand and blow out the door. What can you do? You can't argue with a lady. You can't do a damned thing. That's why they do it. Because it *works*. Once a salesman's been through that, he ain't never comin' back.

After the break-even point is exceeded, managers screen trainees at the larger firms through inattention. Being left alone ensures that all but the most motivated will conclude that they lack the requisite abilities. A trainee described his experiences over lunch: "I'm going to split. Man, it was just me and the phone. I just sat at my desk looking at it! Man, the time crept by. I couldn't sell anything. I couldn't even get through the pitch. No one can say all those things you are supposed to say."

"What we do is simple," the sales manager commented on that trainee and others. "I pay a man as much as I think he's worth, offer the training, and leave him alone. People quit, and I don't have to fire them. That saves me a lot of headaches. You might say that either a man is cut out *for* phones or he is simply *cut out*, period. Overall, it works out. If a man can write business, I'll give him the chance. If not, we part company."

Regulars who are terminated, however, can find themselves psychologically devastated. "Let me tell you," a salesman said. "My wife almost left me. I was with Better Parts for five years. I was fired on a Friday afternoon. No warning. No severance. No nothing. The manager says, 'You will be leaving this evening. Clean out your desk.' It sort of blew me away. It was totally unexpected. Hey, they didn't even have the decency to give me advance warning." Concerning entitlement to back pay and his impressions of the boiler room, he observes:

> I'll be lucky if I get to see 20 percent of that money. You know company policy: "Back pay is held against outstanding accounts." Now, you know that they will always find a number of mysterious returns. They make them up. You can't prove otherwise. They know that. To be honest, the money is not that important. I can always make more money. It's that I thought I had a place. Better Parts is not too far from where I live. That's why I went to work there in the first place. But it's nothing. That's what upsets me. I don't really have any friends there. All my buddies have been fired. Now I am fired. Hey, I spent a lotta time going out of my way to talk good about the company. No one likes to admit that they have been a fool. It's a bitter pill. It's not even the manager. True, he is a sonofabitch, but they all are. What have I got to show? That is the real problem. Look, I am forty-nine years old. Where I am going now? I missed the boat, I guess . . . I was stupid. I waited too long. I should have left [the industry] immediately after my draw was cut.

Most who have been on the telephones for a few years have a small network of fellow boilers with whom they keep in contact. This can provide some psychological support after a firing, or it can serve as a source of encouragement during hard times. A pro says:

> Well. You know how it is. I can pick up the phone right now. All I have to do is talk to the owner or the sales manager. I get an instant appointment. Cheer up! Good phone men are never out of work. Making a decent living? Well, that is something else. A phone is a phone. They are all the same. Sometimes you get lucky. . . . An industry is hot, like chemicals a few years ago.

Then it dies out. It comes and goes. It's like life—ups and downs. Don't be a floater, though. Stick with where you are. Keep on the phones. We all have a bad day. A bad week. A bad month. Hey, I even had a bad year! Do what you have to do. Look, in sales it's all attitude. Make of it what you can. Things will work out.

Working the telephones in large shops or small, those who survive the many hurdles come to understand that the activities in a boiler room represent an intense, concentrated, version of a sales process that has been abstracted to the point of phonic technique and a series of punch lines strung together to form a workable harmonic.[24] The pitchman prepares for the next outgoing call as a chess master awaits the moves of his opponent—as his manager dutifully attends to the business of calculating how long this will be permitted until a replacement is sought.

One result is a trickle of workers being constantly fired. This becomes a torrent when a boiler room is shut down, thereby temporarily bringing into public view the nature of these operations. Such visibility occurs when the glaring discrepancy between what is touted and what is delivered makes news. The notion of an enterprise carrying a corporate charter to manipulate, fabricate, and disseminate illusions is beyond the consciousness of most.[25] It is likely to remain so.

After a period of intense negative publicity, calm is typically restored. A boiler or two with some resources, ambition, and an account list will start the cycle anew. In a passing comment concerning a recent telephone call, an owner known to pros as "Phoenix Jack" (so named for his knack of emerging, more or less unscathed, after his companies go out of business) reveals the intrinsic fascination many have with the industry:

They shut down Americhem. They closed its doors. I just talked to Ron Wilson the other day. He offered me a job! [Laughs.] We used to work together. Now they blow him out the door because the wolves [the authorities] blew the whole damn company down! [Laughs.] Now he's going to run his paper [work his accounts] out of his house. He's calling the operation "Wilco Chemical," and he's looking for an office. Hell, he's a heavy-hitter. He's got to have over five hundred active accounts. That'll keep him busy for a while, I bet . . . I've been there myself. You know, you get to thinkin': The suckers are still out there. They're only a phone call away. Why shouldn't it be *my* phone? It's not like the suckers have been shut down. The mooches still have Master-Cards.

The Illusion of Services:
Scams That Fly by Night

I thought I'd seen it all. . . . But, I just came back from a place where they have a room full of pros, and they give out hundred dollar bills: they pay in cash. It's unbelievable. I just had a talk with the owner, and I listened to them pitching. They are really good, the best I've seen. Hey, it's life in the fast lane. I'm all excited about the phones again . . . I start Monday.
    —*first impression of an owner of a product house upon visiting a different type of telephone operation*

Service Shops: Scam Operations

Scams are frauds. While product houses are marginal distributorships run as businesses, scams are marginal businesses run as confidence games, where a pitchman's skill matches the level of financial rewards available. A sense of genuine urgency forces both skill and reward to race to closure. Scams are designed to shut down; the critical issue is when. Concealing that fact from both clients and operatives, however, requires a high order of competence. At their best, the owners of these businesses are, simply put, charming—engaging enough to coax reluctant dollars from the pockets of unseen marks and smooth enough to train a room full of boilers to work the most complex of pitches.[1] They are also confident enough to maintain a generally positive working environment and mysterious enough not to reveal the true nature of their operations.

Charm, after all, is a quality known by its suggestiveness, not what is demonstrated in a performance. The skilled are those who stand in relation to some measure by which their performance is compared. The charming, however, are always elusive. Their art and appeal lie precisely in the fact that they never have to reveal all that may be revealable. They thereby create the illusion of potential and being perpetual catalysts of surprise, innovation, and discovery. The socially inept, though, always fail to reveal other than the obvious, which is why they are typically seen as being boring, leading uneventful lives, and being dominated by routine matters.

"Life in the fast lane" of a service operation represents a distilled version of familiar procedures. A pro in a gas house captures the sense of the quick-paced achievement there: "ALL RIGHT! [Intense emotion.] ALL RIGHT! It's steak tonight! The bank wire just cleared, and forty-five minutes of pitchin' out my guts just put THE BIG TWENTY-ONE [$2,100] in my pocket. I can't explain it. Maybe it's luck. Maybe it's skill. Who knows? The fact is that when you're hot, you're hot, and I AM Hot! There is nothing else I can do that brings in this kind of bread. That's why I play. It's the only game in town."[2]

One informant, whom I met in a context far removed from the jail where he had served some time for having masterminded a number of scams, described the logic of the industry as succinctly and eloquently as is perhaps possible:

> It's all life in the fast lane. . . . The best way to understand what's actually going on is to imagine a slot machine: What we do is get a lot of people to play. . . . Sooner or later the mooch is looking for his reward. So, you buy back the heat. You fine-tune the pitch, and you load them up [get them to invest more]. . . . There *can't be* a payout. Not for most who play. So, you skip town, take your profits, and move your action elsewhere. . . . People play for the kill. Making a hit. It's the excitement of being a winner. . . . Suckers want the thrill of the sure deal, the illusion that they are *masters* of something. That's it, really, they want a line that they can believe in.

Service shops link the illusion of expertise to a client's revealed need for advantageous offerings. These may be coverages (insurance and credit) or varied kinds or business opportunities, investment tips, betting advice, personal betterment strategies (diets, dating, or training), travel services, employment possibilities, or franchises that come to define the type of scam involved. All involve a very generous notion as to what constitutes a reasonable investment or opportunity.

Although the everyday world may find the meaning of these terms problematic at best and vague at worst, the scams deal only in statistical likelihoods and sales. A claim is true in direct proportion to the number of sales it generates. If too many potential customers disagree, the wording of a pitch is modified until the program sells. Scams work in those areas of social and economic life where effortless profit or a quick fix to an otherwise intractable condition of circumstance, spirit, mind, or body is thought possible if only a golden opportunity were to present itself.

Scams promote an idea: The means to achieving a desirable financial or personal goal is programmatically available. The plan for doing so is for sale to a select few, for a limited time only, *if* one qualifies. Service shops compose the second tier in the world of telephone rooms. At the top of this stratum, only the very skilled are permitted access to the sales floor. At the bottom, almost any scheme is possible. Most scams are put together with greater care than the "Fifth Marine Division, Inc.," which failed quickly. As a salesman recalled, "An operation that called itself the 'Fifth Marine Division, Inc.' was soliciting for contributions [over the telephone] in the name of the U.S. Marine Corps. One of their marks, however, was a real Marine Vietnam veteran who became suspicious [explains]. . . . The operation recruited collections men who looked like they might have been Marines, but they weren't. When the collector came to pick up the donations, the Marine followed him back to the boiler room and settled the matter physically."

In addition to being pure sales organizations like product shops, the scams are centers of pure entrepreneurial activity as well. With no physical product to deliver, there are fewer constraints on the imaginations of those who concoct these schemes than is the case for any other type of telephone room. While a product shop pro is a craftsman, a pitchman in a scam operation is the working magician of the boiler room, creating wealth with some of the most creatively designed pitches to be heard on the telephone and then vanishing to places unknown. In this context, the universal, initially mystifying "two-line ads" placed in newspapers by scam operators are revealing when interpreted correctly. A pro explains:

> I'll tell you what it means. It means what it don't say. There is no mention of a salary. That means it's a straight commission deal. They only give a phone number. That means it's a boiler room. Has to be. No other way. There is no sales manager named. That means it's a smart shop [a small operation run by the owner himself]. . . . Talk about silver-tongued thieves [laughs], notice that there is *no kind of name* mentioned at all, not even some phone name. That means they don't mess around. It's going to be pros only. No managers. No staff. No secretaries. You've got to wail on your dime [start pitching with little training and be able to sell over the telephone]. Plus, there is no *deal* [terms of employment] advertised. That means these guys don't believe in up-front money [a draw or a salary]. . . . Lastly, there's no address given. That means that they don't *need* an address. It means that they don't want tourists, you know, people who don't know the score: reporters, time-wasters, and lumpos, or those who can't make up their minds. It also means that they are new to town. It's the feeler ad: They only need to actually hire *one* pro, the rest are referrals. . . . If there is money to be made, word gets out. People will jump shop. That's why they only run the ad for a day or two. Hey, they can tell in a minute if they've got a real pro on the line. These guys are the best of the best.

A Scam for Every Nature

That scams work all economic classes is a point well driven home in a conversation over lunch with a commodities pro (a boiler who assembles limited partnerships for the purpose of investing in stock options) who had just left a recently shut-down shop where the minimum play (investment requirement) was $25,000. We were both simultaneously interviewed for positions with a plot operation (a scam selling cemetery plots).[3] After the interviews, he offered his interpretation and a comparative assessment:

> Do you believe that place? I was interviewed in the vice president's office, they called it the "war room." They had a huge map of the city that covered almost the entire wall. It was a router [a detailed street map often used to plan delivery routes]. It was a pure *ethnic sell deal.* I've never seen anything like it: an equal opportunity rip-off [laughter]. The blacks sell to blacks, women to women, Hispanics to Hispanics, Asians to Asians. There were three recent immigrant crews that I'd not known were here in sizable numbers [names them]. . . . They pitch 'em cemetery plots. It's a fear pitch [a presentation designed to raise anxieties and promote insecurity]. You work the phones, and then you do a house sit [visit the prospect in their home, by appointment]. . . . And did you hear the loader [the pitch used to increase the size of a sale]? A special deal on multiple [family] plots. Then there is the financing, where they balloon 'em after the fifth year [a sales strategy featuring low initial payments and then larger, balloon payments after a certain point]. Hey, I've sold some pretty wild things over the phone [explains his past experience], but I've never *busted* anyone before, I mean where they *lost it all* due to my deal. I've never ripped off poor people before. . . . Can you imagine? You're new to America and you break your ass cleaning floors or driving taxis or whatever. And then you die, and guess what: *There is no grave!* . . . Did you catch the insurance rider [a scheme offering overpriced life insurance to cover the cost of the cemetery plot in the event of the insured's death]? They get 'em both ways. If they live, they pay bilko rates for an overpriced plot which may or may not be real; then, if they die, their family has a questionable insurance policy and maybe nothing at all. The fine print I saw on the policy was a front-end job [extremely high commissions extracted during the first year of the policy]. These people get ripped off, and death *doesn't* do them part. They get ripped off on their graves.

Whether or not a boiler room scam can function and thrive is primarily an artifact of prevailing market conditions. In a perfect market, a customer has access to comparative data on services, and the distribution system functions optimally. There is no psychologically compelling reason to buy over the telephone. Under such circumstances, overhead costs alone would drive boiler rooms into the history books as an archaic social form.

In certain product markets this process of being driven may be beginning, but its final resolution does not appear imminent on the "scam phone," as service shops are sometimes called. Scams can only work when clients are persuaded to act on what they envision to be real for them, absent serious scrutiny or objective analysis. They operate in what may be considered a phantom market, where hard cash is exchanged for illusions alone. They are in direct competition with conventional investment companies, charities, and self-betterment industries.

Virtually all scams—badge operations are the exception— require financial literacy on the part of pitchmen, many of whom typically read the business press at the start of the workday. This is so because whatever is being sold must be presented in a comparative sense. A knowledge of the language surrounding the generalized operation of markets is the most effective way to make a fictional service appear to be an opportunity of some kind.

Investors of all kinds are also familiar with the direct relationship between risk and gain, and the host of folk adages surrounding speculative ventures are easily adapted for boiler room use.[4] Scams are sometimes known by the type of client, mark, fish, or customer they seek and sometimes by the nature of the service being vended. Thus, there are investment scams that target those who have the requisite levels of disposable income and specific promotions that may tap a wide variety of groups.

Some scams provide intangibles, such as contracts, betting advice, and telemarketing expertise; others vend whatever they think they can get away with. One informant, for example, ironically sold bogus advertising space in never-published fraud prevention handbooks as part of a fake tele-fund-raising effort. When the brief spate of publicity surrounding fraud subsided, he shut down the operation, moved, changed his corporate name, and opened another company.

In the phantom market, new classes of nondeliverables are constantly being created. Maintenance contracts can be sold that will never be honored; lawn and home care services feature an imaginary work force; and promotions for vacation travel, credit, time-shares, contests, investments, and fund-raising result in offers where what is received is worth less than the cost of the telephone call needed to close the deal.

On the scams, a telephone name serves as an alias to protect a pitchman from revealing his legal identity. Some telephone salesmen have more than one. A pro, for example, may assume different telephone roles (the "operations manager," the "comptroller," or the "bank wire manager"), with a different name attached to each. A scam can theoretically thrive in any area of perceived need, and pitchmen create whatever is seemingly required to fulfill it. For example, many consumers have become increasingly annoyed by the sheer volume of unwanted (junk) mail and telephone calls they routinely receive. That annoyance has produced a discrepancy between the needs of customers and vendors. Scams are remarkably innovative; this single example of a conventional annoyance spawned a new type of service room. A pro explains:

Oh yeah, people hate unwanted phone calls and junk mail. One [telephone scam] solved the problem. For a fee, they will take your name *off* of all mailing and telephone prospect lists. Major credit card only, please! It's a contract shop [a service boiler room]. It's a beautiful pitch! Unbelievable. A phone call announcing the end to all unwanted phone calls! They claim to be survey brokers. They've got the kill codes [an imaginary program that deletes names from computer files]. They make a ton of money. The room lists the names on a computer and sells them to other boiler rooms at a premium. They are called "snucker lists." It means silent sucker: people who've got big bucks or resources they want to hide. . . . Look, it's simple. Information ain't safe. Somewhere they code it, sort it, manage it. That means that it's *for sale*. Somewhere out there there's a mooch in the supply line. There's gotta be. There always is. They want privacy? No problem! It's a perfect deal. The phone room makes out twice. They get paid up front from the customer, then they sell the customer's name. Scams thrive on mooches. Some people are moochie [greedy] for money, others for privacy. People can be moochie for a number of things.

There are also different levels of scam operation. Some work multiple scams simultaneously, whereas others specialize in one particular function—fund-raising, for example—but may come to represent many different fictional entities, and some may be run as adjunct operations to a product boiler room. It must be remembered that the scams work in telephone environments where fantasy is readily available. That is a relatively new phenomenon. Although society's two master fantasies (fiction as "literature" and science fiction as a product of the technologies associated with industrial development) have been available in print for many years, widely consumed telephone versions of fantasy materials have only been popular since the mid-1970s.

The porn phone (the vending of erotic fantasies) is in a class by itself, because what is sold can be conceptualized in terms of pure fantasies of response. There are two kinds of porn telephone operation: the sex phone, which uses women who work on commission, and the tape show, a service operation using prerecorded tapes. The former uses credit cards for collecting money from clients, whereas the latter uses a 900 telephone number and extracts a commission from the telephone company.

The sex phone is a boiler room providing a service: Women are paid for their skills in meeting their customers' needs. Tape shows use recordings. They are not boiler room operations, although they use boiler room techniques. Two tape show operations in New York in 1985, according to one informant, received more than ten thousand calls daily. With tape shows, however, the fee for the first minute of telephone connect time is sometimes not specified (it can be a few dollars), and the fee for each additional minute can be quite large. One company uses a "low-ball come-on" and charges 80 cents for the initial minute and $3.95 for each additional increment. A variation of this technique is to bill for a minimum number of minutes without regard to actual usage—"Only $2.09 per minute, twenty-five-minute minimum," for example.

Skin operations (sex and porn telephones) are important, for the purposes of my analysis, because of the fact that the owners of these businesses sell their customers' names to other scam operators. Such lists are called "dirty paper" and command a premium because pornography fans (most of whom are men) often seek other kinds of fantasies as well and tend to be secretive people whose names would be otherwise unobtainable. A sports betting pro observed of dirty paper:

> Hey, I used to think that porno guys were weirdos. Maybe. Maybe not. I got some dirty paper from a flick distributor who had gotten a list of names and phone numbers. . . . I figured, "What the hell, I'll give it a shot. Who knows?" Anyway, I never talk about the porn, but some of these guys are *players:* they make big bets [on sports contests]. I can't figure it out. Maybe one kind of fantasy sleeps with other kinds! I don't know. I do know that I could never get a hold of that guy again to buy more names. He never stopped by again. I wish he would! That was a good list.

Some scams are product-related, although the products themselves are not sold. Industry-specific contract operations, for example, work the consumer durables and electronics fields by offering warranties that ensure customers that items, in the case of manufacturing defect, are covered by a service contract. Their existence nicely illustrates imperfections in a market and the inabilities of conventional salesmen to service a need. The need concerns assurances of product reliability that are readily suited to telephone presentation. All products vended where a customer did not purchase a service contract at the point of sale are thus eligible for a boiler's telephone call. In most cases, however, those with the technical knowledge to make the necessary repairs lack the telephone skills and technique to vend the contracts. Enter the boiler room's outside closer, a professional skilled in closing person-to-person sales.

Chain stores commission-out service contract accounts to local service providers. The boiler room, in turn, contacts these and sells the contracts on a commission basis, charging what the market will bear.[5] These are short-lived because the market quickly becomes saturated. When a goodly number of customers who have made electronics purchases from a given store, or chain of stores, in the past six months has been called, the services of the boiler room lose urgency and are no longer needed. Then the boiler room fires its staff or moves on to another kind of account.

I will focus on five major types of scam operations that illustrate the breadth of the market for telephone sales talent: coin operations, the most common type of investment scam; the "cert" (certificate) boiler room, the most complex and many-leveled type of scam; the "Arizona Energy Company," the most creative scam; badge operations, those scams requiring the least sophisticated pitch; and the "littlest boiler room," the smallest operation I observed. Together, these operations cover most of the telephone action available: investments, recreation, speculation, fund-raising, and franchising. New varieties are constantly emerging, but all telephone scams share some of the elements of the five major types.

Coin Operations

Specialty scams in the field of numismatic investments are called "coin houses," "coin operations," or "coin shops." They are the most common type of investment-oriented boiler room that is patterned after the conventional marketplace for numismatic items. All investment scams follow the general principles applicable to coin houses.

In a conventional market, the value of a coin is influenced by the preferences of collectors, speculators, and investors.[6] The level of demand for a particular coin is reflected by three major indicators of the coin's value: the dealer bid price (that price a dealer will typically pay to acquire the coin for his inventory); the dealer ask price (what the dealer charges the retail customer for the coin); and the value quote (some value above the dealer's bid price but below his asking price). Thus, when collectors speak of the "value" of a coin they mean the dollar price for the coin in a specified numismatic condition that another collector would typically pay: the value quote.[7] Investors and speculators are also interested in numismatic items because there is the possibility of price appreciation for certain scarce, rare, or well-preserved pieces. All find numismatics appealing because the supply of coins for a given minting year (the mintage) is always fixed by the government and can only decline over time, because a number of factors operate to generate scarcity for any given coin.

The numismatic value of most coins, over time, thus increases. It is the rate of increase that speculators find appealing, and they provide the largest and most visible outlays of cash into the conventional marketplace. Consider, for example, a 1964 U.S. dime. A certain number of collectors stash them away, many are lost, many are in children's banks, and some are beneath the cushions of the living room couch. Others are destroyed, some are taken out of the country by tourists, and some wear beyond the point of being able to read the coin's date and legend (called "very poor" condition) and are routinely melted down by the government (which replaces them with current coinage).

To the noncollector, of course, a "dime is a dime," and most people would not be aware of the numismatic aspects of a "64," hence some of these coins always remain in circulation. That fact generates collector interest, because there is considerable appeal in locating a "find" in one's pocket change. If, as is true for the 1964 dime, a coin has bullion value, an unknown number may be sold to dealers for melt (a price quote based on the silver content of the coin). Hence, the number of coins from a given year that are in circulation (the population) is unknown and can vary substantially. Moreover, the population of 64s contains an unknown distribution of dimes in differing states of preservation. Some may be brand new (uncirculated), obtained in bags or rolls from banks during the year of issue and held by collectors or worn by the circulation process to varying degrees (said to be in many gradations of "circulated condition").

For a boiler room, the complexity of the numismatic marketplace makes coins ideal candidates for artful promotion. Even among experts there is always some disagreement over the state of preservation of a given coin because coin grading is a subjective art. One collector's "green tarnish" on the surface of an uncirculated silver dollar (caused by oxidation and certain contaminants in the air) lowers the value of a coin. To another collector this self-same quality may represent "original mint patina" and serves as evidence that the coin was never chemically or mechanically cleaned—and the piece will command a premium as a pristine specimen. The state of preservation is one important determinant of a coin's value.

Even if experts could agree on the numismatic condition of a given coin, however, most coins are not sold by experts but by dealers. Boiler rooms acquire inventory from dealers, and there is no consensus, nor can there even theoretically be, regarding market price. Like diamonds and art, coins have too many variables for precise specification. Although there are rough guidelines, the value of a coin is what people are willing to pay for it. That seems simple and straightforward enough until one asks, Which people? Coin buyers vary by region, age, income, and degree of interest and include dealers and the curious. The value of bullion coins is also dicey because fluctuating metals prices likewise cause the value of bullion-bearing coins to fluctuate if a great deal of speculation occurs in the future price of their main precious metal component.

As with any area of investment, it usually takes an uncommon amount of knowledge and years of following the markets to gain an understanding of pricing dynamics. In fact, the quick fix a boiler room provides to these troublesome issues is welcomed by many who seek only quick returns and are willing to avoid spending the time and energy required to gain true numismatic knowledge.

Tiny variations in the condition of a coin can amount to price differences of thousands of dollars. Using the September 1990 issue of *Coin Prices Magazine* as a guide, for example, page 54 shows that a genuine 1883-S silver U.S. dollar in mint state (MS) 65 condition, DMPL ("deep mirror prooflike"), is valued at $63,000. The same coin, one fine gradation of condition less (MS-65 without the DMPL qualities), is valued at $31,500. The price difference of $31,500 lies in the eyes of those who can distinguish a near-perfect (MS-65) coin more than a hundred years old that has never been in circulation with a never-circulated coin that has DMPL attributes. It is not a game for the timid or the uninitiated. It takes considerable expertise, much study, and the examination of many examples of the coin to be assessed to have enough skill to discern fine differences. Although a boiler room does not (and can never) have such knowledge, it merely must imply that it does—precisely a task within a pitchman's range of skill.

Coin shops trade in what numismatists call "overgraded stock" (coins with inflated values). That is accomplished by labeling a coin's true condition as being higher than is the case. One need not touch or modify a coin to accomplish this; one only need change its packaging.[8] Nor need boiler rooms deal in expensive coins to make windfall profits, as another example from the same issue of *Coin Prices* illustrates. The very popular Kennedy half-dollar of 1964 is a 90 percent silver coin and has a value of $3.75 in mint state 60 condition but a $7.50 value in mint state 65 (a higher numismatic grade)—a $3.75 difference.

Coin Prices reveals that this particular coin sells in rolls of twenty for $50 ($2.50 each). Such an "uncirculated roll," as it is called, would contain mostly MS-60 specimens, perhaps a few nicer coins, and some sliders (coins not quite up to MS-60 grade). This is how a boiler room owner buys, and he gains the dealer as his supplier and access to his expertise.[9] Buying a coin for $2.50 (in quantity) and promoting it at a higher grade and price ensures sufficient profit and disreputability.

Once a supply of coins is located, a boiler room sets up shop by designing an alluring corporate name—for example, "Millennium Numismatic Properties"—and a logo and by creating literature, culled verbatim from the numismatic press. It also advertises in distant newspapers and by conducting direct mail campaigns using reply-mail postcards and/or an 800 (toll-free) telephone number. Less-organized coin houses call investors from leads provided by brokers. If investment advice (a service) is to be offered, a 900 number is used.[10]

One set of boilers typically handles incoming calls on the 800 number, and the less experienced make cold calls to those who have sent in reply-mail postcards. Once a hot item (a type of coin that sells well) is located by trial and error, pitchmen work on promoting varied "investment packages" consistent with the financial climate of the day. The language comes from both the numismatic and the financial presses and is modified accordingly in tune with whatever market pundits find timely.

Pitchmen are free to invent their own scenarios. If the Dow Jones industrial average is climbing, some will talk confidently of the "coming economic boom," whereas others will see a "triumph of the bears" in the same basic information. Some boilers use a "two-pronger"—a pitch with both bullish and bearish connotations—and let the prospect's response determine the style of the presentation. When boilers begin spending a larger fraction of telephone time buying back the heat, it signals the ownership to begin firing cold-callers and concentrate on loading (increasing the size of the orders made to previous customers).

Pros unleash the "acquisitions pitch": a "spectacular hoard" of (whatever they are selling) that has just been made available from the estate sale of an important collector. Pros invent the names of collections, such as the "Wilson Estate Holdings" or "the Newberger Hoard"; and some like to link celebrities and personalities in the news with imagined numismatic holdings, the "fantastic Elvis dollars," the "California Reagan pieces," or whatever catches their fancy. Many tap into news headlines to create fictional acquisitions such as "Russian defectors' coins," the "South African gold traders' stash," and the like.

When complaints continue to mount, pros are increasingly diverted to entertaining them, and regulars are fired. This signals the last cycle in the life of a coin house before what is called "the send"—when the boiler room's prime customers are contacted after their previous orders have been studied carefully. In the send scenario, select customers are offered discounts of up to 50 percent of what they previously paid for a given type of coin. That generates a last pulse of income before the boiler room shuts down.[11]

Coin houses rarely sell to coin collectors or investors, however, but only to those who would like to imagine that they could profit by being so engaged. If a prospect, for example, knows about the American Numismatic Association (ANA) or is familiar with the Sheldon Grading System (i.e., the use of mint state [MS] numbers), he or she is typically not pitched but rather treated courteously, pumped for information, and thanked for their time. Someone who knows anything about numismatics is not a likely phantom market candidate.

The knowledgeable are avoided for two reasons. First, they cannot be sold because they base their investment decisions on actual data. Second, they can complain to the numismatic press, to coin dealers, to local newspapers, and to television shows such as "60 Minutes," thus increasing the visibility of the boiler room. Although such complaints may shut down a particular operation, they do little to influence the industry. The reasons for this are cultural: Americans often tend to view certain types of investigative journalism as entertainment. Unless celebrities or the politically powerful are implicated, the effective message communicates a current reading of American mores: only the stupid, the greedy, and the gullible get stung in a capitalistic society. Those in the know are presumably too smart to be conned.

Because the structure of a boiler room remains invisible and the problem is typically reported as an issue involving the personal shortcomings of wayward individuals, it is easy to see why most Americans, given the terse nature of news reporting and the shallow training most reporters receive, would rather experience revelations that testify to their own implied levels of sophistication than address the more troubling issue of systemic fraud.[12] The fiction of "lone scamsters" and "greedy victims" is much more appealing and comforting than the reality in boiler rooms.

Although cutbacks in government regulatory activities may delight fiscal and other conservatives, they are also "wonderful news" (a line used in many pitches) for those who run boiler room scams, because there will be less heat in the future. Moreover, because the type of attention generated is typically sensationalistic rather than analytic, and news of "boiler room busts" must compete with other financial news, the nature of the industry will typically be ignored unless some hapless victim happens to be interviewed on a slow news day, when not much is happening.

Simple publicity, however, more often than not is just so much heat that must be bought back. For a single publicized event—say, a widow who gets burned—the remedy is simple: a refund is offered. Whether it will be honored depends on the boiler room's "closing schedule." The promise of a refund, in the case of a media event, however, can generate publicity and more orders. In any event, by the time the press gets around to doing a follow-up story, the coin operators have typically long since fled.

Cert Operations: Travel in the Mind's Eye Only

Travel scams, called "cert operations" (after the certificates they vend), are among the most sophisticated of boiler room scams because they operate at many levels, although most are headquartered in Florida. "Feeder shops" are set up across the country and use a wide range of talent. "Road boilers" set up the operations and manage them, and sales managers are hired locally, as is a telephone sales force composed of regulars and trainees. Cert operations require a great deal of planning and logistic support in commercial real estate, accounting, list brokerage, administrative assistance, telephone and furniture acquisition, and office fabrication.

Cert operations also use some salesmen who are trained in outside closing but are hired locally to work certain kinds of commercial accounts. Few remain in business for more than a year, the minimum length of a commercial lease in most parts of the country. Cert operations are organized in four stages. The first stage consists of locating a target city and then dispatching road boilers to locate a working site, set up the operation, and hire and train the outside sales force.[13] The second stage involves building the boiler room itself, hiring workers, and promoting travel contests of varied kinds, which are serviced by the out-of-state company. The third stage involves the promotion of franchise opportunities.[14] The final stage involves shutting down, returning to home base, and then moving on to another city, leaving franchisees, customers, and workers without payments or services.

Stage One: Setting Up Shop

Road boilers are telephone sales pros who have typically been trained in real estate, as stock brokers, as automobile salesmen, as "book men" (encyclopedia salesmen), or as travel agents before they connected with the headquarters boiler room (HBR), where they specialize in travel promotions. They work as a team. Typically, three or four pros are assigned to a selected city, and the team may include a husband and wife pair. Like pros in product houses, they are craftsmen. Unlike them, however, road boilers are confidence men in the fullest sense of the term. Not only can they sell over the telephone, but they can also train others and close outside deals (those involving face-to-face contact).

Most enjoy doing so and have extremely high levels of interpersonal competence. They dress fashionably and seem to be selected for their ability to project confidence and business acumen. The ones I have met are universally trim and fit, and their ages range from the low thirties to the mid-forties. Their skills will ultimately be used on four kinds of marks: customers, most of whom will never receive services; the outside sales force, most of whom will be fired; the inside sales force, all of whom will be cheated out of wages and then fired; and franchisees, all of whom will pay for useless territories and rights.

Only a handful of such teams work the entire country. They constitute an elite in the boiler room world because they are extremely articulate, geographically mobile, and very skilled. Moreover, because they specialize, full-time, in starting and closing feeder rooms, they are somewhat unattached to the conventional world.[15] Divorce is common, and none have children with whom they live. Unlike other types of boiler room operatives, cert operators are ultimately and genuinely hated by most whose paths they cross because they prey on virtually everyone.

Leaving a home state has three advantages: First, any heat generated remains at the satellite site. Feeder shops only express receipts to the HBR, and its only traceable physical location is typically a rented business services box where mail can be received. Second, working out of state, satellite sites can be locally promoted as franchise opportunities that investors can see in operation. Finally, when the shop folds, road boilers get on an airplane and remain invisible to clients, angry workers, and defrauded franchisees.

The operation is functional when road boilers select a suitable site and hire and train salesmen to work local automobile dealerships, nonprofit organizations that need to raise funds, and big-ticket retailers who can offer "free vacation trips" as promotions to bring in customers. Salesmen are recruited with the offer of paid training seminars, given a base salary, and promised generous commissions (usually in the range of 10 to 20 percent of the price of the cert package). The first stage of a cert operation is to sell vacation travel certificates (sometimes called "vouchers") to businesses.

Marketing the Cert

The boiler room is a front for a travel broker. That is, it will contact travel agencies—owned and/or overseen by the HBR in Florida—to provide what little travel that they select to offer to a very small percentage of the deals covered by outstanding certs. The certs sell for roughly 10 percent of the prevailing market value of a true vacation travel package to Florida-centered destinations. Three cert packages are usually vended. The Bahamas cert features a boat trip from Florida to one of the Bahamian islands and hotel accommodations for three, five, or seven days (and two, four, or six nights), with optional meal plans costing extra. The Orlando cert features similar hotel accommodations and optional meal plans, costing extra. And the Disney cert features paid admission to Disney recreational facilities in Florida, with or without hotel accommodations on the Disney site.

Each cert is for two adults and up to three children, but some operations sell a "bumper cert," where a fee is charged for special arrangements, for example, three adults and no children or a party of four adults and four children. "Combo cert packages," which include some mixture of the basic three cert options, may also be sold: a trip to the Bahamas, for example, or variably sized packages that include trips to the Disney facilities (two or three days, with or without hotel accommodations and with or without admission to MGM Studios). All cert packages also include a discount coupon book good for selected auto rentals, air transportation, gifts, boat travel, clothing, recreational activities, and meal discounts and valued at more than $1,000.[16]

Certs are initially sold as premiums, something designed to be given away as contest prizes or promotional awards. The logic behind the low price is that numerous limitations and qualifications must apply before a cert will be honored. Businesses are sought as clients because the cost of the cert can be written off as an advertising expense, and nonprofit organizations can have their patrons donate the cost of the cert, thus achieving significant tax advantages in both cases. A pitch given to automobile dealers follows:

> Look. It's a laydown deal. You buy the certificates [certs] in blocks: twenty units, ten units, five units. Your cost is $100 per in the twenty block, $120 per in the ten, and $135 per in the five-lot. Your discount is already built in [pause]. . . . And each cert is worth from $600 to $750, each, to your customers. *Guaranteed.* It's all in writing. You decide on the effective date. We give you a three-month window. Your customers have a full year *from the date you select* to use the cert . . . and for *each package* they get the discount coupon book with over $1,000 of TRAVEL DISCOUNT coupons. So each cert it worth about $1,600—and that's the low end. . . . And we're talking MAJOR HOTELS, not unheard-of places. Your total cost is less than $1/10$th of that. When your customer wants to travel, they merely mail the cert back to us with their date selections, and we mail them their tickets. It's that simple! Each cert is numbered so no one can fake them. WE DO THIS, BY LAW, FOR THEIR PROTECTION. *We do it all,* so you can concentrate on your promotion. I even have a promotions package for you, included free of charge, showing how other dealers have used our promotions. It's full of camera-ready art. All you have to do it take it to your printer. . . . And we have a special bonus for your customers, *the fantastic one-year extension rider,* free of charge. If your customer doesn't use the cert within one year, they simply mail in the rider, and they get another year in which to use the program. So they are not pressured to act in haste. . . . Why, this is the best deal in the industry. . . . We can do it because we are brokers. By guaranteeing that our sponsoring hotels will be full, our tour boats booked to capacity, and our sponsoring airlines filled, we pass the savings on to our customers. It's all in the planning. That's the secret.

In a few months, salesmen typically exhaust the local area's supply of potential clients, and most of the outside sales force is fired. The best are offered positions in the boiler room itself, which, during the length of their training period will have acquired local presence: telephones, business cards, bank accounts, a working business address, letterhead, and a trained secretarial staff and receptionists who have been busy processing the cert orders made by the outside sales force. Selected outside salesmen are offered the chance to become sales managers and trainers for the boiler room proper.

Stage Two: Setting up the Boiler Room

Retained salesmen are trained and paid to run the boiler room under the tutelage of the road boilers, who now become general managers. Road boilers use what are essentially colonialist techniques. They train a few salesmen to take charge of the cold floor, reward them with incentives, and let them manage the operation. Control thus emanates from locals but is overseen by the road boilers. These managers must be taught how to use the telephones, and the boiler room now changes its tone and style. Instead of selling to businesses, it offers contests to a selected mailing list of customers who are informed that they may have won a "vacation travel package [the cert] to the Bahamas!" If they call the 800 number, "They can find out all the details."

Incoming lines are now routed to the telephone stations staffed by the former outside salesmen, who read a pitch designed to build anticipation on the part of prospects. After being placed on hold by the pitchman to verify "their names with our winner's registry," prospects will be greeted enthusiastically with the "news" that they, in fact, have *won* a free trip to the Bahamas! The pitchman runs through one of the cert offerings and explains all of the qualifications: how to use the cert, the time limitations, and how enrollment takes place. Here is the eight-stage close (which is a printed script):

That's right. Congratulate yourself! You have *really* won! You are going to THE BAHAMAS! Now here's what you have to do:

1. Get ready for your orientation package to come in the mail. It will include your travel vouchers, your $1,000 worth of gift certificates, your itinerary request, and your guarantees. It's all in writing. For your protection. We also include a free travel video which shows your hotel and describes the [package you have won]. It will come to you by one of the national courier services, and by law, you have to sign for it. So plan to be home or leave word with the neighbors!

2. Here's the bad news. To guarantee that everything I said is true, you will have to send us confirmation that you have read and understand this promotion. Only then will your vouchers be given an *authorization* number. BY LAW, you MUST write this number on the vouchers as they are worthless without the approved authorization. THIS IS FOR YOUR PROTECTION.

3. We request a service fee of $75 to secure your voucher package. We are brokers, and this covers our administrative expense. We accept all major credit cards.

4. I need your correct address [pause].

5. Now your phone number [pause]. Remember, you called us! And no, there is NO CHARGE for this call. It's a FREE CALL!

6. Now, BY LAW, you have a full thirty days to read all of the materials. Everything is in writing. If you are not completely satisfied, just send back our materials, and you will get a full refund. No questions asked.

7. If you don't want to go to the Bahamas, you may elect to have your vouchers transferred as a gift to anyone of your choosing. [Goes into the gift pitch]. But, BY LAW, this must carry YOUR signature. The general public may not participate in this promotion [goes into the promotions pitch]. Fair enough?

8. I just need your credit card number, and you are *on your way* to THE BAHAMAS!

As salesmen become more proficient, the boiler room expands its mailings, and new salesmen are trained and hired. In about three months the boiler room will be filled to capacity, and selective predation guarantees that it will be filled only with the enthusiastic. The former outside salesmen appear to be in complete control of the management of the operation. The third stage now begins.

Stage Three: Selling the Franchise

After roughly nine months of operation, the road boilers announce that, having been so successful, they will soon be offering shares in the company to interested parties. Advertisements are placed in newspapers to attract interested investors. The road boilers present the program to the new managers first, however, to get "their feedback," as they are told. Here the "master plan" is revealed. They will sell ten shares of the operation, at $5,000 per share, to the first ten investors who are sufficiently liquid, and qualified, to come on board. A share buys 5 percent of the net yearly profits and carries rights to future expansion. Payout occurs semiannually, beginning six months after the effective date of the sale.

This presentation is a front to get the newly hired sales managers to buy into the operation. It is offered in the style of the classic take-away ploy; that is, the offer is implied and then withdrawn. Advertisements are placed in the "business opportunities" section of newspapers, and seminars that feature a catered brunch are given at a local hotel. Serious candidates are then screened, and a $100 deposit is collected for a "prospectus seminar" to be offered at a later date to invited investors only and to some of the sales managers. The fee is generously waived for the sales managers.

The HBR then dispatches a shill to be the first interested buyer. The shill, and any recruited investors, are then free to tour the boiler room at appointed times. The road boilers assign the shill to one of the former outside salesmen (now a sales manager) and encourage "honest discussion." The shill's conversation drifts toward concerns that the operation will be managed properly, and that sets the stage for the final pitch. After that, the sales manager invariably asks if he can buy in. The shill and any recruited investors agree that this would be a good idea. Money changes hands, typically a month before the boiler room's lease runs out, setting the stage for the final curtain.

Stage Four: The Shutdown

After all checks clear, the road boilers have a special meeting with the newly acquired franchise owners, the shill, and the sales managers who have just become owners. At the meeting, they explain how the system makes money. This is called the "procrastination pitch," the double meaning of which is only typically understood by pros. It is full of enthusiasm and apparent honesty wherein the shortfalls and opportunities of the company are "realistically" discussed. Here is one rendition:

> Look. This is a sleeper deal. It works because at each stage in the program there are qualifications and limitations. When we sell to dealerships a good percentage of the certs will never be redeemed. That's our margin. It's pure profit. The dealers buy because they want to sell product. They are not in the travel business, they just want a promotion that brings in the customers. Certs require timing. First, the cert package has to be sent out: that's thirty days. Then the customer has to read the contract and acknowledge the program: that's another thirty days. Now, when they elect to travel they have to request a date-frame. This requires approval. If we have the dates they want, we issue the tickets; if not, we have to request another set of dates.[17] Most people won't travel immediately when they get their certs; most will procrastinate. So you have to be patient. You won't be able to please all of the customers all of the time. That's all there is to it.

Before the meeting ends, recent levels of revenue are announced. The road boilers mention that the "big bosses" are so pleased that they will be personally coming up from Florida to inspect the company. A catered party will be held in three weeks, on a Thursday afternoon, and everyone will have the next Friday and Saturday off. "A real celebration, we'll even shut down the telephones for a two and a half days," one of the road boilers typically announces. "The big bosses will come on Monday, and we will get paid that afternoon." A road boiler then gives a "celebration pitch" wherein he confesses that this has been the best year in his life, that he really loves all the people who work here, that he really loves the town, and that he is very grateful for the hard work put in by all the loyal workers in the shop.

It is typically the last sales meeting before closure, and bonuses for the sales managers and salesmen with the most tenure are announced ("building the bite"). The shill and the new franchise owners are typically present at this "good news" sales meeting. The HBR expands its mailings to ensure that the telephones will ring off their hooks for the next few weeks. When the long-awaited Thursday afternoon finally arrives, a catering company serves a delicious meal, and the road boilers bring champagne to a festive office party that lasts a few hours. Everyone gives each other a long-weekend round of parting gestures. By Monday morning the office will be stripped bare and locked. The road boilers, the shill, and all of the corporate assets will have relocated to parts unknown in Florida.

"Green" Road Boilers: An Ecology Scam

The entrepreneurial talents of scam operators often exceed their organizational skills, so some scams evolve as they progress. In what follows, a pro describes how changes in tax laws during the early 1980s resulted in a team of four boilers promoting energy-saving franchises targeted at small business owners. The scam evolved in seven stages: initial planning, picking the site, placing newspaper advertisements, creating a fictional investment company, giving qualifying seminars, going for the money, and dissolving the company.

Initial Planning

Well, it all started over the holidays, the owner [of a gas house] got together with [names pro] and some of his friends to discuss a possible venture. They were convinced that some bread could be made out of the new energy laws. So they came up with the idea of the "Arizona Energy Company" (AEC): a deal to be promoted as a speculative business opportunity. They would need some investors and a hook to bring them in. The target market was picked to be small moochie businessmen, you know, guys with some venture capital and a big dream to pursue. They hit upon "Arizona Energy" because of all the sun in Arizona. It's a nice image. They have a logo with Ol' Sol turning dreams into green cash [laughs]. That's all they got out of their first meeting: a name and an idea.

Site Selection

It was decided that Kansas would be the target state because it is nice and square, and the territories could be easily assigned. So, they spent a couple of weeks acquiring geological maps and working with yellow magic markers and divided up the state of Kansas into twelve parts. That's the number of investors they decided on: twelve. The program was designed to pop [sell] at $3,000 per territory.

Placing the Advertisement

Then they got the 800 line for the AEC, made a recording, and ran newspaper ads in [a major city in] Kansas. They put them in the business opportunities section of the paper. They first worked with a number of different headings until they found one that worked. They settled on "energy-saving small business opportunity," as that got the most responses. So, now they had a few interested people, an outline of what AEC would be, and they had to figure out what it would do, and how they would promote it. So they ran more ads, this time soliciting for *investors* who may be interested. That was because [laughs] the first calls that they got were from people interested in opportunities but who had no money! It was a really dumb original choice of words.

Creating the Arizona Energy Company

They still needed a pitch and some literature. They decided that AEC would specialize in contracting for the installation of name-brand, energy-saving materials and devices. The targets were heating, air-conditioning, and insulation. So they needed some equipment and stuff to talk about. They used [a well-known directory] to locate equipment and product manufacturers and got literature on a number of devices and insulating materials and [installation] procedures. They picked the ones that offered the most potential for energy savings. This became part of the lit[erature] package to be sent to potential investors. Then they went to a graphics firm to design the company logo, letterhead, and prospectus for the AEC. They opened an AEC bank account and used a fake address and the 800 number on the literature. . . . The stuff was well done, real professional, but they still didn't have a pitch. So they sent out a few feelers [calls made to get a sense of the market]. The pros took notes and found out that the prospects that they called were indeed looking for a hot investment opportunity. . . . So they kept running the ad until they got fifty interested people. Then they worked on the pitch and ran more ads—as insurance, you might say—and kept qualifying and screening both old and new callers until fifty hot prospects remained. . . . Now they were ready for the seminars.

Pitching the Seminars

Bear in mind that all of this stuff is part time. I mean, they kept at working Kansas until they got their fifty mooches, perfected the pitch, modified the literature, and worked the prospects until a sufficient number of them were ready to go. . . . Then they made arrangements for four suites, a conference seminar room, and catering at an airport hotel in the state of Kansas for three days and two nights, four months in advance. The target month is August. They ran another set of ads in Kansas newspapers and worked on a pitch designed to attract more investors. The close was an invitation to attend the wealth-building seminar at the hotel, a chance for prospects to send in their allegedly refundable check for $75 to cover seminar expenses, and included the description of a raffle [tickets to be given at the seminar] for $5,000 worth of business computing equipment. Most of that will be won by the shills, of course. Now they have to create the seminar close, whereby after the seminar they actually go for the money. This would be done, it was decided, by setting up a screening committee to select prospective investors who qualify for the program.

Going for the Money

Look. When they've got their fifty seminar attendees, that's $3,750 [50 × $75]. That about covers the hotel, transportation, and incidentals. They still have to work out the warmer pitch. That's where they really qualify the mooches. So about two months before the seminar, they plant the enticer, a pitch given to the prospects that informs them that by special arrangement officers of the AEC development division will actually be there after the seminar to screen potential investors in two-hour sessions. . . . You figure they've got four suites, two hours per screen, for three sessions on Sunday after the seminars. That's twenty-four screening sessions. They only need twelve investors at $3,000 a pop, so they can eliminate twelve candidates or they can accept conditional deposits [if a number of selectees "otherwise qualify" but must undergo further screening]. So they telephone-pitch the fifty prospects, assemble all their contracts, documents, and seminar gear, and the four pros and two shills set their schedules to work Kansas. Now the seminar itself is a business opportunities pitch . . . they've given it dozens of times. All it does is hype up the room and get the prospects excited. Then they have the raffle, the shills win most of the prizes, and the screenings are scheduled for the next day at the hotel. The prospects have already been priced out [i.e., told to have their $3,000 "good faith" checks, or cash, in hand]. The program really works because of the screenings. That's where the investors have to prove that they qualify. So they bring bank statements, credit reports, and all the formal stuff that investors are supposed to have. . . . The enticer pitch qualifies them for having the necessary documents. At the end of the day, the operators collect $36,000, get on the airplane, and go back to the "AEC Corporate Office," which is, of course, the phone room.

Dissolving the Company

After all the payments have been banked, the pros develop a loader pitch that says to non-selectees who attended the seminar that there has been an unexpected dropout from the program due to a death in the family of one of the prime investors and that this slot can be filled by prompt action. . . . Of course, they first tell a tall tale about how the money was immediately refunded. You know, the standard buy-back [of the heat] pitch. Then, they offer to have a courier pick up the client's investment for immediate entry into the program. . . . So they turned down twelve people, maybe they'll pick up four or five. . . . This must be done quickly, so they make offers to all twelve and see what they can get the couriers to pick up. . . . The loader, for those who have already bought into the program, is the unexpected acquisition of the "Nevada Territories" [imagined additional territories offered for only the fictional cost of filing the paperwork]. "They have first pick," they are told, and that there's a $250 filing fee for each territory, and there are four territories open.

"Our courier will pick up your check," they are told. . . . So you figure, maybe, of the twelve, six or eight will come on board for some additional territories. Who knows how many? I mean they make all of this up. They can sell four territories, ten times, or whatever works. . . . Then there's the con-dis [pronounced *con-dees*—the conditionals].

Well, that's simply found money. They cash their checks, and then they finally launch the smoother, that's the next-to-the-last pitch. They call all of the investors, the condis, and the newly signed-up [after all checks have cleared]. First, they tell the condis that they have been accepted and arrange for courier pickup of the balance of their investment; then they call the regulars and announce that all paperwork for the franchise is moving in good order and that they will receive all documentation and permanent territorial assignments [the grid maps of Kansas] in ten working days. Then they wait for the condi money to come in by courier.

The last pitch is made when they pretend to explain the delay in the arrival of the maps and paperwork. It's WONDERFUL NEWS! They give a very energetic pitch and announce that a major supplier of energy equipment has just been signed on to provide AEC franchise-holders with *exclusive distribution rights* in Kansas. . . . So, they are told, a special courier will be dispatched. That's the solidifier. It gets them hot for their documents to arrive and throws them off. I mean, are they going to get the documents first, or the documents and the news, or what? Then it's all over. They simply disconnect the 800 number. It's a real clean cut. The checks have cleared, and there is no way they can be reached. All the literature has a fake address and an 800 number. All the fish will be waiting at least another ten days for the major supplier news, which never comes. Of course, once the basic pattern is worked out, they can become the "Boston Energy Ventures Corporation" or the "Nevada Energy Development Group" or whatever.

So figure it out [runs through computations and estimates]. . . . That's around fifty-six grand. Figure four grand for phones and other stuff. Maybe the other stuff would be some money for the shills. That's fifty-two grand split four ways, including the cost of the trip to Kansas. Call it a working vacation [laughs]. That's about 13K, net, each. . . . Not bad for a few days' work.

Badge Operations

Because most state laws are nebulous regarding the percentage of gross receipts that a fund-raising enterprise must legally provide to a nonprofit organization, many boiler rooms literally or figuratively associate themselves with fire, police, and emergency service departments. These are called "badge operations." The boiler goes out (makes a call as) representing a public service sector benevolent association, charity, union, or other a voluntary association. An informant explains:

> Yeah, I did some badge time about two years ago . . . I went out as "Sergeant John Smith" with Ladder Number 12 of the local fire department or the 87th Precinct for the police—whatever numbers made sense. . . . Hey, it's the best opening [line] in the industry! No one hangs up the phone when there's a cop on the other end. . . . The hard part, well, it's *not really a pitch* [emphasis added] that they use, I mean, it's just sort of demands. You say hello and ask for the money and make up stories. It's short and to the point. . . . So we get donations and give a portion to the fire or police department. No one had the balls to ask if we were legit. I mean, did you ever ask a cop if he is real? We even had a line in the pitch that we were members of the BBB [Better Business Bureau]. No one ever checks . . . I then worked days and made some money for a while. Businessmen are the easiest. They are hungry for the tax write-off . . . I got paid. It wasn't a bad gig, all things considered. . . . It was OK while it lasted. I didn't make as much as he promised in the newspaper ad. . . . But he didn't cheat me. He even gave me a few bonuses when we had a good month.

An owner considers his badge operation:

> It's real simple. Everybody loves the cops when they need them. No one gives a damn when there is no problem. Cops can't raise money. It's illegal for them to solicit in uniform. These guys get wasted every day in the line of duty. Who gives a damn? Some small precincts can't pay for uniforms, and some cops get $5 or $6 an hour. Can you believe it? It's true. So I get on the phones for [policemen's annual] balls and special events to raise money. No one wants to do this kind of work. My pro makes $1,500 a week. . . . There's money in this. All you have to do is say "police," and we dispatch our couriers for the bread. No organization turns down donations, so there's no problem there. The cops smile at us, but they take our checks sure as shootin' [laughs]. It's that simple. . . . Between you and me, I make 65 cents on the dollar. Then there is overhead. . . . Maybe the cops get a dime. Hey, a dime is a dime. Nobody is fallin' over themselves to give to the cops. . . . It's hard work yellin' and beggin' on the phone for the cops, but we bring in the bucks. It's money that they otherwise wouldn't get. Now, I'll tell you one thing. We have a corporate charter. . . . Right here [shows charter with pride]. We don't fake it. . . . Fund-raising ain't illegal.

The Social Organization of Badge Operations

Badge operations are created and financed by companies located in Florida, New York, and Chicago and serviced through autonomous local boiler rooms that may spring up in or around major metropolitan areas. The headquarters operation (HO) remains totally invisible except for its logo, corporate insignia, and the printed materials it delivers to its contractees: boiler room marketing companies, sometimes called "satellites" or "local shops."

HOs require a communications network with aligned vendors, access to a printer, and a mailing address. They typically rent a mailbox from a business box retailer, which provides a street address to which to assign the corporate name, fax machines (if needed), and a courier recipient drop-off point for collecting receipts from participating boiler rooms.

HOs are named in a nebulous manner to provide the illusion of being a public service, benevolent, or charitable organization, for example, the "International Association of Charitable Associations: Police, Fire, and Health." The variable acronyms (IACP, IACF, and IACH) are then used in a pitch. HOs provide the initial conceptualization of the service to be vended: a charitable contribution ultimately to be made to a named local or regional benefactor. HOs gain access to, and information concerning, legitimate charitable and benevolent organizations and associations by monitoring the activities of their lobbying groups in Washington, D.C., because these regularly and publicly provide literature, background, and levels of current need. Five market imperfections permit HOs to operate within gray areas concerning the law:

1. All legitimate charities and benevolent organizations are in constant need of funds and thus are never fully funded by public support.

2. All charities provide a means of public justification and documentation of their tax-free status through their national organization's literature, which can be used for purposes beyond its original intent: to provide legitimacy for genuine acts of charity and philanthropy on the part of the giving public.

3. Most centrally organized national charities and worthwhile causes cannot possibly monitor all of the fund-raising activities in all of their branches or affiliates, all of which have variably staffed levels of administration which, although producing no income, must nonetheless be supported and financed out of voluntary contributions. This creates both autonomy and overhead expenses.

4. All accept anonymous donations. Thus, when the HO gives some small portion of its collections—to stay within the letter of the law—to a bona-fide, registered charitable or benevolent organization, the money is typically welcome.

5. Although society is the ultimate recipient of fire, police, and emergency services, in any particular community there is only a generally recognized need that is served when catastrophic circumstances dictate. Because only a small percentage of the population uses emergency services at any given time, few get to know members of the local fire house, emergency squad, or police

department or have any clue about how these organizations are run and funded, although most citizens generally acknowledge their importance.

An area of generally worthwhile activity, supposedly sponsored by or
affiliated with good people (fire, police, and health personnel) and aimed at a
local community need, which can be orchestrated to cater to widespread mores concerning philanthropy and widespread fears and anxieties over fire,
crime, or emergency, sets the stage for a boiler room. The boiler room inde-
pendently contracts with the HO to solicit donations, from which its ownership is usually paid a commission equal to a percentage of the gross collections plus expenses, which may include, depending on the arrangement, the
costs of producing literature, courier fees, a percentage of company overhead,
and a percentage of the telephone bill. It is the responsibility of boiler room
ownership to arrange to "sponsor" a charitable fund-raiser, to which the HO
contributes and which boiler room owners attend.

The badge shop, being organized and sometimes chartered as a marketing
company, also gains its local street address, faxing capabilities, and mailing and
courier drop-off privileges though a business box company. The telephone room
is housed in a rented office. Thus, for example, "R.H.O. Marketing," the corporate name of a hypothetical boiler room, would establish a commercial identity, a corporate bank account, and a business presence in and through the rented
office, but its business box would be one of the acronyms for the HO, perhaps
IACP, to which donations are ultimately sent. Local couriers deliver to R.H.O.
Marketing, however.

Some of these operations provide employment to boilers previously discredited by run-ins with the law (called "priors" because they have previously
been incarcerated, probated, or paroled for some prior offense) and thus provide a boiler room irony: those with criminal records soliciting for the police.
A badge shop is one of the few sites where middle-class income options are
available for work, although temporary, where previous work history is irrelevant. "Badge boilers" are not especially skilled, but they are well paid.
Most know little of sales techniques, and few see themselves as salesmen. Only
the owners possess the skills of confidence men. Boilers use a very crude pitch
and badger prospects into submission, an effective tactic when used on business enterprises owned by recent immigrants who are often fearful of offend-
ing the police and on the well-intended elderly, who frequently fall victim to
charitable requests.

Seasonal variations (the Summer Camp Program, the Spring Ball, the
Holiday at the Hospital) are used as the year progresses. When sufficient
objections bring inquiries to and possible investigations from authorities, the
badge shop fires its boilers, closes down, vacates its office, and assumes another identity. The HO is never identified, and the boiler room's address is a

business box. Some of the more sophisticated operations use a "trunk network" to prevent telephone calls from being traced.[18]

The Littlest Boiler Room

Sometimes the technique of establishing a boiler room is used for reasons not directly related to the process of generating sales over the telephone but rather for creating the illusion that this is possible so other types of investment programs can be promoted. I was able to observe such an operation when informed by a salesman who had taken an outside job for a multilevel franchise operation that a (telephone) room was being started up to promote water purifiers.

I had dinner with the owner at a celebrity-owned bar and restaurant. The man was impeccably dressed and paid for our meal with a $100 bill. I scheduled an interview at the job site. A few days later, I rode an elevator in a recently constructed office building. The general opulence was apparent. Heavy carpet was everywhere; oil paintings were on the walls; and steel, chrome, and glass were artfully mixed with rich dark woods, out of which were fashioned the corridors. White stucco separated the offices. The air-conditioning system produced welcome shivers on this hot summer night. As the elevator stopped at my appointed floor, it opened to two massive secretarial/receptionist desks. An attractive woman controlled the security panel that allowed the outer corridor doors to open electronically after my presence was announced over an intercom. I walked past a number of rooms. One contained a massive wood conference desk, another housed a modern mail room, and a third was a computer room to which all offices had corridor access. My final destination was a small office (roughly ten by ten) where the owner was making a few telephone calls. He invited me to the conference room, past a refrigerator stuffed with snacks, wine, and carbonated beverages.

After an introduction to the product (a water purifier wholesaling in the $30 range), the marketing strategy was discussed ("house-sits," where an outside salesman presents the product while the potential customer views a company-provided video on their home's VCR), and the need for the telephone room emphasized (to generate qualified leads and raise the fears of the customers over the quality of their water supply). The sales technique would be to use a chlorine indicator that turns a drawn sample of the water to be tested the color of urine.

The operation was conducted in three waves as part of a franchise vending scheme. The owner had just come into town and rented the plush office complex. During the day, "business opportunity seminars" were conducted where the outside man (my initial informant) served as a roper. This salesman presents the water purifier deal as a business opportunity to interested investors. Three types of purifiers were for sale: sink-mounted (retailing in the $160 range); an under-sink model (which cost about $90 and retailed at $750); and a home system model (which cost about $250 and retailed at $1,450).

The impression given was that the pitchman owned the entire floor of the modern building. In actuality, he paid rent for a small room and a monthly surcharge for each ancillary service (conference room, seminar room, photocopying room, mail room, typists, or computer room) used. During the day, when the seminars were conducted, the "technicians" (salesmen with no technical training) would conduct house-sits previously scheduled by telephone to demonstrate the purifiers. The conference room (unused in the evening hours) also had two telephones that were used to make calls. As new clients were recruited to the seminars, the owner wanted to be able to show them that a telephone room would be generating leads.

All leads, in fact, were given to salesmen already in the field. For a small investment ($500), a potential investor could purchase a stock of purifiers (marked up 100 percent) and then presumably use company resources to place (sell) the units. The potential customer would then "be in business for himself" and could, at a later date, buy into the franchise, set up his own operation, and acquire his own sales force after first learning how to perform these functions on a part-time basis.

In the scam, appointments are made with potential customers by offering a free water test. By making cold calls to those in affluent communities—identified by list brokers who provide this information—fronters soon discover someone displeased with the color, odor, or taste of their drinking water. If (the qualifier) a homeowner is concerned over the healthfulness of the water, a free water test is scheduled. A technician is then sent out with a purification unit, a videocassette documenting the hazards of industrial pollution and the virtues of clean water, and a chlorine test kit. Both husband and wife are expected to be home for the presentation, a strategy that virtually ensures a placement, because once the technician is in the home, few refuse what is presented as a "free trial." Encouraging both homeowners to be present is pitched as a "safety precaution against having strangers come into the home."

When the technician arrives, he or she instructs the homeowner to put the videocassette in the VCR while the other, unencumbered spouse accompanies the technician to the kitchen to install the purification unit. This takes about a minute. All present then view the twelve-minute tape on "Clean Water: An American Right." After the viewing, the technician talks about the quality of the water in the neighborhood, checks off items on a list intended to look like a water survey, and then all parties go into the kitchen for the water test.

In the kitchen, the technician extracts a sample of unpurified water from the tap and waits for it to change color after adding a test chemical. Because all municipal water is chlorinated, the color change produces the expected visual response in the potential customer. It does not take much sales skill to equate a murky yellow color to the possibilities of disease and contaminants.

The technician then diverts an incoming water stream through the purifier unit (The Puppy, so-called "because it is cute and will likely find a home," notes the owner of the operation) that has been previously attached to the sink. Because the purifier filters out chlorine, when the prospect is invited to taste the difference between the filtered and unfiltered water a difference is observed. The sample of murky yellow liquid, left on the table for dramatic effect, enhances the comparison. The deal is then sold using an effective version of the take-away ploy. When the customers are led to expect a sales pitch for the purifier, none is given. The homeowner is instead told:

> Oh, yes. It is true that we are manufacturers of water purification units, [Mr. Customer], but we are providing a public service for the community. We are new to this region and are trying to test out the market for water purification. I certainly *don't want* to sell you a unit. That wouldn't be fair. You didn't ask for a salesman to come to your home, you asked for a water test. Am I right? I could sell you the unit, but I am not a salesman. They do cost [gives price]. But what I suggest that you do is *use* the unit for ten days. See if it works. Use the water to cook. Make coffee [goes into the pitch]. . . . It's actually cheaper than bottled water![19] We will call you in about ten days [makes appointment] to remove the unit for you after your test. If you want to purchase a unit you may do so at that time. Let me leave you the literature so that you can make a decision. There is no charge for this demonstration or for the information we have provided you. TO YOUR HEALTH, Mr. and Mrs. [prospects' surname].

The salesman leaves The Puppy connected to the sink. The deal is closed with a telephone call from a salesman offering a small discount for payment when a major credit card is used, and a lifetime guarantee is given. If the customer is "hot," the larger units (under-sink or home system) are offered. If the customer seems unwilling to pay the highly inflated price (about $160) for the unit, a drop close (deferred payments) is used. If the customer refuses, a high-pressure salesman is sent to retrieve the unit and force a sale. He is instructed to again offer a twenty-payment plan (roughly $8 per month) or a ten-payment plan (roughly $16 per month). If that fails, the salesman produces a contract and aggressively offers to waive the company's policy of sending letters to the credit-reporting companies, because the fine print signed upon receipt of The Puppy turns out to constitute a bill of lading. Customers who elect to use the payment plans are also billed a $15 service fee, which they discover after the first payment is sent in.

The owner of the Littlest Boiler Room (a name suggested by an informant) produces three income streams: one from the income from the "business opportunities" seminars; one from the gross profits derived from the sale of the units to salesmen who are paid at two prevailing commission structures (one if they have bought into the franchise and a different one if they have not); and a third resulting from an override on all outside sales of the units. The latter income stream is also sold as a right to franchisees, who, after paying an initiation fee, are entitled to a small residual from the sales generated by each member of the sales force in the tier immediately below theirs, hence the multilevel aspect of the operation.

How long the owner remains in town is determined by the responsiveness of the general public to the idea of purchasing overpriced water purifiers. The market is the upwardly mobile and marginally educated, those who have income but not the comparative knowledge of water purification devices. How fast the operation expands depends on the size of the franchisees' social networks. The scam operator taps into three markets: that of workers displaced by recession who seek self-employment as salesmen and technicians, small businessmen who seek a franchise opportunity, and customers concerned over the quality of their drinking water.

Shutting the operation down is simple. When his lease expires, the scamster simply leaves a rented office. All corporate symbols, letterhead, telephone numbers, and materials produced (warranties, franchise rights, and contracts) become meaningless, as do any outstanding checks for commissions, wages, or sales bonuses. Although the purifiers are promoted "to last a lifetime," the instruction sheets sent by the manufacturer recommend that the cartridge elements be changed every six months. Thus, the long-term buildup of any filtered contaminants and the ensuing bacterial growth that may be trapped in the filtering element because of extreme concentrations pose a genuine health threat that would not exist if the purifiers were not in place. If the operator of this scam is still in business, I assume that he has a deal on replacement cartridges.[20]

Service Rooms as Opportunity Structures

Service shops occupy the most profitable, and the final, rungs in the boiler room profit hierarchy because they require quick-thinking pitchmen, and the accession cost of what they provide (certificates, warranties, contracts, or documents) involves only the fee charged by a good printer. Service rooms afford new opportunities for traditional product men to pick up new skills as they moonlight, and many boilers stumble upon those operations that compose the lower end of the industry when they are fired from their parent shops.

A good number of service operations have a night shift and place calls when most residential customers are at home. This type of part-time employment can offer alternative, extra, or different telephone work for those so inclined. A service shop can also be run in addition to other boiler room activities because an innovative product house owner can sometimes acquire a "service line" by being attentive to the potential in markets currently being served. A salesman describes the "stolen baby scam" that one chemical house used successfully to increase its revenues and temporarily change its customer base:

> Well, it works like this: One of the pros in the back room over at Sandy Chemical gets a-talkin' to one of his regular customers who, it turns out, is a southern sheriff. You know, the guys that they sell Gold Bond Delousing to.[21] Well, it turns out that they have this list of kidnap victims for the entire state of [_____]. So, the salesman cuts a deal for the list. Then they run off a circular called "Things That You Can Do to Get Your Child Back." They go out as a research service, and the guys in the back room pitch mothers on how the program is successful in recovering stolen babies. Listen to this: They charge "only $29.95" for a sure way to get stolen kids back. It's pure profit. They only accept charge cards. Talk to a nervous and frightened mother? It's a laydown. They made a lot of money for a few months. You remember when they started to advertise all the missing kids on the milk cartons? Well, that's when they made a killing.

A service shop always contains a number of boilers who have been displaced from their parent houses through shutdowns and firings and some who may have jumped shop through the referral network. It also contains a number of rippers: entrepreneurs who only seek the training so that they can start their own companies (so-named because, in the eyes of the owners, the sole purpose of these men is to rip knowledge from service room operators). The mixture of talent on the sales floor—some of whom have worked for product houses, some of whom have worked other scams, some rippers, and some who have only worked for conventional firms in sales capacities—permits a number of evolutionary possibilities. These generally follow, and are inherently constrained by, prevailing occupational stratification patterns. Investment operations are typically started and staffed by those with previous experience as brokers or agents (real estate, bonds, mutual funds, stocks, or insurance); franchise operations have their origins as business opportunity ventures that are later adapted for telephone promotion; and badge operations have their origins in other fund-raising activities.

Boiler room talent only enters the equation when any of these conventional operations seeks to expand. Because this often mandates placing advertisements in newspapers, it invariably attracts those with telephone sales skills. Sometimes a hybrid organization can result if the chemistry of the room, the talents of the boilers, and the personalities of the owners match. In that case, there are two emergent possibilities, one direct and the other indirect. A direct outcome may be that the boiler is made a part owner of the company; or, more commonly, he will assume the role of the house pro. An indirect outcome results from the quality of the contacts the boiler makes on the sales floor, which may prove useful in the future.

Another indirect outcome involves a salesman's incorporation into the boiler network, an informal, mutual self-help and referral network which, after a scam shuts down, may help the boiler secure alternative employment.[22] In most cases, however, the boiler is as victimized as are the scam's clients. Typically, only the owners and the rippers benefit—the latter taking the knowledge acquired, and perhaps some commission income earned before they quit, to start their own companies.

Rippers represent the next generation of scam boilers because they may take their service-shop skills in idiosyncratic directions. Some may modify presentation and closing skills learned and develop new markets. Two informants, for example, started their own coin shops, but one used investment money from his coin marks and expanded his chemical sales company—feeling more comfortable with products he had a proven track record of promoting. The other boiler had the insight to invest a good portion of his profits in the commodities market. Thus, when his coin operation folded he had a financial cushion upon which to fall back and thus could buy time for planning his next enterprise.

Only rippers and, to some degree, fronters escape the pull of the scams (which might be likened to the black holes of the boiler room world), because they alone use them for their own ends and leave the scene before they become victims. The general pattern of social mobility in the world of boiler room scams depends on the social context wherein a particular salesman receives his initial telephone experience. One may, perhaps, start as a telemarketer (chapter 5) and move up to a product house or begin in a sales position of some kind and move on to a product house floor. Those who follow telephone sales careers move through product houses, which differ in sophistication, until they develop a "phone personality." Recruitment to the scams occurs by achieving pro status in a product house or, in some cases, through lateral movement from a conventional brokerage or fund-raising firm. Scams typically have no trainee positions and require a half-dozen or so years "on the phone" for a candidate to make it through the initial screening.

Downward mobility patterns are not symmetrical. People leave the scams only to retire, become a conventional businessman or permanently leave the world of telephone work, or go to jail. They also leave through death—hence the black hole metaphor. The scams are the final destination in the boiler room world "for those who qualify." Age-grading is notable because those who are young, trainees, or new to the boiler room world are typically absent. The scams contain some of the boiler room's oldest and most experienced personnel. One can move, however, within the scam world for many years by becoming a floater.

Life in the fast lane has its advantages. It typically pays more than conventional work and more than what is earned in most boiler rooms. But the pay is neither regular nor patterned nor progressive; it comes in waves, each filled with a pulse of excitement and income. The knowledgeable learn to quit before the operation folds.

The nonentrepreneurial play a special role in service shops. They become fronters and leave closings, sales meetings, general excitement, indoctrination, and disappointments to others. Fronters are the existentialists of a boiler room. They are left alone to do their jobs, are typically well liked, reasonably paid, and are treated decently by the owners. The secret of fronters inheres in the fact that they have internalized the craft norms of pros but do not seek to be magicians. They do not enter the boiler room with great expectations. They know the score, they are proficient, and, most important, they are not part of the social control structure.

Fronters are typically the only people who leave boiler rooms in the good graces of all parties. An informal norm ensures this: The fronter's leaving signifies the first stage of the boiler room's (always unannounced) shutdown. Fronters leave when it is no longer profitable to open new accounts. At such times, the volume of complaints is typically escalating, which diverts the use of available talent. Fronters are typically awarded severance pay at a time when many are being fired and remaining boilers are being put under great pressure to load remaining accounts. The fronter's absence signals those with experience on the scams to begin to look elsewhere for work. The rest, who may be innocent of the clues, are typically too consumed by the level of action in the room, their own confusion, or their own greed (or ignorance) to note minor changes in personnel.[23] The owners extract every ounce of energy from those remaining on the sales floor before they, themselves, flee. Because front-ers are well aware of this, their silence commands a premium.[24]

The Social Cost

The scams, excepting those vending water purification devices that must have their filters changed regularly, cause no physical harm to those who buy into the phantom market. Rather, they are vehicles for redistributing wealth from the vulnerable, the misinformed, and the greedy into the coffers of pitchmen ready to "fly by night." The social organization of scams, however, has im-portant implications for the evolution of the boiler room, because scams tap some of the most capable, innovative, and creative individuals and put them into a structure that is both predatory and cannibalistic. That thins their ranks constantly while making survivors ever more skilled in the requisite tech-niques needed to manipulate clients as well as other boilers.

The scams cannot be said to practice elite deviance because their location in the social structure grants them no political, military, or economic power; they have a discredited social status; and they are not affiliated with the state.[25] Nonetheless, they form an elite deviant group among boilers. Scamsters ben-efit from society as it presently exists. Their redistributive function carries no political agenda, and their energies are wholly devoted to hunting down the deals and thus supporting, and in some cases enshrining, the culture of business.

Absent from personal conversations with such boilers is any hint of dis-affection, the politics of dissent, or social injustice.[26] Capitalism's siren song of unlimited opportunity is at its highest pitch in service operations, where state intervention in the economy of any kind, especially regulation, is whole-heartedly condemned, taxes are cursed, weak individuals (those unwilling to take risks) are jeered, and the commonly accepted nature of man is that of a creature who is "lazy, stupid, and greedy." One pro in a coin house captured these sentiments well when he said:

> We are sharks. Pure and simple. At first I took offense to that. . . . But it's true [smiles]. We are the best at what we do. We feed on mooches and those looking for a quick buck who are too lazy to do what it takes to really make a killing. . . . And that, my friend, is hard work. It doesn't matter what the killing is, name it. If you're *good* at it, you had to *work damn hard* to get there. Sure, there is no free lunch, but I can still sell tickets to the buf-fet. I can take this phone [holds telephone in the air] and, from a cold start, in twenty minutes, I'll have some mooch in California ready to wire me a few thousand dollars. That's because the shark ain't no slouch. The shark is

always movin'. . . . Hey, it's not my fault that people are moochie. They are also stupid. I mean this is an impulse deal: you come on board if you are a player. I like to take on those with cash businesses [explains why]. . . . Now, you'd think that these guys would know better. But no, they want the easy deal. Well, that's why I'm here. Mr. Easy Deal, that's me [smiles]. But let me get back to the sharks. Do you know what happens when you deprive a shark of his action . . . like when you put him in an aquarium? I'll tell you what happens. He becomes a *fish*—tired, lazy, looking for a handout, seekin' out the easy deals. Just like the people we sell to.

Common ideologies of the shop floor can be deduced from the manner by which the deals are closed, that is, by observing the kinds of social imputations promoted to make a deal sound appealing. The prospect is seen as "decisive," "quick-thinking," and "sharp"; "the kind of man who knows how to grab 'an opportunity'"; and "the kind of investor who *takes advantage* of the situation," who "strives to succeed," and who does not engage in "stinky thinkin'" (being pessimistic or overly analytical).

If contemporary political issues and social problems creep into a sales presentation—as they sometimes can—a universal retort is to depict the opportunities being vended as economic "solutions," via untold wealth or personal power, to be unleashed by "the program": a metaphorical ticket to an imaginary land where one's loved ones will live free of crime, insecurity, and want, and where one can enjoy leisure.

When a shrinking elite contains creative, innovative, and entrepreneurial individuals and predation patterns keep these people socially isolated, a group, of necessity, will never form, and thus it will be unable to socially reproduce itself. After having literally created a "means of production" that resides in the power of illusion alone, these men become trapped and isolated in the very structures they have created by din of their sheer effort and intelligence. Although scam artists have mastered the techniques of domination, secrecy, manipulation, and extreme interpersonal competence, they exist in capitalism's purgatory, where success is perpetually elusive and awaits the judgment of the next deal, in the next operation, at the next site. When a shop folds, the owners are isolated individuals, literally on the run, and all others, immediately after the point of greatest profits, find themselves unemployed.

No elite can sustain itself under such conditions. Thus, although scamsters have high levels of skill and social organization, they compose an individuated elite which, like the services that they sell, exists only at the conceptual level. This differentiates these men from most other criminal groups which, being deeply grounded in the social order, need only select alternatives to conventional means to solve the economic problem and can thereafter return to the comforts of kin, class, clan, or neighborhood to live out their conventional roles in most other regards.[27]

Thus, but for the conventionality of the means selected, most police are amazingly similar to criminals of the same socioeconomic class. Most white-collar criminals, but for their misfeasance or malfeasance, otherwise live in a white-collar world; most political criminals, but for their ideological differences, share the same universe of discourse with their opponents minus the willingness to agree upon political means; and most prostitutes, but for their prostitution, are remarkably similar to other women. Most deviants lead lives organized around their deviance, as in subcultures, or in spite of it and thus spend a good deal of time among conventionals, neutralizing the possibility that their norm violations may become public knowledge.

Scamsters, however, live in a netherworld; they are linked to the economic part of the social order but not quite permanent residents. This particular pattern of social isolation has been noted by students of deviance in other settings: among check forgers, compulsive gamblers, embezzlers, horse track bettors, and those who engage in certain forms of homosexual exchange.[28] The critical difference between the "lone wolves on the scam-phone" and others who may face social isolation stems from the structure of boiler room operations themselves rather than individual whim, misfortune, good luck, fate, or personal preference.

Unlike lone individuals who experience the identity problems associated with most forms of deviance, a scam artist cannot typically resolve these through symbolic realignment with one or another competing groups or interests. A boiler room, being a set of structural conditions, produces no remediable role that can be modified or changed or to which alternative identity props, gear, and personas can be assigned. Those in other discredited occupations may artfully employ all manner of rationalizations to sustain a day's work, but when a scam folds its owners and workers stand alone. Society assumes that selves can be restored, changed, or otherwise modified, but people pay scant attention to the structure of the roles that individuals play.

In a scam operation, the owner's unsharable knowledge of true corporate goals and strategies, of float values, of the true economic costs of the operation, of suppliers, of the markup and the firing sequence (who will be terminated and when), and of the shut-down date (when the operation will be closed) isolates him from both his marks and those in his employ and therefore from the benefits of either a subculture or rehabilitation. There is no local social group, save perhaps one's family, into which a fleeing telephone scam artist is welcome. His workers are likely owed money; his clients are likely angry; his pros are out of work; his staff must seek employment elsewhere;

his investors are out their time, money, and energy; and the law may be looking for him. To the best of my knowledge there are no families (i.e., groups
bound by blood or social organization) of boiler room owners.[29] Each operation is conceptualized and run as the product of a lone entrepreneurial mind.

In service shops there is no legacy to be passed on to the next generation.
There is also no genuine subculture. Scamsters take their secrets to the grave.
If scam operations were integrated into the larger boiler room culture, one
would expect to observe the diffusion of personnel and techniques. That does
not occur, however, at the level of the scams because of the insularity of the
operations and the character of the personalities therein.

The transfer of boiler room techniques to other types of sales operations
is quite common (chapter 5), but these are not initiated by those who own,
or work, service shops. Rippers, the only trans–boiler room migrants, typically use their knowledge to set up other scams or make some supplemental
short-term cash, not to enter the working or managerial ranks of an operation other than their own. Fronters move from scam to scam, not into other
sales jobs. Moreover, the very notions of hands-on management, working for
a wage, or empowerment—the most recent ideological props for justifying
the existence of a management class—would likely be considered contradictions of terms to most scam operators. One owner, who runs a mineral rights
scam, captures the sentiment well:

This stuff sort of gets into your blood, I guess. Right now the [mineral
deal] is working OK. I can never go back to chemicals, though. Too many
problems with the pros, hiring workers, meeting a payroll, getting suppliers. . . . Too many headaches. Of course, I would never work for anyone else,
that's even worse. I've thought of working a job, you know, where they do
something real, but I was *there* ten years ago when I worked for the government. The government is OK, I guess, if you're dumb. All they've got is
job security. . . . Hey, when I'm six feet under, *that's* security too
[laughs] . . . I was offered the management of a chemical house, for example, about six months ago. Management! That's a joke. That's even more
headaches. For what? To blow people out the door? To make up pitches to
give to morons? To steal paper [accounts]? It ain't worth it. When you boil
it down, hey, pardon the pun, it's the money. I know that sounds simple, but
it *is* simple. Look, [explains the mineral deal]. . . . There is just no way I can
make this kind of bread by being a small cog in some big machine. I don't
like working for somebody else. . . . But I always keep my eyes and ears open.
You have to. My latest deal is a racehorse. I'm goin' in for a one-third interest. Hey, now that's somethin' I love: the races! So, why not, right? I've
been thinking: even if the horse doesn't win, I'll have a nice ride, right?
Something I can follow, like a hobby. Who knows, if the horse wins, I'll *work*

up a pitch [laughs]. Maybe this time next year I'll be into selling racehorse shares over the telephone! Why not? I've sold just about everything else.

When a service shop folds, the rugged individualism that characterizes the industry plays out to its logical outcome: owners on the lam, looking to set up the next "golden opportunity," and dislocated boilers searching for more telephone action. One informant reports the following conversation with a scam operator who was on his way to jail to serve time for fraud: "Hey, I lost this one. The truth is, I made my play and wailed [on the telephone] with the best of them. Life ain't always easy. But it's like any investment: you take your shot and do the best that you can. We all make mistakes. Sure, I shouldn't have been so damn greedy and should have pulled out sooner. . . . Well, you live and learn, right? I'll have some time to study the situation carefully [laughs]. I won't be so foolish next time."

Variations on a Theme:
The Use of Boiler Room Techniques

I just do wholesale now. It ain't so bad. I teach my class and pump the
phone two afternoons a week, maybe three if I need extra money. . . . It
pays better than the grad school does. It's workable. I guess you might
call this a telephone assistantship [laughs].
  —*a graduate student, frustrated by the heat, work, and pressure in*
  boiler rooms, who started his own parts brokerage operation

The quest for sales through the use of deceptive practices, predatory management styles, and varying degrees of fraud defines a boiler room. Some companies, however, lack the social organization of boiler rooms, whereas others function as boiler rooms in limited ways and for short periods; a few begin with boiler room talent and change into other types of businesses; still others are run as conventional businesses but contain elements of a boiler room operation.

These operations are best understood as quasi-boiler rooms because they are linked by the vast turnover of personnel in all telephone rooms and the fact that a small cadre of boilers always remains on the telephones at any given time. Thus, some innovators create new schemes and discover new markets wherein to practice their art. How that happens is the subject of this chapter.

Adaptation

A quasi-boiler room is highly specialized and typically only has one product or service to offer in a narrowly defined market. It has two social sources. One lies in the personalities of the boiler room progenitors who establish them, and the other arises when conventional businesses turn to the use of fraudulent telephone sales techniques.

Although it is theoretically possible that any company that uses a telephone staff could come to be run as a quasi-boiler room and, conversely, any quasi-boiler room could evolve into a full-blown boiler room operation or into a conventional business, it is more likely that some boiler room techniques will migrate to conventional businesses and a larger number of fraudulent businesses will seek out boiler room techniques to become more disreputable than they presently are. The reason for this essential asymmetry lies in the fact that boilers are trained to achieve sales at any cost, and their skill is known and defined by that standard alone.[1]

In some quasi-boiler rooms, however, the dialer is irrelevant. Most work part time for slightly above the minimum wage, few receive any benefits, and employment is sporadic. Profits derive from providing the basic service, not as a result of the sales skill of the practitioner. In a strict sense, boilers cease to exist, and "phoners" take their place. Although a classic boiler room is an all-male preserve, women are common in quasi-boiler rooms, where they experience all of the frustrations associated with telephone work but reap few of the rewards.

Three types of quasi-boiler rooms are known by their increasing social distance from the genuine article. Phone scams, closest to the boiler room and often part of it, are set up as adjuncts to another business; transformers (operations using boilers in a conventional business setting) have their origins in a boiler room that mutates; and "conventionals," farthest from the boiler room, are companies engaged in telephone sales or servicing that come to use boiler room techniques. These three compose most of the telemarketing industry and constitute the largest single source of all annoying telephone calls to both residences and businesses. An unemployed boiler, reflecting on his impressions of one such scene, captures its spirit:

> You wouldn't believe it. It's like a church or something. Everyone was so well dressed. Nice office building. . . . So I figure, "Hey, is all of this worth $5.25 an hour? For twenty miserable hours a week? Who can live on that?" But I shut up. I need a gig, right? So check out the phone room. It smelled like a flower garden. Honest to God! There were little pots of dried leaves on some of the desks. There were maybe thirty computer terminals in cells and a training room that had maybe six phone cubicles. I swear, cells with padding on the walls. No smoking. No eating. No drinking. No talking. I counted four clocks on the walls. There were *two guys* there. One was a cripple. . . . You don't even do your own dialing. The computer does. Man, you don't even control *time*. Blew me away! So I visit the manager's office, and he is busy looking over a bunch of computer stuff. Hey, a three-piece suit, you know, "Mr. Madison Avenue." "Hmmmm," I say to myself, "What's this guy doing?" Then, listen to this, he shows me the printout. Holy shit! They have *everything* recorded: time spent on each call, sales, unauthorized calls [out of calling area], shift hours, time not spent on the phone, disconnected numbers, "no answers," hang-ups. It's like being a goddamn robot. . . . All of the women were dressed nicely. Well, there was no problem with the people. Absolutely no "seed factor" [laughs meekly], I'd say. I tried it, but I just couldn't afford to work there. There was no money to be made. . . . Funny thing, though,

when I collected my pay there was a shoe box full of envelopes with the pay-
checks for people that they *fired*. Do you believe that? . . . Turns out that Mr.
Madison Avenue blows 'em right out the door, pretty babes and all! It kinda
shocked me, really. It's a goddamned boiler room in prince's clothing. . . . True,
I was down on my luck, so I figured I'd give legit a try. I mean, this place was
so *respectable*-looking, but hell, no one there made more than $150 a week.
Freaked me out. Hey, that could be *my wife* workin' there. Kinda makes me
mad. These guys are makin' a livin' off of girls.

A quasi-boiler rooms differs with regard to the degree that the seven disreputabilities that define a classic boiler room are present: fraud, deception
of the sales force, marginal employment, account manipulation, deception by
the sales force, corporate organization as a pure sales organization, and secrecy regarding the corporate rationale for being. When none are present, the
operation is not part of the boiler room scene. When some are present, the
operation (however conceptualized by those present) can be empirically identified as a form of boiler room.

The dilemma inheres in the basic incompatibilities between sales talent,
capitalization, operating expenses, and product markups. One variable alone,
however, cannot be changed without influencing the others. Long pitches
require skill but consume a great deal of telephone time. Insufficiently skilled
phonemen are not cost-effective. The largest component of overhead in any
telephone room is the telephone bill, but if fewer calls are made, fewer sales
result. Talent on a boiler room sales floor, however, is defined by heat, work,
and pressure. Remove the interactive skill of a pitchman and what remains is
a script. Reading a script will not move highly marked-up items.

Remove the ruthless competition for economic survival, and the chemistry, tone, and style of a telephone room changes notably. The predatory nature of boiler rooms assures that only the skilled survive—if only for a while.
Remove the varying degrees of effective task orientation, coercion, and deception, and what remains is not boiling but merely telephone work: account-
servicing, information dissemination, data collection, and order-taking. That
is, when all the discrediting factors are removed the social organization of the
company shifts as well. What remains is a company where what is presented
over the telephone is actually provided to the customer. Examples are magazine subscriptions, telephone-polling, voter registration activities, political
campaigning, customer service functions, and certain fund-raising activities.

As a telephone room loses its ability to function as a boiler room, however, it loses those qualities that make it profitable. Boilers, literally and figuratively, cannot exist in a low-markup environment because their skills are manipulative. With reduced profit and markup horizons, an operation must
change its reason for being. The quasi-boiler room is one such evolutionary

accommodation. It offers "side-bets." By running for short periods of time, it produces supplemental revenue and then shuts down.

I have organized the next section of this chapter in terms of examining those quasi-boiler rooms that emerge from the fluidity that results when telephones, profits, pitchmen, and opportunities are assembled in one place. Boiler rooms can shift the amount of emphasis they devote to their ancillary activities, quasi-boiler rooms can become conventional businesses, and conventional businesses can become quasi-boiler room operations.

The "Hope School House" Scam

One form of short telephone con involves recruiting salesmen to the cold floors in certain types of product houses. It is common in chemical rooms but is also known to occur in sports betting and some badge operations.[2] The Hope school house is run by boiler rooms that have learned to turn a profit by eliminating a time-consuming and costly training activity faced by all but the most sophisticated operations: acquiring new sales talent. The scam is sarcastically called the "Hope school house" because, like a Hope diamond made of glass, only the students, so states the lore of the boiler room, hope that the scam will turn out to have real value. It runs by creating the illusion of a training program, collecting money, and filling the cold floor. The program is then terminated. A pro explains:

> Well, I got hired by this chemical room in [name of town]. A few months go by. . . . So, one day the owner asks me if I want to be a floor manager and also an instructor. So I say, "Of course." I mean, pay me some dough and I'll be anything you want me to be. Ain't that right? So he busts out a wall into the storeroom and installs eight phones where there used to be nothin'. In two weeks he has a new room. So then he places an ad in the newspapers under "Training Opportunities." Here, I saved a copy of the ad [shows copy]. The ad reads [verbatim]:
>
> $$ LEARN CHEMICAL SALES $$
> 30 HOUR TRAINING CLASS
> Learn to talk on the phone to people from all over the country! Use WATS lines to sell chemicals. Earn Big Bucks. Our Top Salesman made $1,400 last week. This is for YOU! Training and "hands-on" experience in the world of telephone sales. GUARANTEED JOB upon completion of the program. Cost: $200.00, if you qualify. Phone now for a confidential interview. Classes start [date] for those selected. Make the move. Step up to training that you can use and will get you in on the ground floor. Pick up the phone. Do it now!
> Telephone: [given].
> $$ LEARN CHEMICAL SALES $$

So, here's how it works. He [the owner] takes in $1,600 from "those qual-
ified" [laughs], and I get to run the floor. I give classes from nine to noon; then
from 1 P.M. 'til 4 P.M. for four days. Then, on graduation day these guys get to
make cold calls for six hours on a Friday. If anyone sells anything, or sounds
halfway decent, they get offered a job on Monday. Those who don't get job
vouchers good for six months. Hey, it cost him [the owner] absolutely nothing to run his floor for a week! I ran the extra room; he cleaned out the wood
and has some enthusiastic students. He also eliminated a big headache in having to train the new men. Heck, I made 30 percent on the deal [$480]. It was
sort of like a vacation for me. Hell, any phone man can talk about the phones
for four days at $480 a pop, right? I also get the accounts of the wood [incom-
petent salesmen] they fired on the cold floor, and I get the paper on whatever
the new guys sell.[3]

The Hope school house modifies a common industry practice: paying
newcomers lower wages, salaries, commissions, and benefits.[4] The boiler room
adds deception. This general technique works well in other areas and is especially potent when the vulnerable young can be conned. Two fraudulent industries have evolved to exploit this possibility: school house operations and
"beauty shop scams." Both use a quasi-boiler room to generate clients who
are seen to be, and are self-defined as, students.

School House Operations

The 1980s witnessed a vast expansion of self-improvement schemes of one
kind or another. Included in this growth were those companies vending imagined vocational skills to a narrow demographic band of clients: youths from
the ages of roughly seventeen to twenty-four. School house operations work
only a segment of this population that contains those members of the underclass who have not totally given up on having a conventional future.

The key to the scam lies in the fact that the young are especially vulnerable to manipulation from those in adult roles, and boiler room techniques
are successful among those who lack the experience that would sensitize them
to the possibilities of fraud.[5] To capitalize on this potential, the quasi-boiler
room school house only seeks young adults who, for whatever reason, have
either failed to complete high school or, upon completing high school, have
been unable to find or keep a regular job with any reasonable expectation of
a stable career.

School house operations typically flourish in the aftermath of war, when
hundreds of thousands of veterans can be soon separated from their benefits
through ruses presented as offering an occupational bridge back to civilian life.
In the absence of war, these operations thrive on inner-city youths who en-

dure higher than expected levels of unemployment and virtually every other contemporary social problem.

The failures of the conventional school system, which produces dropouts,
semiliterates, and those with extremely low levels of language and interpersonal skills, represent a target population ripe for a scam involving education,
and the school house assures that they will pay dearly for this particularly
cruel type of quick fix to the enduring problem of educational deficits created
by social stratification.

Boiler room techniques work because the general idea that education is
some sort of magic key to success is part of the conventional wisdom. Of
course, boiler room techniques have a natural affinity for promotable magic
keys of any kind and success by any definition. School house operations use
salesmen (called "counselors" to the marks and "screeners" to the staff) who
work the telephones trying to entice young men and women to enter the next
available training class, which is always in the process of formation. For some
reason, perhaps related to the need for peer support, adolescents like to feel
special, a word that is commonly used in promotional literature.

The salesmen work tear-out cards enclosed in newspaper supplements and/
or respond to the yield of potential prospects derived from mass mailings and
television commercials. Some operations use telephone men to screen new recruits and set up appointments and leave the counseling to other staff. As the
president of a school house operation that sells (subject) training said, "We
want young people who are interested, and who have the money, or can get
the money, to take our classes." When asked about the cost of the programs,
he responded:

> Well, it depends. We have full-time and part-time programs. We also have
> evening classes. We are fully accredited in [name of state]. Our courses run
> from $2,000 to $3,800 [tone becomes belligerent]. But that depends on the
> program of study and is none of *your* business. [Assumes an aggressive pos-
> ture that is most similar to that of a drill sergeant in the military.] It's your
> job to qualify them for interest and make an appointment with the counse-
> lor. Counseling is *their* job [points to staff offices], not yours. All we are hir-
> ing *you* to do is to work the phones. There is no selling here. Just qualifying.

Years of cultural conditioning, vivid memories of basic military training, a
desire to complete my research, and perhaps luck allowed me to contain my
rage and prevented me from walking out upon hearing what I was sure would
be his next words: *"Do I make myself perfectly clear?"* They were, but somehow the subject changed to lead acquisition and administrative matters.

One school house operation is located within five miles of a major regional
university. A quarter floor of a three-story office building is occupied by a

businessman and his wife, who serve as president and general secretary, respectively, of the school. All of the instructors and staff are white. A half-dozen rooms are filled with as many part-time staff and serve as classrooms, counseling rooms, and work areas where projects meet devices (tools, hardware, and machines) common to the trade. The teaching staff is recruited from local high schools and from the ranks of retired shop teachers. Two larger classrooms in another part of the building are filled with students. Most are black males. All are well dressed and energetic. It is typical for two or three students to work on common projects. The tone is purposeful. There is no sense of boredom or restlessness. The bathrooms are graffiti-free.

The main office is decorated with the school logo, and photographs of graduates fill a good part of an entire wall. Under each photograph is the name of the company allegedly employing them, neatly and uniformly stenciled in black ink at the bottom of a paper frame. The layout is consistent with that of a school, replete with a large American flag to the right of the president's desk. This scene and setting are likely duplicated in dozens of other cities where the lure of jobs in the electronics, drafting, construction, and food service industries is appealing to young marginalized men looking for permanent work and some kind of productive future.

Management, interior decorating, accounting, and English-language operations have joined the ranks of school house operations. A quick look in telephone directories for most urban areas (or on the insides of matchbook covers, in comic books, and on early-morning airwaves of local television stations) will typically reveal a host of operations offering courses on a wide array of subjects, from "How to Drive the Big Rigs" to "How to Start Your Own Business." The latest "hot school houses," according to informants, are those featuring VCR and computer repair.

"Language houses"—a relatively recent addition because of shifts in immigration patterns—are especially effective. By definition, their marks are not native speakers of English and thus the easiest to con. That immigrants are more likely to think both optimistically and uncritically of their new homeland is also an important factor, assisted by the marketing reality that these operations bill themselves as "schools," "institutes," and "learning centers." Most operations have professionally designed brochures and catalogs that lend credibility to the scam.

What is actually vended I would classify as training in "obsolescent trades"—skills whose time has passed but whose image continues to carry allure among the uninformed, the young, and the vulnerable.[6] Language houses aside, most offer alleged technical training of some kind. Readily available photographs of devices such as VCRs, televisions, microprocessors, or laser-beam generators coupled with inexpensive NASA publicity photos easily create the illusion of participation in the "knowledge society," an especially

ironic phrase (used in many pitches) when school house operations are instrumental in artfully conning those with educational deficits.

High-tech images come to embody the target industry. Students are not
told that former graduates billed as "working for the U.S. government" may
be in the army or in jail. School houses work the backwaters of the educational system. Many of these businesses began when federal authorities closed
down the larger electronics and trade school scams in the early 1970s, thus
leaving entrepreneurs looking for some other kind of action that could be
operated on a smaller, less-visible scale.

Just as the breakup of Florida real estate scams resulted in making that
state what is perhaps the boiler room capital of the world because unemployed
salesmen turned to the telephones to make a living, school houses attract those
businessmen who can combine and facilitate the merging and orchestration
of educational props and hardware with boiler room techniques.[7] Like the real
estate scams that prey on the desire of urban folk to own land—and sell worthless parcels—school houses work the generally perceived value of education
and hope that their marks will confuse substandard fare with the genuine article. They are one result of what can happen when pure market behavior is
unleashed upon the vulnerable young. It is perfectly legal to provide bogus
training as long as it can be documented that training is, in fact, provided. If
the outcome of these ruses does not result in gainful employment, it is commonly seen as an unfortunate market artifact rather than something for which
entrepreneurial businessmen can be held accountable.

Entrepreneurs and educators who are in business are ultimately responsible only to the corporate ethos by which they keep their jobs. Because neither has any great love for poor students (the scholastically incapable and the
economically disadvantaged), and the underclass has nowhere else to go, apol-
ogists for substandard educational alternatives will always be able to make
the case that they provide a useful service. Although warehousing the young
to extract their money and loan entitlements pushes the definition of "useful" beyond its ethical limit, none can argue that these are not profitable
business ventures.

Such scams thrive on the huge pool of resources waiting to be tapped in the
form of the availability of state and federal loan money as well as on the hopes
and dreams of students—all of which are subject to manipulation. The scams
stay within the letter of the law by focusing on the easily refuted premise that
the training offered is clearly inferior. Once critics agree to focus on the premise
of curricula integrity alone they are quickly disarmed. School houses, in fact,
offer extremely rigorous training that few students actually complete. A school
house is a scam of attrition. Featuring rigidly constructed curricula, authori-
tarian techniques, and the liberal use of manuals and educational props, it breaks

no law when its students flunk out, elect to leave prematurely, or switch programs. School houses dutifully collect tuition, and students amass a substantial amount of debt and are tracked into useless programs. This end is facilitated by salesmen who, in many cases, are boilers.

The system works by establishing a complex and demanding syllabus that is segmented into blocks of study. The cognitive demands of the first half-dozen or so blocks (the bait) may be at the elementary school level, whereas subsequent blocks are demanding. The school house, however, gets its money up front (the hook), and its managers are as capable of becoming masters of fine print in designing contracts as state and federal loan program bureaucrats are in being nebulous in their administrative definitions of approved curricula.

The curricula of the school house are typically flawless, a fact that permits these scams to continue to rip off the young. As in any system of education, curricula are only formal statements. As any undergraduate who scans college catalogs is no doubt aware, the merits of a given course do not inhere in its brief description—designed, more often than not, to comply with administrative requirements—but ultimately reside in the credibility of the host institution: in its quality of instruction; in the dedication of its teachers; in the total educational experience it makes available; and in the taken-for-granted assumption that there is some value to be realized by conforming to academic routine and rituals.

Absent these assumptions, it is functionally irrelevant that there is some degree of bureaucratic consensus regarding the content of curricula. By the time school house students have paid the bulk of their nonrefundable tuition and fees, however, they notice that the curriculum begins to change: It tightens up at an escalating rate. More reading is required, and less shop time is available. Homework becomes more demanding, and technical terminology and higher computational skills are increasingly required. The lessons become longer, more difficult, and more complex.

At this stage counselors play a more important role in stressing the difficulty of the tasks at hand. They begin to generate heat: to suggest and imply that students should perhaps rethink the seriousness of what they are undertaking. What follows is a counselor (a salesman) describing what is called the "block 12 pitch," a talk designed to weaken the will of students to remain in the more demanding programs:

> Before block 12, we give 'em pep talks about the industry and their careers when they finish the program. We talk about successes. After block 12, it's sink or swim. Their tuition is paid. We have our commissions. If they make it, beautiful! If they drop out after block 12? Well, that's up to them. We now

tell them the truth: This stuff is hard. Now they find out for themselves that it is! Look, our programs are accepted by the state of _____. The program is tough. The instructors know that. Hell, they work hard for their money. But the kids just can't, in most cases, do the work. That's not *our* fault. Look, these assholes spend all of their lives in bummed-out schools to begin with. Yeah, man. They can shoot great hoop. Big goddamn deal! Know what I mean? When they get to the electronics section they begin to realize that all that shit that they teach you in the tenth grade *is* important after all! These kids don't know that. If they did, they wouldn't be *here* [laughs] . . . I used to feel sorry for them. Not anymore. Sometimes, however, we do get a few bright kids. They do fine. They actually learn something. I had one ten months ago. Hey, this guy should have been at the local college. You should have seen his homework! He was from Russia or something like that. . . . His problem was English. I mean he actually worked in the field of [_____]. Real sharp. Let me tell you something. When the instructors saw the work this kid was doing, they cheered him on. Everybody did. It was almost like a school is supposed to be. But, look, that is one in a hundred. Half these kids have trouble reading. Heh. Heh. Of course you know who the *school hero* is, right? That kid. That keeps the company legit. All they need is one or two successful graduates. For him, at least, the program works.

When many students respond to the block 12 pitch with the anticipated second thoughts about completing their courses, they are usually "cut a deal" where a small partial tuition refund (for noncompletion) is offered. Operations that wish to maximize earnings by producing graduates (some states require completion of the courses for full tuition-loan eligibility) modify their techniques. They use the counselors to direct the students to switch tracks from the advanced to the service levels of the program. That effectively limits the use of expensive equipment and the need for highly skilled instructors. A counselor explains:

Here's how it works: We pull a switch track. The high-tech stuff is only for the advanced-level students. Just about everyone *starts out* in the advanced-level program. That is, before they pay all the tuition. Once the bucks are in, well, we use a switch track pitch. We get the kids to change from the advanced-level to the technical-level courses. The instructors grade the courses, not us. Tests don't lie. . . . It's not the instructors' fault if these kids are numbskulls. When these kids get a look at the advanced training material manuals and textbooks. . . . Hey, I never saw so much math in my life, it's all formulas and technical stuff. They *freak out*. So that's where we come in: We give them a chance to switch tracks.

Absent from the ranks of the students are those who have taken night courses at local high schools or junior colleges, where the training, in both cases, is more affordable, and better.[8] Absent also, it would seem, are those from families that place a great deal of faith in the conventional educational system, to the degree that previous failure in that system may breed contempt for, and suspicion over, its methods. The half-dozen or so students with whom I spoke were receiving substantial degrees of both financial and emotional support from their parents, who expressed (in the words of one informant describing his mother's attitude) a hope that maybe "this time" school would work for her kids.

The pitch that draws students to the initial school interview emphasizes that they will have a chance to "take charge of their lives." Upon seeing those very much like themselves in dress, manner, and ambition hard at work over desks, projects, and study, the illusion of a school is constructed. The work at hand is presented as serious educational business.

The salesman leads a discussion with the more successful students followed by a break. Prospects are free to engage in anticipatory socialization. They may leave when they wish or wander around the premises. The counselor shows off the classrooms and the students and then concludes the presentation with an invitation to attend a free orientation session. No pressure is used. No deposits are collected. Coffee and doughnuts are made available. A roster is left at the door, and the counselor leaves the room—a classic version of the take-away ploy. The boiler room, of course, is off-limits to all students. On its door is a sign: "Professional Staff Only."

Some school house boilers work as fronters, and others become more deeply involved in the manipulation of students. After the class quotas are filled, the fronters typically quit or are fired, and the quasi-boiler room shuts down. The best are offered sales positions as house pros, where they work as counselors, screen inquiry calls, develop introductory pitches, and await the next recruitment cycle, which will find a new group of prospects and temporary positions for new fronters.

Beauty Shop Scams

Beauty shop scams are school house enterprises that rely on two kinds of telephone talent: telemarketing screeners (who possess "telephone voices") and counselors who close the deals and are recruited from the ranks of screeners. These salesmen work the pool of young women aged eighteen to twenty-six who are interested in beauty training, cosmetology science, hair design, wave sculpting, and the other glamorous-sounding titles by which contemporary hairdressing has come to be known.

By working the responses to advertisements placed in local newspapers and through mailings, screeners solicit interest in beauty programs and receive the minimum wage plus a bonus for each qualified lead (appointment with a counselor) that they generate. By asking background questions (part of a telephone script), the screeners practice a form of what might be called "applied business demography." With knowledge of a student's age, type and age of automobile, address (to be plotted on a router map), formal education level, number of siblings, and employment status, a screener qualifies ripe candidates and ascertains eligibility for vocational education loans, entitlements, and benefits.

Screeners give this coded information to the counselors who, in turn, will meet prospects in a face-to-face presentation.[9] Counselors wear stylish clothes and work out of offices separate from the telephone room, where dress codes are less relevant. Most counselors are single males in their twenties. The opportunity to meet single women in contexts where they can do so in positions of authority is appealing to many. Counselors are younger than most boilers and more physically fit, athletic, and well groomed. What they lack in the area of telephone sales skills they make up in the area of interpersonal competence.

A counselor serves as a confidant, mediator, and covert salesman. This latter role is never directly acknowledged, however, and is only revealed through an astute reading of newspaper advertisements placed for sales help. During the initial interview prospects are taken into special meeting rooms that feature track lighting and walls covered with what are called "celebrity faces" (photographs of movie stars) and advertisements for hair products. One informant calls the initial presentation the "Hollywood pitch." He explains: "Catch this. The room is filled with photographs of every Hollywood celeb you can think of. We try to pitch a group. It's easier that way. Remember that all women want to be beautiful. We sell the idea of beauty: That they can make themselves beautiful while they get paid to make others look beautiful. Pretty nifty, right? It's an easy sale. These babes come in here and think that in a few months they will know all the Hollywood secrets. The babes are into faces, you know: hair styles, the eyes and proper makeup, the cover girl look, the fashion model style."

After the prospective students get their "trip to Hollywood," as the pitch is also sometimes called, and take a tour of the facilities, they are then sent away to think about their experiences and read the school's literature describing tuition (between $600 and $1,300 for the basic program), the refund policy (most of the money is up front, few refunds are actually given), and vocational education options (add-ons). Many beauty shop operations adapt their sales materials to whatever customers find most appealing.

Smaller beauty shop operations are located in the suburban belt of metropolitan areas and larger ones in the core of large cities. They have numerous contacts with local salons—where some of their graduates can get entry-level jobs. These businesses also hire aides to assist the beauticians who serve as instructors. The basic courses of instruction are usually between sixteen and thirty-eight weeks long, depending on the program selected and amount of time spent in the classroom. Classes are held in the evenings and on weekends. Aides work in the afternoons where, in addition to serving the general public for a reduced fee, they groom and cut, manage, and style the hair of the staff, counselors, and owners.

Because of this, all who must make a public appearance in the organization are assured that they will possess a stylish haircut to complement their acceptable personas. Those who work the telephones as screeners can typically purchase beauty services at half price, as can all categories of help. One informant said, "Well it's sort of a perk. They do our hair. We always look good for work. I'll have to admit that. They'll even do your nails. It also makes the operation look real. You know, students training to enter 'the glamorous world of cosmetology' [a line from the pitch]. It also helps sell finis (pronounced *fin-eys*) to the students."

Question: Finis?

Counselor: Yeah. Those are *add-ons*. We teach them. They sell for an additional $60–$150. We can earn as much as 30 percent commission on each student. It's additional training. We set up seminars to teach the girls how to write a resume, how to conduct a job interview. They are sold in blocks [weeks of training] along with, or after, the basic course. One is called "Basic Business Skills" and teaches checkbook balancing and beauty record-keeping. We also offer advanced courses in nails, popular hair cutting, and in electrolysis. You know, all the beauty gadgets. But we don't teach those, we just sign them up as part of "counseling hours" [each salesman gets to pitch the students on different aspects of the programs offered]. We also use *loopers* to pitch 'em on a consulting basis.

Question: Loopers?

Counselor: Sort of like shills. They are our former graduates who have jobs at beauty parlors. We give them coupons for free or discount services, which they can distribute to their girlfriends, and some cash. The coupons have the looper's name on the back. When a customer presents the coupon for discounts, the looper gets some kind of bonus. It's a numbers play: give away some freebies and you get referral business. If this results in new students, the loopers get a spiff. Some take the cash and/or a combination of tickets and cash. It makes our jobs much easier. . . . Sort of like testimonials. We bring the loopers in for scheduled counseling sessions. They tell the girls how good the school was to them and how the training pays off. The loopers have instant credibility, you might say. Right now they are pushing the fini on "Unisex," it's the hottest fini around. It costs $65 for three, one-hour sessions. If the looper "plants the seed" on my counseling time I get the commission if I can sign the girl up. It works out real well.

A former counselor, whom I met in a boiler room, assessed the value of these programs to the students:

> Gimme a break. What value? They pay aides a half-a-buck over minimum wage. That is the job that most of the graduates get: an *aide* to a beautician. . . . And no one can work over thirty hours a week as an aide.[10] Aides do the shit work: washing hair, cleaning up the floor, using the hot towels on the men, and doing a facial prep [applying the first in a series of cleaners and moisturizers to the face after the initial wash]. The instructors are also all part time. They are also looking for work. As soon as a better job materializes, they quit . . . I mean, they are all beauticians but they can't make a decent living at it because in this business the shop is the key. It's not how skilled you are. If you work in a high-priced beauty parlor, you make out OK. If you don't, well, then you teach at the school to try to make a few extra green ones [dollars] being a looper. Anyway, back to the students. After working as an aide for a number of months, the students with the best personalities can sometimes assist in cutting hair. Like, it's not automatic, you know. The beautician has to ask for help. If you don't ask for the better deal, you wind up just doing the dirty work. Actually, what goes on is that the sharper ones teach themselves and the school gets the credit for it. The problem is that most of the students don't have the personality for dealing with the public. Those that do, seem to do fine. I mean, the aides work one-on-one with the beautician. It's an apprenticeship . . . I'll never forget this *hog* [an overweight, unattractive girl] who was in the last class we had. She even had bad breath! Hey, I sold her three finis—but she won't work out for anything other than maybe taking out the trash. But we did a *good* selling job. . . . Even the hogs thought that they were going to "get jobs in the beauty industry" [a line from the pitch].

The size and duration of the quasi-boiler room depends on the capacity of the school and the length of its programs. When class quotas are met, screeners are fired and the best are retained as counselors. Periodically, the counselors are also fired because, with age and experience in this line of work, it is thought that they will counter the illusion of schooling being presented. A fired counselor explains:

> Well, it was nice while it lasted. Actually, what happens is that you get to know the babes [students]. At first, it's neat 'cause some of these girls are really knockouts. Real lookers. I mean, you're gonna score with some of them 'cause you're their counselor. It's an ego trip. I'll admit it. . . . Of course, after the thrill wears off you begin to realize that these babes are being used. You know it. Management knows it. Some of the babes get to know it if you date them. So management doesn't want you datin' the babes. Right. So you can

get around that, but after a while most of the guys just sort of grow out of this line of work. I mean, if you're a real salesman you want to get some real *commish*, not just finis. If you're a phone man, you want to pitch the big deals, not just impress a bunch of kids who are dreaming of Hollywood. . . . And hey, the owners aren't going to cut you in for a piece of the action. You know how it is. So, sooner or later you get fired or some sharp phone guy takes your job.

Contract Telemarketing: Spawning Scams

Were it not for the generative role of certain types of quasi-boiler rooms, the telephone sales landscape would soon be reduced to a number of historical accounts of defunct companies and burned-out scam artists. That is not the case, however, because contract telemarketing operations serve the latent function of assuring that boiler rooms and their techniques will continue to evolve and thrive.

Contract telemarketing is a particular variety of scam that embodies the most adaptive characteristics of the form. It is, in the words of one informant, "The mother of all boiler rooms." These operations evolve in boiler rooms whose owners wish to cash in on the appeal of the lucrative telemarketing (TM) industry by promoting ventures that target small businesses unable to afford the services of the larger, more conventional TM firms. They do so by placing ads in the "Business Services" section of newspapers and using a part of the boiler room, and some of its sales talent, to work the scam.

Quasi-boiler room contract TM operations are involved in "business-to-business" cons. The scam operates when the client contacts a quasi-boiler room to provide services for a fixed number of hours (called the "contract"). Both conventional TM firms and quasi-boiler rooms, in effect, sell telephone time at a variable hourly rate that depends on the duration of the contract and the number of tasks required. The quasi-boiler room, however, has two assets that conventional TM firms lack: the ability to slash prices well below the prevailing market rate to secure an initial contract, and pro boilers who make the initial presentation and work the telephones, at least part of the time.[11]

A contract TM deal is sold as a package that usually includes, first, an initial consultation (to assess the needs of the client); second, a service run (where, for the initial part of the contract, a specially trained group of boilers performs some of the tasks required); and, third, a trial run (where the staff of the service provider spends a fixed number of billed hours accomplishing the specifically requested tasks that compose the contract: account servicing, sales, lead generation, market analysis, and data collection and dissemination).

After an initial contract, the client may renegotiate, terminate, or extend the obligation to the service provider. The quasi-boiler room adjusts its work force accordingly. If it turns out that a new market is discovered, it may be serviced by boilers on the sales floor at a later time. Commenting on the fact that all contract TM clients are small businessmen, a pro responds:

> Of course they are businessmen. All that means is that they want to make a buck. . . . They say to themselves, "You know, *my* company could expand its market just like the *big guys.*" So, they respond to our ads. These guys are all small-fry with their ideas on how to make a killing. Hell, we've got inventors, distributors, doctors . . . [he goes through a list].[12] These mooches are going to sink a few grand into a dream. Then they are going to discover "it ain't for them." When *we* tell them at the end of a hundred or two hundred hours that their marketing schemes won't work over the phone, they, in fact, won't work. Who knows, maybe they'll get lucky. . . . Look at our track record [smiles]: Out of sixty accounts, we have two successes. Those two *love* us. True, the salesmen add a little charm to what they sell, but they are delighted. No one was selling over the telephone in their markets. Ask our two successes about the fifty-eight failures. Let them decide.

Contract TM operations parallel the growth and expansion of the conventional TM industry that began to flourish during the early 1980s coincident with the almost astronomical growth of personal and business computing in the United States and the changes in the telecommunications business. The three huge industries support the computerization of many aspects of contemporary life and have produced an "information explosion" wherein digitized data delivery systems have transformed the marketplace.

This transformation has created an almost irresistible set of symbols in the small business community: the power of the computer linked with the amazing capability of the telephone to provide instantaneous communications. As a general rule, scams always thrive where there are imperfections in a market. Lack of knowledge concerning the business implications of technological innovations is one such imperfection.

Transforming technical information into the quest for profits among small businesses requires a sales effort. Because boilers are used for this purpose, it is one area where a boiler room has a comparative advantage. It works the backwaters of the TM field when it sets up contract TM operations and hires out its services to small companies with a product or service to sell.

Many of the sales calls that most homeowners receive in the evening likely have their origins in a quasi-boiler room. This is one measure of the success of the contract TM provider in successfully pitching local businesses. The operation has the additional advantage of being totally invisible. Because it places calls on behalf of its client, it can never be identified, reported, or made part of the public consciousness other than as a generalized annoyance traceable only to the industry that contains the client. Nothing has yet to appear in print concerning these operations.

Each broad category of client, however, often contains businesses that are run fraudulently. If so, the quasi-boiler room is said to have "found a winner," and the pros in the host boiler room may acquire a new line. If not, the small business that hires the contract TM company simply loses the cost of the initial (failed) contract. In the first case, a new boiler room type may emerge; in the second, another kind of fish will be revealed. The quasi-boiler room wins in both cases and thus ensures that the host operation will constantly evolve.

What follows is a catalog of fraudulent business types that use contract TM houses. Each is transformed (sometimes immediately, sometimes over time) into a working line in a boiler room, a "list of winners" as it were. Those businesses rejected, that is, "losers," of course continue to ply their trade through means other than by using the telephone. For purposes of brevity, I list only the most common scams and elaborate upon what pro boilers call the "pivot point": that part of the operation especially amenable to a pitchman's manipulation. A quasi-boiler room only acts in those areas where the target businesses have an identifiable pivot point. Lacking this, it is not likely that the scam will be telephone-promotable. Thus, after the initial contract is vended, the mark is cooled out, and no further action is taken if there is no pivot point to be discovered.

The Boiler's Catalog

The building trades (pools and decks): List brokers provide the names of prospects. An appointment for a free, or reduced cost, safety inspection is offered. What is sold is a contract for overpriced services, some or all of which may not be provided. The pivot point is that those with children are safety-conscious and can be readily identified.

Heating and air-conditioning: List brokers provide the names of prospects. An appointment for a seasonal tune-up, calibration, or inspection is offered. A service contract is sold, along with overpriced equipment. Both are likely not to be honored and/or delivered. The pivot point is that air-handling systems require regular maintenance. The very young and the very old have health concerns that can be easily amplified by concerns over pathogens supposedly bred in the air ducts and the fact that heat pump technology is interpreted socially. Thus, air heated to 92 degrees by a heat pump feels cold to the human hand.

Home restoration (roofing and siding): List brokers provide the names of prospects. An appointment for a fire and safety inspection is offered at reduced cost, for free, or as a refundable option. A "courtesy" gutter cleaning and inspection is provided as a hook. Services are sold at highly inflated prices. Financing is sometimes offered. The pivot point is that most homeowners find "free" (or reduced price) gutter cleaning offers irresistible. This puts a salesman on a ladder, because few people have the opportunity to examine areas of their homes above the gutters. A creative salesman can invent many "conditions" in older housing stock and offer overpriced remedies. Chimney repair is a popular problem area. Its merit is that most customers will not climb a ladder to examine imaginary problems. The very creative can also stage accidents. The elderly are most likely to be successfully conned.

Lawn care (seeding, weeding, and insect control): List brokers provide the names of prospects. A free "soil evaluation" or "care estimate" is offered. A perpetual contract is sold (i.e., the number of applications continues indefinitely), and inferior materials applied by untrained labor is delivered. The pivot point is that middle-class homeowners have uses for their time other than lawn care and are often ignorant of the principles of agronomy. Most people fear insects and the diseases they carry. Most "brown grass" results from lack of water rather than from disease. Watering is never a service that is provided, however. Many people are proud of their green lawns.

Basement maintenance (sealing, waterproofing, and draining): List brokers provide the names of prospects. A free or reduced price safety inspection is offered. An expensive repair or rebuilding contract is sold. Such contracts are paid for but typically not honored in full. The work is begun, funds—"depos" (deposits)—are collected, and the contractor never completes the job. The pivot point is that most people are uninformed about the actual medical and structural consequences of dampness. A creative salesman carries a packet or tin of desiccant which, with the clandestine addition of saliva, turns blue, green, or yellow. The pitch follows.

Secured credit cards: List brokers provide the names of bad credit risks. Secured credit is offered at outrageous rates and sold as a package that includes service charges, fees, and overpriced annuity insurance offerings.[13] The pivot point is that the poor are often unable to obtain credit cards.

Insurance (for bad drivers): List brokers provide the names of recent automobile insurance cancellations. "Free coverage," for a limited time, is offered. A balloon policy is sold (i.e., the rates and fees escalate monthly). A security deposit is required. The pivot point is that canceled drivers are often desperate and embarrassed. A creative salesman can arrange direct payments, made monthly, from a checking account. A bounced check results in excess fines and fees and automatic cancellation. The comeback is reinstatement for an additional fee.

Imaginary tax write-offs (energy conservation): List brokers provide the names of prospects. An energy audit is offered, for a fee, which is guaranteed to save clients a specified percent of their taxes, and a retroactive refund is assured. It does not; the boilers lie. The pivot point is that some small business owners and homeowners take great pleasure in the illusion of being able to "beat the tax man." This is readily discerned through the use of an artfully designed pitch.

Bogus business opportunities (vending machine deals, fake franchise rights, and imaginary placement opportunities via fictional "location brokers"): A business opportunity is offered. None exists. Overpriced equipment, fictional distribution rights, territories, and prime locations can be sold "to those who qualify." The pivot point is that distribution routes and merchandising are appealing to many middle-aged men who are unemployed or experiencing a midlife occupational crisis. List brokers provide the names of investors and the relevant demographics. A quick screening call qualifies for interest and liquidity. Pro boilers use the take-away ploy.

Replacement windows: List brokers provide the names of those with aging housing stock while router maps identify poorer neighborhoods. A free inspection and "heat loss analysis" are offered. Inferior goods, often financed at outrageous interest rates, are sold. The pivot point is that babies and the elderly have easily amplified comfort needs. A creative salesman can use winter headlines regarding weather-related deaths to promote fear, and the less dramatically inclined can promote imaginary cost savings. Both will note that a lit cigarette, placed near a cold window, correctly identifies naturally occurring convection currents that can readily be interpreted as leakage.

Fake service contracts: List brokers provide the names of businesses. "Expire houses" send fraudulent bills for nonprovided services on or around the date of expiration (or scheduled maintenance) on legitimate service contracts, vended by other providers, for fire extinguishers, copying machines, and fax machines. The pivot point is that most businesses have safety-mandated fire extinguishers that must be recharged, office copiers, and fax machines. All must be regularly serviced. Three inquiry calls are made (at different times): one verifies the business address; a second identifies the name of the responsible division and/or the name of the appropriate manager; and a third acquires the identification number of the business appliance, the "servicing date," and confirms the payment amount. If the documentation looks complete and the timing is correct, a certain percentage of businesses will pay bogus bills sent to accounts payable a few weeks before the due date of the genuine contract.[14]

Some sense of the ingenuity present in a quasi-boiler room can be deduced by noting that all of the preceding businesses rely heavily on list brokers to provide the names and telephone numbers of prospective clients. The profitability of this linkage should not be underestimated.[15] Induction provides the same conclusion. There are, indeed, quasi-boiler rooms called "slick list operators" that capitalize on the importance of list brokers. An informant explains:

> The *slick-listers* are pretty smart. They are pros who do this as a part-time gig [run a quasi-boiler room]. The prime room [the boiler room] is usually investments. You know, coins [numismatics], art [lithographs], or oil [oil and gas leases]. The guys with the silver tongues. They realize that good leads are essential to any phone operation. Here's how it works. First, they pay top bread to a real list broker and secure genuine prime prospects at maybe $2.50 to $5 a name. If you know how to properly qualify a prospect [explains details], you know that a prime lead is worth a lot of money. So they produce a real [genuine] short list of prospects and call it a "sample." It's a smooth scam. But it can only work on certain type of phone operations that don't know the score. . . . Anyway, if the typical phone room is paying, say, 20 cents for a name, well, you know that the list is being pounded by every damn phone room in the country. I mean cheap leads really destroy the payout ratio [the ratio of deals to calls]. That's why *good leads* are gold: They pay for themselves. So, they get a list of phone rooms [explains technique]. Then, you get on the phone: you promise a minimum 25 percent payout ratio [the bait] and offer to send a sample of twenty-five names free of charge [the hook]. Hey, what the hell, a freebie. No phone room turns down freebies, right? So, they send the sample and guess what? They are damn good leads! That's how the con works. You don't even have to make a follow-up call in most cases. The greedsters call you! It's sort of ironic [laughs]. . . . Well, anyway, you offer five thousand red hots [prime leads] for a quarter a name [$1,250], and a 10 percent "promotional discount" [$125] and send the courier to pick up the check [$1,125]. Even phone rooms are moochie, you'd think they would know better. But they don't. So, it cost you, say, $100 for the sample. Actually, since you can deal with list brokers, let's say it costs $80. Then, let's say the courier costs $10. Oh, go ahead, throw in another $20 for whatever. That's $110. Now, you've got a check for $1,125. So, you simply wait 'til it clears. It's a nice scam. You've outboiled the boilers. Only a pro can do that. Of course, you never send a product [explains stalling technique]. They get burned. They can't complain. *There is no heat.* Plus, the owner will, of course, curse himself for being taken. But this is not something that he won't understand.

Because most people have likely received a call in the evening from solicitors (some with bad diction, most with terrible phone voices, and few with telephone personalities), and the preceding boiler's catalog offers a strong guess about which types of operations are most likely to have your number, an obvious question would be, How can ill-trained telephoners, reading pitches verbatim—and sometimes poorly—and calling the general public generate any business at all?

The answer, of course, is that typically most cannot. That is because the sole purpose of a quasi-boiler room operator is to sell the TM contract, not to deliver on all of the promises made in the pitch. This is subject to modification if a client has something that generates income over and above the cost of the initial TM contract. Then, boilers reappear, telephoners are fired, and pros start working on pitches.

The Transformers: Boiler Rooms That Change

An informant pro and I had a number of interesting conversations that concerned the source of the impetus to change the nature of boiler rooms. Because there are no written materials on this important subject, the bulk of our discussions centered upon boiler room lore, his twenty-five years of boiler room experience, and his philosophy of life. He provided a useful metaphor as a partial insight into my quest for an organizing principle with which to explore how and why boiler rooms change.

His insight originated in a joke about a widely advertised line of children's toys called "Transformers," models of various sizes made up of a number of puzzlelike components capable of being rearranged. Although the initial configuration appears to be a truck, an airplane, or a boat, careful sequential manipulation of the components transforms the toy into a fighting robot, a space vehicle, a prehistoric monster, or a superhero.

He called these toys "scam toys" because they work their magic by not being what they appear to be and because of the fact that one must learn the correct procedures to "make the transformation happen." The toy's basic nature does not inhere in whatever shape it happens to assume at any given time but in its ability to assume different configurations. That is an apt description of social change in the boiler room.

Transformation of a boiler room (changes in the product line, in personnel, or in the type of market served) and its mutation (changes in the type of operation) are part of an ongoing process. New product lines are acquired while old ones are phased out as the mix of skill on the sales floor changes with new accessions and firings. Owners are also sensitive to new innovations in billing (credit cards) and shipping (the use of COD and sly shipping techniques).[16] Skills in promotions can also uncover new needs, trends, and markets in real time (before the raw data can be identified, analyzed, and publicized by industry analysts). Live telephone contact with those from many walks of life can reveal as much as the pitchman's ear is sensitive to encoding.

Sometimes it is possible for a company to transform if the owner has been especially fortunate to have a new business opportunity correspond with an upswing in a market presently being served. That permits possibilities. The boiler room may move in the direction of conventionality and become more respectable, or it may become a quasi-boiler room and new varieties of fraud may be created—or older ones refined and embellished. The corporate fate of a telephone room rests largely on the personality of its owner, the circumstances he faces in the marketplace, and his perception of what his company is to become.

Each of these variables interacts with the others. To state that an active boiler room is as flexible as the owner is willing, capable, or insightful enough to let it become explains the varying fates of individual operations but does not address systemic aspects of change. The notion of a quasi-boiler room offers a structural explanation. These are settings that are most attuned to shifts in the market and serve as halfway houses of sorts. A few evolve into conventional companies if they can acquire enough capital and the proper kinds of accounts. If that should prove financially rewarding, a boiler room may mutate. Two informants made the transition from boiler room operatives to independent brokers in the wholesale business. For one of them, the change began when he happened to make contacts with wholesalers who were impressed by his telephone personality. He explains:

> Well. It was kind of funny. I called one of our suppliers [to the boiler room] for a routine order, and he asks me if I can locate a load of [names the product]. "See if you can round some up for me. Make some calls," he says. So I worked like hell. I finally tracked down a guy in California who had what he needed. Of course, I didn't have any money to pay for the materials even if I located them, so I asked another supplier if he would drop-ship the order and cut me in. Well, it was risky, but he decided to give me a shot. And that was it. My first deal. That's how I got started.

For the second owner, the transition occurred when he started graduate school on the West Coast. He had worked for a product boiler room as an undergraduate and decided to save some of his accounts until he was able to discover the boiler room's supplier. As he explained the transformation of his line of work, "I was working in a phone room out of [name of city]. I'm working hard, paying tuition and gettin' by. I finally figured out who the supplier was. So I said to him, 'Look, I would like to do this out of my house. Would you back [supply] me if I work for you [i.e., sell your line]? I already have the accounts.' To my surprise he says, 'Hell yes. I'll drop-ship for you, under your name.' So, I quit the phone room and started up my own operation and took my paper with me."[17]

At the corporate level, for the period of time required for the transformation, the usual product lines are typically still vended, the old techniques used, and viable capital is acquired. That is usually accomplished by firing staff and diverting the income that would normally pay for them. An owner explains:

> Our bills are more or less current. I've worked a deal with the phone company for the new phones. We will continue to sell [names line]. I'll have to prune the sales force, hold off my suppliers for a while, and begin the new operation. I have a change window of about sixty days. It's a big risk. If we succeed, this will change the nature of the whole business. I've got to *make it happen*. If this works, by this time next year, I can go to the bank for financing. This will be a real company. We will no longer sink or swim based on what our suppliers can provide. We will *be* suppliers.

Another source of capital for transformation lies in the expertise of a boiler room in the general area of promotions. If a group of investors can be secured, the boiler room can tap into their economic aspirations. An ideal group for such purposes are those members of the small business community who have acquired modest amounts of money for investment and/or expansion. These individuals become marks for a quasi-boiler room. This is facilitated by the fact that boiler room owners and their small business customers are strikingly similar demographically. Both have many years of business experience, both need capital to expand their operations, and both have experienced the cyclicality of commercial life. Both may have also acquired dreams in excess of their means, and both are ripe to take risks if the right opportunity presents itself. Both also turn to the capabilities of the telephone as an instrumentality for achieving their goals.

Unable to raise the necessary capital quickly enough to realize their dreams as successful businessmen, boiler room operators and members of the small business community alike are fatally attracted to each other. Each seeks a golden opportunity. By catering to the economic aspirations of businesspeople for "making a killing," "finding a hot market," and "getting in on the ground floor" (lines from varied pitches as well as phrases used by boiler room owners themselves when they conceptualize their own enterprises), it becomes clear that the owners of boiler rooms and their clients share the same universe of discourse.

While strategically advantaged with respect to their marks, however, boiler room owners are not wholly invulnerable to their own ambitions. Thus, it is always possible that the final stage of a transformation can be bankruptcy. A house pro, reflecting on a transformation that occurred in a number of stages, recalls some as successful, others not:

Look, I wouldn't want to be in his [the owner's] shoes. He has to sell these cockamamie deals [via the contract TM operation] to small-time dreamers. . . . So, I go out as the "director of telemarketing." Hey, we have a business lunch, and ya know what? The client is impressed. *Of course* he'll be impressed. I'm *good* at what I do [chuckles]. So then we have the screening committee [laughs] decide if the customer qualifies for our services. Of course, we try to pick a winner, but there are few winners. Most of these guys are crazy. They think that once you make a few calls, thousands of orders will magically appear. They are greedy. So, we get the contracts . . . I *pitch* them. I tell them what they want to hear. But here is something for you to think about: The boss actually *believes* that some of this hype is really possible. He better watch out. I've told him so. He doesn't believe me. In my opinion he is as moochie as some of these wacko customers.[18]

In that case, a quasi-boiler room transformed itself into a multilevel operation using boiler room techniques. Then it went bankrupt. As an experienced informant explained after the company went out of business:

The fish got fat and went belly up. Your friend was a small fry that got greedy. He had a good little operation going for himself. . . . He was smart. He worked hard. But I know *the operator* that took him under in the [names the multilevel operation]. . . . He is probably in Florida by now. He works the entire country. Now *he* is a pro. He is *very* selective. He only goes after people who have experienced a recent windfall in their businesses. Those are the best fish. They see themselves as success stories. That's why the scam works: because they *are* really self-made men. But not for long. That's *all* he goes after. As you can see, he is a very good fisherman.

Solicitor Operations: Conventional Telemarketing

Certain categories of personnel who work the telephones do not always sell over them but rather let a telephone call become an initial contact point for some other activity. These telephoners are called "lead generators" and work in telemarketing shops. TM is a major industry in the United States.[19] As a rule, if something is advertised via an 800 number, it is a safe bet that a telemarketer will answer the telephone. TM operations provide five functions:

1. They *gather* information. This includes conducting marketing research and surveys, estimating grievances in a population (commonly selected by political action committees), and updating data files of varied sorts. Virtually any organization can use TM if it has a need to assemble, update, or gather data regularly. Telemarketers can also serve as adjuncts to an outside sales force

by setting up appointments. All credit-reporting agencies use telemarketers, as do all list brokers.

2. They *service* current accounts. Telemarketers staff the 800 lines contracted by charities, service organizations, television promoters, municipalities, and vendors of all kinds who have a customer base of some kind to service. Telemarketers are order-takers hired by various industries.

3. They *provide* information. Virtually any call to an 800 number that requests information can be handled by a telemarketing company. Most customer service functions in large firms are handled by telemarketers who access manuals and data bases and read out the information requested. Some are hired to provide referrals or access to certain types of crisis intervention (various hotlines in the area of human services). They also provide voter registration information and are involved in many aspects of political campaigning.

4. They *answer* the telephone. Most answering services use telemarketers, as do most paging services. The economies of scale realized by electronic interfacing means that each set of lines can perform a different set of tasks, serve different regions, and work different time zones. Thus, centralization of these functions is quite common. Most telephones staffed around the clock use telemarketers.

5. They *sell merchandise* and *raise money*. Only this group of activities has the potential of becoming a quasi-boiler room operation. Telemarketers can also be contracted to sell subscriptions and make collections, as well as to raise funds for charities, alumni associations, and political action committees. The largest and most profitable use of telemarketing services lies in the contracts made with large businesses (banks, manufacturers, credit card vendors, retail chains, and direct marketing firms) to vend merchandise or services.

The TM industry has grown rapidly since the mid-1980s. A hybrid combining aspects of both sales and marketing, the trade has its own professional association, specialized magazines, and a lobby in Washington, D.C., to further its interests and promote telephone sales, marketing, and data collection for academic, polling, and research purposes. Concentrating on information flow and marketing functions, the industry has access to state-of-the-art electronics, data processing systems, information technologies (fiber optics systems, satellite hookups, and newswire feeds) and can achieve economies of scale with the telephone company.

In a modern TM operation, telephoners sit by their computer terminals, accessing data on magnetic tape, reading a script that appears on the screen, and using the software capabilities of the system to que a prompt that helps answer questions or objections given by survey respondents or potential customers. One set of keyed instructions dials the telephone.[20] Another records data or a sale; another sends an inventory instruction to the warehouse or prompts the next question to be read; and still another prepares a bill or provides a salutation to a script.

The companies typically serve regional and national markets. The annoying telephone calls that most people receive when they come home from work require a sophisticated design and are generated from an equally complex business structure. Whether working inbound 800 lines or performing outbound cold calls, telephoners—called "phoners" in the trade—act as active and passive electronically assisted clerks.

After an initial wave of advertisement (or the preparation of a calling roster) that generates (or targets) the calls, mostly underpaid women sit with scratch pads or questionnaires and read the screens, punch the buttons, and add the human voice that is still required in this line of work. There are few boilers on TM work floors. Absent are the smoke-filled rooms, the heat, and the frenzy of pitchmen—indeed, most men, other than the managers. There is little collective social interaction as is common in boiler rooms. Each phoner punches a time clock, staffs a cubicle, accomplishes a limited work routine, and punches out.

The tone of a TM operation is different from that of a product house or service shop. Gone is the entrepreneurial impulse and the heat; gone are the elaborate comebacks and apprenticeships to the pros; and gone are the sales managers who dialed their first calls on a rotary telephone and who as pro boilers had to survive unbelievable odds just to bring home a regular paycheck.

The chemistry is different as well. There are no visible owners, only stockholders who likely know little and care less about the telephone activities that occur in segregated rooms set up for the purpose of mass solicitation. The TM manager is one of the few involved who has a full-time job and company benefits and is able to lay claim to being able to support a family. There are no thirty-minute pitches and no big-ticket items being touted, only small orders; many times no sales are being sought. There are no premiums, prizes, or bribes. When a deal goes through, there will be no cheers; no one will bring in a bottle of champagne; and no one will even light up a cigarette, much less a joint, and share some lore. The style is also radically different. There are no pros to tell tall tales of a golden age. There are no pitchmen who can command absolute silence in a room full of commissioned salesmen who will gladly forego income and their own time for a chance to listen to a master. In fact, there are neither pitchmen nor masters nor commissions—only cubicles, wages, and scripts.

TM represents the application of the highest orders of technology to the most routine tasks, for small stakes, with the least amount of skill required, with the smallest amount of corporate expenditure for labor. TM operations in this regard are like the huge supermarket chains that thrive on a tiny margin amplified by the tremendous volume of product that passes through the aisles. The big dollars are not in being a checkout operative but in managing such a system. The greater the span of management, the larger is one's paycheck.

Two informants are sales managers for large TM telephone rooms that are parts of divisions of nationally recognized companies that serve multinational markets. One is a newspaper, and the other is a media company providing books, periodicals, magnetic media, and communications products to domestic and foreign markets ("Big Media"). The boiler room techniques used include bilking customers using the latest marketing tricks, turning over the sales force, and diverting accounts to increase profits. Thus, three of the boiler room's disreputabilities are present: fraud, deception of the sales force, and account manipulation. An informant describes the shop at Big Media:

Informant: Stay away. It's gotta be the biggest boiler room on the East Coast. *It just don't look like one.* They run seventy-two phones full burn. They have three shifts. They have made screwing you into a science. It's unbelievable. First they work the phoners four hours a day. That's it. Four hours. You can pick 8–12, 12–4, 4–8. There are no other choices. Get the feeling that you can't make out on twenty hours a week? You got it! Plus, you get to work four hours on Saturday, but not everyone, just "the best of the shifts." Saturday hours are 9–1. Bonuses, however, are only paid for twenty-four hours a week. Guess what? Not good enough to qualify for Saturday work? No bonus! That's just the start of it. That's how they bleed out the people they don't want. They are a very big company. Everyone's heard of what they sell. . . . It's against the law not to hire blacks, women, and other minorities. So, no problem, you *bleed the floor.* You hire anybody. That keeps you legal. The law don't say that you *keep* everybody, though. You simply bust ass. Can't speak English? Sound like you just came off the block? Have a singsong voice? Fine. *No problem!* You don't make many sales? You are *gone.* History. Competition is fierce. Hell, they've got students from the local colleges who will pull teeth for four hours of work a day. For them, it's a verbal game. The work fits their schedule. They're good on the phone to boot. So, the locals don't have a chance. . . . That's sort of ironic, I mean the people who could really use a job doing phoning can't keep one. . . . There is also no full-time work, unless you are a manager. Then they pump the paper and use the back rooms.
Question: Pump the paper?
Informant: You know, age [assign a priority to] the accounts and blow out [turn over] the floor. The product they sell is usually books. Volume 1 goes for a song. Usually the cost of production, overhead, and a coupla dollars. It's a loss leader. Let's say volume 1 trades at $6.95 plus postage and han-

dling. There's no money in that. They use a weekly, tiered commission structure. Say, base [salary] plus 50 cents per sale for the first ten sales per week, 75 cents for eleven to twenty, $1.50 for twenty-one to twenty-six, and $2 over twenty-seven. Then there's the so-called bonus system: high man bonus [per shift], high shift bonus [among shifts], top weekly salesman, top shift [weekly], and the monthly stuff. It looks really impressive, but the heavy-hitters win all the prizes . . . and guess what? All the heavy-hitters are on the same shift. It's planned that way. Prizes and contests look good, though. . . . Now, new people work new accounts. The money is in *the series*, however. Think about it. Twenty-six volumes at $14.95—all of which follow volume 1. That's over $400 when you figure in postage and handling. . . . Of course they ship at book rate and charge for first class, that's another little rip-off. They ship regularly. It adds up. The income stream starts with the first order. They don't pay commission on each and every volume, however, to trainees. For them it's a one-shot deal. . . . But remember, you have to have six months' tenure and be *currently employed* to collect residuals. That's the hook. The salesmen are told to work toward their six-month longevity point to be eligible. Of course, most are fired before they can collect. They're jammed [worked hard, and then fired] and the paper is pumped. Who gets those accounts? The guys in the back rooms. . . . Note that I said "guys"; the broads don't get to the back rooms—at least not to work the phones [laughs].

Question: Back rooms?

Informant: Yeah, the pros. They work full time. They get all the paper [accounts] when the room turns over. They also split the residuals. Pros can also load.

Question: Load?

Informant: Sure. Offer the new product line. They come out with a new series all the time. Name it. Health? Sex? Birth? Afterlife? Hey, they've got a series on any imaginable thing. You, know, if astrology or dieting is hot, they've got it. "Only $8.45 for volume 1. Cancel anytime. No obligation. Subsequent volumes will be sent periodically, for ONLY $19.95 plus postage and handling." Works every time. The pros offer the new products at discounts and earn a nice dollar. . . . They get the hot lists [current customers] and the dropouts [previous customers]. Drops pay a premium if you can get them back on board. So you call 'em, pitch 'em, sell 'em. Only the pros do that.

Question: Isn't that legal?

Informant: Oh yeah. It's not illegal to make books sound exciting. These guys are maybe the biggest in the country. It's a numbers game. They make money on the delay.

Question: Delay?

Informant: Yeah. The idiots who buy the books don't read the small print. The company has a *variable* billing and shipping cycle: Book 1 arrives, then

book 2. Sometimes four weeks, sometimes in nine weeks. It throws the
customer off-track. So they keep on sending in checks. After a while it occurs to people that they've bought a *string* of books. That's why they
spread it [the billing cycle] out. So the customers won't do some simple
math. Those checks add up. . . . Anyway, sooner or later the customers
cancel. But it takes *time*. The average clod gets a volume or two more than
he wanted due to the delay. You say stop, sooner or later they stop. Usually later. All additional books after volume 1 are gravy. There's no advertising cost. It's simply a matter of shipping and billing. None of this
stuff is sold in stores anyhow, so the discounts aren't real. Marketing
makes it all up. What does a "$39.95 *value*" mean? Who knows? You can't
buy the product other than through the company. But then you hook 'em
with another series. . . . People buy this junk for their kids, hoping to get
them interested in books, reading, "smart stuff," you know. It's a dream.
The fanatics [enthusiasts] actually read the stuff. We get a lot who get off
on war: *The Big Media Picture Book of Death and Modern Aviation* [laughs
sardonically]. The next best is glamour series for women, you know, "The
Life of the Stars," "Hollywood Make-up Secrets," things like that really
sell. You should hear the pros *pitch series*. Damn. They could make the
local library seem like a place of "untapped knowledge of the ages" [a line
from a pitch]. People really go for that.

That boiler room techniques are profitable is not overlooked by corporate
finance and accounting when it comes time to distribute rewards at the end
of the year to the managers of telephone rooms. As in the classic boiler room,
however, manipulative techniques that work to the detriment of the company can also be used to further the careers of sly managers. In part, managers
are rotated into unemployment for this reason, as a preventive measure.

Being a telemarketing manager is prestigious as long as the division is
making money. In more difficult times, during downsizing or restructuring
or while fine-tuning—or any of the other popular euphemisms by which
being fired is commonly known—managers are often treated poorly. That can
come as a heavy blow to those with business degrees and illusions of a genuine career. A TM manager with ten years of experience, after being fired from
a very large company, said:

I don't get it. I did everything right. Everything was above-board. I never cheated anyone. My background and training are better than most. My sales
figures were good. I had a good crew. Do you know what the division manager said to me? He said they don't need a *boiler room* anymore. That's what he
said! Honest to God! So they are going to subcontract out the phone operation to some place in Kansas. . . . It's really sort of strange, come to think of
it. I hired a guy last year who worked in a *real* boiler room. I liked him. Real

friendly guy. Good talker. He only worked here for a while, but he told me that I should watch out. "Mike," he said, "you're too good for this stuff. This whole deal looks flimsy to me." I didn't understand what he meant. He saw something I didn't. He was right.

Because the field of telemarketing is quite nebulous for most corporate executives, most tend to overly rely on concepts with which they are more familiar. "Sales generated" is one such concept, an indicator almost universally used as the exclusive measure of the effectiveness of a telephone room. That this perspective breeds the use of boiler room techniques is apparently unknown to many who run large, conventional firms.

Boiler rooms avoid close relations with large, established companies. Only their techniques are exported, to be used by the TM companies or divisions as their managers see fit. When a boiler room becomes involved in TM, its part-time, largely female night-shift employees work for twenty to twenty-five hours a week on the telephone banks. Ironically, such telephoners are likely to fare better (economically and psychologically) overall as adjuncts to a boiler room than in larger and allegedly more respectable TM companies for four reasons.

1. TM is usually a sideline for a boiler room, and the main operation is run by boilers (moonlighting as TM managers) who are likely to be sympathetic, and give larger bonuses, to part-timers because none can live on their own part-time TM earnings.

2. A boiler room can pay more money to its phoners because it gets paid up front for its contracts and only needs to maintain the illusion of having capable talent on hand. Other things being equal, TM managers are also likely to be paternal toward phoners. One reason is that their professional egos are not involved. They do not have to prove themselves in this area because it is inconceivable for a boiler room to fire a TM room manager. The TM activity is not central to the main operation.

3. The temporary nature of the work attracts women from higher social classes, and they are more interested in supplementing their income ("pin money") than they are reliant on this line of work as a prime means of support. Boiler room TM managers spend less time indoctrinating such workers than do the full-time managers in conventional TM rooms who have a career stake in the activity. Because they screen for adequate self-presentation, diction, command of the language, and sociability, training typically involves only teaching familiarity with a script. Moreover, the work is presented as temporary work, so there is no need to sustain the illusion of a career.

4. The purpose of a boiler room TM operation is to discover new kinds of accounts that may prove profitable while extracting money from the bulk of

its accounts that will fail. Thus, personable phoners are hired to lend credibility to the con. This permits room managers much more flexibility in what might be called "stage design." For example, prospective marks will have intelligent conversations with those working on their behalf if the phoners are college students. One woman, a college student who had worked as a telemarketer for both boiler rooms and conventional TM companies, explains the difference:

> [Laughter.] Actually, I like telemarketing for [the boiler room]. It's more fun. First, the manager is great. He jokes a lot. Second, he runs the sales floor during the day. Those daytime guys are really good on the phone, so the manager really knows his stuff. But the most important thing is that he pays good bonuses. . . . Lots of telemarketing companies that I worked for in the past, all they know is tired sales meetings. It's really demeaning because they have dozens of stupid make-work things, you know: telephone logs, time sheets in triplicate, accounting for time on the phone, time off the phone, break time. Now Bob [the manager], he comes in and says, "Ladies, did we have a good day today?" He sounds like a television announcer. . . . And then he tells us what the nightly bonuses will be and gives out prizes. The important thing is [that] when you have a problem, he's right there. He *shows* us how to do the job. Plus, the pay is better here, and I like the flexibility. Bob doesn't care if you take a break, or about how you keep your desk, or really about anything very much as long as you write business. . . . When it's time for midterms [at college], Bob lets us rearrange our schedules. It's pretty good for a part-time phone job. I like it here.

The addition of a TM telephone bank to a boiler room helps the management use fixed costs more effectively. Telephone rates are cheaper in the evening than during the day, and the marginal expense of the added shift is covered by the profits generated. The giants in the TM industry are effective at what they do best: making distribution systems more efficient and reducing advertising costs.[21] Many of a boiler room's potential customers are easily lured by extensive advertising campaigns conducted by the telecommunications and computer industries.

The message communicated is simple. At its heart is the assertion that virtually any company with a product or service to sell can realize enhanced sales, expanded markets, and increased profits by adding a TM program. Executives at larger companies, however, who are intrigued by the capabilities of TM for expanding markets, servicing customers, or enhancing the movement of product, usually do so in-house by hiring, training, and controlling their own TM staffs to work on extant telephones in existing facilities. In such a manner risk is tightly monitored and incorporated into the long-term planning of a firm. If the in-house TM operation proves unsuccessful, it can always be contracted out to one of the TM giants. A telephoner who moves "up" to one of these, however, moves into a dead-end, part-time job. Thus, TM at its most respectable, conventional best offers telephoners a chance at becoming members of a growing, part-time, pink-collar army. For most, there is only the grinding pattern of conventional telephone work, absent a decent wage, unions, a forty-hour work week, health benefits, some job security, and virtually every opportunity for advancement that operators had in an earlier age with the telephone company.[22] The nemesis of the phoner does not lie in the boiler room but rather in the banal nature of the technology itself and the unseen managerial machinations that dominate this line of work.

A pro boiler captured the difference between boilers and phoners when I asked him to ponder that issue. After a few minutes of thought, he responded:

> I'd say that a boiler *works* the phones. If you do it right, you get commish, and maybe you learn how to sell something. If you're really good, you can work the scams. That's the basics: selling on the phone and earning commish. The better you sound, the more you know, the more bread you make. I mean, that's assuming that the company stays in business. . . . Now, a phoner gets *worked by* the phones. There ain't no *spread*. Bad phoners make $5 an hour. Good phoners make $7. Bad phoners and good phoners can't support a family on twenty or twenty-five hours a week. It's for ladies. There's no *room* [margin]. It's an industry thing. . . . Think of it this way: What kind of *deal* are you tryin' to move? If I can understand it, and you can understand it, and the customer can understand it, what's to *promote*? There's nothing to promote. That's when you use a phoner. You only use a pitchman when you've got a deal that has to be pitched.

An Ear to the Tune of the Times

A quasi-boiler room is a flexible social form. It plays a critical role in aligning markets, customers, marks, and telephones because it can exist in the world of the boiler room, in the more conventional world of routine business telephoning, and in the gray areas between the two. The direction of the transformations involved, however, remains problematic because refinements and accommodations can emerge from shake-ups in an industry, technological innovation, economic dislocation, or some combination of them all. The forces of innovation, entrepreneurial impetus, economies of scale, and opportunities shift constantly.

A new quasi-boiler room called a "cable phone operation" is used by some cable companies to work new territories. Telephoners set up appointments with installers for the services being made available. After a territory has been sufficiently developed, however, the operation shuts down. The best are kept on for customer service jobs. The remainder get burned, some experience in the quasi-boiler room, or some skill in reading newspaper advertisements for telephone salesmen.

According to informants, smart shops vending fraudulent biotechnology opportunities and tax write-offs—widespread scams in the late 1980s and early 1990s—have been upstaged in notoriety by "job card operations": quasi-boiler rooms wherein for $350 to $750 billed to a major credit card the white-collar unemployed can receive the promise of career advice, networking contacts, state-of-the-art resumes, and a guaranteed job "in the field of their choice" (a line from a pitch) within thirty days of payment, up front, at the time of the "initial [telephone] screening" that is part of these programs.

The pitch is strategically timed to correspond to the statute of limitations for holding credit card companies responsible for unwanted purchases that can no longer be charged back to a vendor's account. All the marks receive, of course, are promises. The persistent are stalled until the shop relocates. This new version of an old rip-off (fraudulent job placement agencies and techniques) has its origin in quasi-boiler rooms that unexpectedly formed as one result of the "Crash of '87," when an entire cohort of previously successful head hunters (professional job placement service workers) came under hard times. Some of those executives began working out of their houses. An informant explains:

> I was a head hunter, you know, a job placement counselor, at the time. All I knew was placing bankers and brokers. When the market went bust, many in my office were laid off. I didn't know what to do, I mean here I am, a *job placement officer* who is unemployed! All I know is how to work the phones. . . . So I get this phone call from an associate. He and his wife were also in the business, but they figured out an interesting twist: running an operation with no jobs! They're doing it out of their house. It's a scam. That's not my cup of tea, but I never heard of such a thing until after the stock market exploded.

The hottest growth market in the telemarketing business is "personal conversations," where lonely or bored teenagers who watch the advertising aired during late-evening time slots on local television stations can listen to real or simulated peers exchanging jokes, simple conversation, or fantasies for 99 cents to $1.99 for the first connect-minute. Their elders, for a few dollars more, can interact with astrologers, card readers, other telephone mystics, and imaginary loose women. Such operations began as telemarketing firms, where the basic infrastructure (telephone banks, line hook-ups, dialing multiplexers, cubicles, scripts, and telephoners) was in place and needed only a shift in emphasis, which was provided by the quasi-boiler room.

Whenever anything on the telephones is hot, boilers usually take notice. While economies of scale and increased competition are constantly driving down the price-per-minute for varied kinds of "fantasy phone" operations, a New York operation offers what are called "skinvestments": a "golden opportunity" to buy (fictional) shares in the allegedly major pornography production companies. The scam is run as a quasi-boiler room working out of a coin shop where the marks (previous customers) are carefully selected and screened, sent some free porn (the bait) and offered "options" on the distribution rights (the hook), which are touted as exclusive investments being offered "to those who qualify" for a chance to "cash in on the increased demand in the Latin American and Asian growth markets" (a line from the pitch).

The secret of the operation lies in the comeback and the carefully designed load (the size of the sale). Shares trade in blocks of ten for $500, an amount small enough to be charged to a credit card, large enough to make the pursuit profitable, and, apparently, "heat-free." An informant explains:

> This scam is still new, but [name] just started up a small phone room in the Big Apple where he learned the ropes in a coin shop. He ripped 'em good [worked in the parent house, learned the techniques, and quit]. Here's the scoop: They screen for married geeks [pornography enthusiasts] and pay the [list] brokers for a sort [an arrangement of marketing data] on religion and property values, as well as for past porn purchases. A sharp idea. This way they know they've got a pillar of the community. . . . So, they send the free porn and then pitch 'em on the investment angle of the deal. Then, they load 'em for the nickel [$500]. 'Course they are air-tight, and you can't trace the operation [explains specifics]. . . . But if some objections should arise, they put a pro on the phone and give 'em "the fright": they threaten to send a copy of the porn and the credit card receipts to the wife and the priest, or the holy man, or whatever. It's *heat-free*. Most geeks are so embarrassed that they simply eat the nickel and don't make any noise.

Product houses are on the decline and await the next pulse in the economy for resurrection. Boiler rooms, their techniques, and their various incarnations, although as American as apple pie, are no longer limited to exclusive growth in the United States, however. An informant who visited Great Britain brought back an advertisement that appeared in the *London Times*: "Telephone Sales Professionals. Starting Salary: 20,000–30,000+ Pounds. Call [name, number given]." Thus some pitchmen now speak the Queen's English and, no doubt, others will soon be speaking other languages as well.[23]

Conclusion: The Future of the Boiler Room and Other Speculations

Populus vult decipi, ergo decipiatur. [People want to be deceived, therefore let them be deceived.]
—early Roman saying (Kaku 1994, 53–54)

Only the owners benefit. Look, take this [radiator] hose. There you go: Hong Kong's latest insult to what used to be a decent job for some guy in Detroit. . . . Now, what happens when some lady out there in Bumfuck, Texas, gets this beaut installed in her car? Nothing at first, 'til she's drivin' home from work and this sucker blows. . . . For what? An extra buck that goes into the owner's pocket? For the 48 cents I made in commission? For the benefit of the two dozen guys who've been blown out the door of this place in the past six months? Gimme a break.
—a salesman, over lunch, on the "who benefits?" question

Once the basic nature of all telephone operations is understood, speculation regarding the possible futures faced by the various kinds of boiler rooms and their clones can be provided. The analysis begins by examining one strategic research site: The Silver Company (TSC).[1] The firm was studied during a process of evolution and transformation that required different kinds of dialers (boilers, brokers, and phoners) at different times, and to different degrees, thereby bringing the relationship between dialers, markets, and structure into the sharpest relief.

Before I proceed with an analysis of TSC, I will shift my emphasis, temporarily, from the familiar typological examination of the different kinds of telephone rooms to an overview of the properties they all share. All are guided and driven by four elements concerning their etiology, social organization, management, and operation: the postulate of social construction, the business imperative, the management mission, and the role of dialers.

The Four Postulates

1. A telephone room is a social construction. People and telephones must be brought together to produce telephone calls. The necessary technology

must be available, culturally understood, and viable. A telephone room is animated by an exclusive, repetitive purpose.

2. Telephone rooms are socially organized as businesses. These are the primary objects of study: companies, or parts of companies, which rely primarily on the telephone. It is the telephone bill in telephone rooms that determines whether that being said or done over the telephone will be permitted to continue.

3. The mission or purpose of a telephone room is a managerial decision. Methods of implementation; selection of products, markets, services, and projects; remuneration programs; and the techniques of operation and control result from an agenda dictated by those in management positions. Workers may or may not be aware of that; they may or may not agree with it. They are, however, rarely consulted, and they never have the power to alter the corporate mission from whence all managerial authority flows.

4. Telephone rooms contain a least one dialer (someone paid to make calls). A dialer engages an occupational role that is routinely assessed. The exclusive purpose of the calls is to acquire revenue: Calls are understood, and socially organized, toward this end. There is no requirement, however, that they need be presented as such. A telephone room dials for profit. Revenue is then distributed in accord with prevailing norms grounded in, but not exclusively defined by nor limited to, those of the larger business culture. The allocational decisions (over the terms of employment, the account base, assigned tasks, and the commission structure) made by managers, however, do not create a dime of income for the firm.[2] Income derives from dialers, who add value to wares, contracts, and promises. This is best seen by exploring the origins of TSC to gain a general understanding of the essential postulates of dialing and how these may combine, recombine, and change.

Andy's Dream

TSC began as a dream in the mind of Andy—a pro boiler and entrepreneur—who is a college-educated Vietnam veteran in his mid-forties. His serious interest in the world of business began in a trench somewhere in Southeast Asia, where, he vowed, if he ever got through his ordeal he was going to get back to school and study something that would allow him to "do something" in the business world. His childhood fascination with business took the form of flights of fancy that often involved the images of a large machine tool factory near his boyhood home. What impressed him more than the noise of the machines, the rhythm of the work, or the size of the company was the idea of directing those engaged in productive work. His comments:

> You know, I've thought of that owner of the machine tool company for

most of my life. Think about it: Owning a company where you make something, meeting a payroll and having all those people depend on what's in your head, on the decisions that you make. . . . When you get old you can point to that factory and all those people who work in it and say, "It was my idea. I turned a lot and some walls and tools into a way for people to make a living. That's my company." Really something, no? I've always wanted to do that.

Andy's dream is as characteristically American as his struggle. After getting through the war in one piece and getting his business degree, he was ready to settle down and begin his career. He took a position as a buyer in the fabric trades and started out the late 1960s in what he saw as interesting work: cutting deals and making the rounds to various wholesalers. Andy's charm, ambition, and good spirits made him welcome in an industry dominated by older men who were nearing retirement. He liked to "talk and cut deals," and he was well suited and apparently well paid for this.

After a few years spent learning the ropes, Andy married and began to enjoy what he called the "good life": a fine home, a nice car, interesting work in the sales field, and a social life that revolved around parties and "good times." His father was proud of a son who had entered his field, and the war became a distant, easily forgotten memory. Andy could not foresee that his line of work—and the life that he knew as a buyer—was soon to become obsolete because emerging world trade patterns would virtually decimate the American garment industry.

The cutbacks and slowdowns of the early 1970s saw Andy's boss retire and give up the business. Andy was unemployed. Being resourceful, personable, and a self-characterized "gabber," he looked to find "something, until something better turns up." He saw an opening in "telephone sales" at a small product house started by an owner who was once himself a wholesaler out of work. Andy paid his dues in boiler rooms for almost a dozen years, moving around and chasing deals before winding up in a large product house in the automotive field.[3] There he worked as a general sales manager for roughly five years.

Andy liked management because "you get to see the big picture." He began to rekindle the dream of running his own company, where he could "run the whole show." As he put it, "Look. A small show of your own is better than a piece of someone else's action." He began TSC from a telephone booth: a testament to his entrepreneurial and sales skills.

The Birth of TSC

Andy contacted a small number of his regular accounts from the product house and arranged to sell them automotive parts. He initially had to hand-carry the cash to finance the orders, because no supplier would give him credit.

He worked for a number of months, secretly, on the side. With rolls of dimes, he cut his deals from a pay telephone on Saturdays, masterfully inserting sufficient coinage so as not to trigger the bells that would indicate that his time was up. Should he miscalculate, his comeback was that "he was on the road," which, literally, he was.

This awkward arrangement ensured anonymity, and Andy knew the importance of that. All boiler room owners know about the "bleed," in which choice house accounts are diverted to other companies. Life can be made difficult for those caught diverting paper.[4] Andy patiently worked a small portion of his account deck until he could obtain a line of credit from his supplier. That done, he took his savings, quit his job, took two salesmen with him, and rented a small office that became TSC's first incarnation: the Silver Boiler Room.

Managing his own business, however, proved difficult. He encountered most of the problems he had hoped he could avoid: his pro stole house accounts, his regular ran up high telephone bills for personal business, and his suppliers caused problems (one did not ship the agreed upon orders, and another was on his heels for back payments and threatening to limit his line of credit). Andy's room began to turn over. There were fights over pay and commissions. Valuable time was spent training people who would ultimately leave the company.

Andy did it all. He was a salesman, a bookkeeper, a pro, a boss, and the shipping department. Many nights were spent alone, trying to run the business after everyone else had left for the day. The effort trying to grow his company, intense isolation, increasing debts, and a withdrawal from recreational activities slowly took their toll on his personal life. Starting a boiler room is more than a job. It can be a defining point in one's life. At such times, "free time" is seen as a luxury that other people have.

His marriage dissolved. His company was shaky. If Andy were a younger man, the company would have likely folded. Andy saved it by pitching his suppliers and renegotiating his debt. He also became more attentive to locating alternative sources of supply. Over time, his business began to grow. With growth came an improved cash flow, credit, better terms with suppliers, and bankers became more open to, and supportive of, his perceptions of emerging opportunities.

After about a year Andy was successfully running a parts-brokerage business that he created from his old accounts, his new suppliers, and his own innovative efforts. It was, however, still a boiler room; there was still distrust and secrecy. Six months later, he shut the business down, kept one man, rented a new office, and slowly began to transform his line and his self-image. His new corporate mission was to build the business and eliminate all reminders of "this goddamned sick world of selling on the telephone."

The Silver Cloud

Andy's first month in the new quarters was spent being attentive to its lay-out. New carpets were installed, and desks—as opposed to cubicles—were purchased for the sales room. Andy would ultimately hire a handful of care-fully selected salesmen. The Silver Cloud was his corporate and spiritual home.[5] He hired an interior decorator to design his personal office, and the front office featured large new desks, artwork, plants, and vases for the flow-ers that he envisioned would someday be for his bookkeeper and a receptionist.

Andy now had what he called a "real company." Although he never used the term *boiler room*, The Silver Cloud would have no back rooms, manag-ers, or trainees. Andy would only hire experienced telephone salesmen and "let them go at it," as he is fond of saying. The tone of the operation was set by Andy, and he saw the new company as his chance to "do it right."

His first full-time, non-sales employee was a bookkeeper. After six months he had hired another salesman and had one more in the wings who was pres-ently working at a large product house. With time came more salesmen and a receptionist—and flowers for her vase. Andy systematically removed all vestiges of a boiler room by changing the chemistry, tone, and style of the company.

Style is important. Nothing in the external environment had changed, and the industry was as it always is: competitive, uncertain, and ruthless. Andy decided that all his people would work full time and that they would get full medical and dental benefits. "Look," he rationalized, "if a man can't provide for his family he's gonna go elsewhere. If he's a good phone man, and he can't pro-vide, it's comin' out of *my* hide. . . . Hey, you can't cheat a good salesman. Not really. Oh, yeah, you can steal from him, for a while, but there is no free lunch. He's got the accounts. Burn him, and he winds up burning you. . . . Anyone who works for me is going to get a fair shake. I pay what I can pay and set a fair commish. The rest is up to the salesman."

Short-circuiting the Boiler Room

The Silver Cloud offers no premiums, prizes, or bribes. By eliminating the role of manager there is no incentive to turn over the sales floor, and accounts are not diverted. Salesmen receive a base salary based on projected commis-sions, which are a percentage of net profits on sales. Those who work for Andy shake his hand to affirm the terms of employment.

In the parts-brokerage business, it is possible for a salesman to know what is called the "true in-cost" of a product—the accession cost plus freight and overhead. Salesmen can then determine a markup based on the size of an an-ticipated order. In a boiler room, such costs are always kept secret, as are the names of suppliers and the markup. In fact, the boiler room's ability to manipulate these costs defines the disreputability pervasive in the industry.

The Silver Cloud thrives precisely because boiler rooms working the auto parts and accessories industries have saturated this market with junk and promises. A salesman—who had the basic economics right but became somewhat carried away by his metaphors—explained:

> Silver Cloud is like the "Star Trek" episode with the "Doomsday Machine."[6] You know, where this renegade device goes around eating planets [laughs]. . . . Well that's what we do with the customers of the goddamned boiler rooms where we used to work . . . I *love* being the "boiler room eater" [tells angry tales of previous experiences]. . . . Now when I go home at night, I've made a fair dollar over the phone, I took away business from my old company, and I know that the user of this stuff isn't going to have their damn car explode because most of the price that they were charged went to pay for some guy in a back room.

The chemistry of the room at The Silver Cloud is oriented to selling products that constantly change as a function of the shifting markets. This permits the flagrant violation of two assumptions upon which a boiler room is based: that there must be a required circulation of accounts from the cold floor to the pros, and that new accounts must be opened constantly. Moderate pricing eliminates the need for successive tiers of salesmen to renegotiate the deal as part of a comeback routine. Moreover, because the quality of products is backed by suppliers, exchanges, should a defective part be found, are made as a matter of routine. Thus, there is no heat to buy back. Because salesmen are paid a percentage of the net profit on a sale, it is not necessary to open a constant stream of new business. Salesmen can and are encouraged to share accounts, because each salesman's expertise and product knowledge typically exhibit a comparative advantage relative to selling a particular item. Natural abilities and product preferences among salesmen permit an emerging natural division of labor.

This type of corporate design eliminates many antagonisms between management and workers and all of the secrecy common to boiler rooms. As a salesman describes how an informal discussion resulted in the company's acquiring a wholesale load of car wax, "From what do I know about wax? So I asked Andy about wax. I got the 'wax pitch' [laughs]. . . . So, I'm talkin' with my customer that afternoon and, what the hell, I ask him about wax, just something to chat about. Turns out that they got a liquidation deal [describes]. . . . So, I put the guy on hold, and tell Andy, and he says, 'Make a bid on the load.' So, I made a bid. We got the deal and own the load! And I get a commish on 'the buy.' I love this job. I made some money on something that only this morning I didn't know a lot about."

The conversation is important because it provides a good, unobtrusive measure of the level of cooperation on the sales floor.[7] The tone of the room is convivial, the chemistry is cooperative, and the style is supportive. Similar events do not occur in boiler rooms where accounts are guarded jealously, where information about suppliers is secreted away in hidden files, where only the company's buyer is authorized to make purchases, and where the purchase price of a product is never discussed publicly.

The case of TSC aptly demonstrates that when dialers become brokers the internal logic of a boiler room can self-destruct. The telling questions for the future of product houses are twofold: Why is this so rare, and can such arrangements ultimately be profitable for both management and workers? The answer to both questions is suggested by the insightful analysis performed by an informant who was the sales manager of the Silver Telemarketing Group.[8] He was trying to explain why TSC was doomed and ultimately would go out of business:

> Look. The Silver Cloud is an oddity. Andy created it because what he *really* wants is a small, respectable, growing company that he can call his own. He pulled it off. Look at this place! It's clean. It's well run. It's a nice place to work. . . . This ain't your average phone room, though. Let me tell you why. He made a smart shop *for products*. Look at the salesmen. These guys are great. They're intelligent, hardworking, they have unbelievable product knowledge, *and* they all have telephone personalities. How come? Because he hand-picked them. . . . To replace one of these guys would take at least a year. That's *not* how you run a phone room, it's how you run the back rooms [laughs]. He eliminated the manager. That's his secret. . . . Look, let's say the house nets sixteen bills [$1,600] a week after paying Andy, the staff, and all overhead expenses. Well, how can you split this up? Andy pays on a salesman's contribution. . . . Now, what I would do is throw out the four desks and put in twelve cubicles, pay twelve people $100 a week, and hire *a manager* for $400. That's how you run a phone room: Twelve phoners at twenty hours a week, each, is 240 phone hours. That's eighty *extra* hours, over four men at forty hours, each. Then you turn the room [over]. . . . You don't *need* brain power in a phone room. That's why you have a manager. He babysits and turns the room [over] . . . Andy's guys can buy or sell *anything*. That's not how it's done. You want your phoners to sell a few things. Then you blow 'em out [the door] and let the manager work the paper. . . . Look, a boiler room is there to make money. That's the only reason for it to exist. Now, what's the most profitable thing for the ownership to do? That's easy. *You want a profit machine with replaceable parts* [emphasis added]. That keeps your costs down and it keeps you in control. Those extra eighty hours a week, that's pure profit. . . . Andy is living in a dream world. It's beautiful, but I've been on the phones most of my life. I'll give him two years, tops.

The logic of such cost-benefit analysis is both irrefutable and descriptively accurate. This raises two dilemmas concerning skill and the role of management in product houses. First, given the constraint of profitability alone, increasing the level of skill in the sales force creates a diseconomy. Skilled workers are difficult to replace and costly to develop and train. Second, careful selection of such personnel shifts the burden of their development onto other companies, part of the external environment. This is neither predictable nor does it assure a steady flow of workers.

Selective predation is always more cost-effective than spending time and energy actually training workers, and there are many ways to fill a sales floor by seeking compatibility with the chemistry, tone, and style of the room, personal qualities, product knowledge, interpersonal competence, race, religion, gender, age, intelligence, and education. According to one informant, a sales manager in a chemical house hires on the basis of a potential employee's zodiac sign.

The reason for this blatant triumph of ritualism is clear but never articulated: selecting the criterion of pure profitability makes managers themselves expendable. That is why it does not matter at all what they do so long as they are sufficiently occupied and perform long enough for a company's account base to grow. Their function is purely motivational. They are liquidated when they lose enthusiasm, when the pros in the back rooms tire of their style, or when it is time for a house regular to be promoted.

In smaller product operations the range of flexibility regarding corporate goals of the ownership is substantial. Some owners have "bought themselves a job," which is perceived to be more rewarding than working for others. Others have alternative sources of income and/or seek the benefits from tax advantages granted to corporations, the most important of these being that life-style amenities (meals, travel, drinks, a company car, dry cleaning, health insurance, and retirement investments) can be written off as expenses. A few enjoy the role of being the boss—having a staff, hiring and firing, and having a corporate expense account. Because of the varying personal interpretations of these factors, the chemistry, tone, and style on the sales floor of a small shop can be idiosyncratic. The mission of smaller firms is more directly dictated by the whims, preferences, and values of owners than is true in larger operations where these are transformed into "corporate policies" interpreted by managers. Thus, smaller shops have the potential of being more humane in certain regards, more oppressive in others, or, in some cases, both more humane and more oppressive because the standards being used can rapidly change. In one small chemical house, for example, the owner gave Christmas bonuses to some salesmen and then fired them after the first week into the new year. A pro's explanation: "The boss changed his mind."

The Fates of Product Houses

To understand the possible fates of product houses, reflection on their historic origins and a generational metaphor will prove useful. Product houses are distributorships. The first generation of owners comes from the ranks of employees in a particular industry who go into business for themselves. If telephonic means are useful for facilitating distribution, they are used. Most distributorships do not advance beyond this level.

If the company expands, it is faced with hiring new personnel. Most simply hire salesmen from the industry, or sometimes those with telephone skills are sought. At this point a nascent telephone room may develop. That is, when the first telephone salesman is hired, the chemistry of the group changes. These men form the first generation of dialers. Most distributors, however, can have both salesmen and dialers working alongside each other. A dialer, however, never leaves his desk. If the company thrives, the ownership expands the sales force. The dialer simply continues to perform a sales role over the telephone. If another dialer is hired, however, the chemistry and tone of the group may change again because for this hire a new possibility exists. He now has one colleague working as a telephone man, not as an industry-specific salesman.

Ownership is now at a critical juncture: Should it expand the telephone room? If it does, a third generation is born. The last dialer hired becomes part of what is defined as a telephone room, whereas before the new configuration there were only outside and inside salesmen. From this point on, the telephone bill will assume greater importance in determining whatever is said, or done, over the telephone.

The mission of a telephone room, however, is a managerial decision. Acquiring one dialer simply means that a distributorship has sought to use another tool to move product. That is quite common. Hiring a second dialer, however, introduces training and experience that are qualitatively different from that of the first generation of owners or from those of the first dialer who stood alone in relation to other salesmen. If that dialer should be bitten by the entrepreneurial impulse, his company will likely be a telephone room that happens to sell product rather than a distributorship that happens to use dialers.

Whether the dialer becomes a boiler is a managerial decision based on an assessment of the cost-effectiveness and desirability of using deception. Deception is always cost-effective in the short run, but it may not be desirable for many reasons. The choice not to defraud must be absorbed by capital. To sell reputable products and treat salesmen fairly requires that the ownership must be willing to sustain a relative loss or to forego disreputable gain for some other value choice not expressible on a balance sheet.

The Product House as an Investment

Product houses are the most conservative of boiler rooms from an investment standpoint because they require that capital be tied up in inventory. By the time an owner is ready to liquidate the company, the cost of the initial investment will likely have been recovered many times over, and the list of house accounts is an asset tradable on the black market.

Although owners must deal with the psychological factors involved in terminating workers, they typically do not lose money when this happens. They simply convert the usable portion of the account base into sales, reduce the size of the payroll, and move on to other corporate scenes. Whether or not the boiler room "goes down in flames" (selects to ship and bill fake orders) is a management decision determined, in part, by the relationship the owner will have to his present customer base when he closes the firm.

Workers are treated with the same logic. An owner may offer a pro or two a partnership or a job in the new operation—if there is to be one. If not, the pros will liquidate the room. There are no hard and fast rules, but the level of predation in a boiler room always escalates before a shutdown. A pro explains the liquidation of a small chemical sales company:

> Jim [the owner] packed it in about three months before they shut the doors. That's when he knew we would close. Actually, for me, it was quite profitable. . . . Firing the trainees was easy. You just blow them out the door. But the manager had to be cut in. No problem! [Laughs.] Jim made him some big promise about a closeout bonus. 'Course he ain't ever gonna get a dime. That's OK. I hate managers. They are slime. . . . We let go of some of the regulars flat out; they were simply fired. Others who had been with the company for a long time were given a small bonus. That bought back some of the heat. I mean, why create anxiety? . . . So we creamed the crop [describes pitches]. It wasn't too hard. With basically no payroll to meet, and by reducing the administrative staff to part time, it was fairly easy. . . . He sold the remainder of his lease to some other phone operation. It was a perfect deal, since the phone system was already installed. He even cut a sweet deal on the office furniture.

As an owner gains experience in shutting down a company it becomes easier to repeat these procedures in the future, and he is less likely to view this as something other than a normal cost of doing business. Shutting down also gives the owner some space and a chance to act on his next business venture somewhat cushioned from a sense of urgency; it also reaffirms his sense of being a businessman. Capital is always treated more favorably in this regard than labor. Financial assets can, after all, be reinvested.

An experience-cohort of product room pros provides the next generation of boiler room owners, while others may move to service shops, and some cushion from downward income mobility is available because a pro can sometimes find work in other types of boiler rooms or assume management functions. Some become fronters in certain types of scams, and others can find ready employment in contract TM houses because their knowledge and interpersonal skills are highly valued.

The fate of product room managers is influenced by the nature and size of the company that contains them and is most industry-specific. Lateral mobility is only possible if an industrial sector is growing. During contractions, however, managers have little value to other firms in the same industry and virtually no value to boiler rooms elsewhere. Regulars in product houses are least influenced by industry trends because their fate is the most site-specific of all boiler room workers. Thus, after a product house shuts down, regulars become floaters, where the cycle repeats. They learn the ropes, build an account deck, and face termination. Trainees are irrelevant to the investment aspects of product houses; they are a necessary cost and an expendable resource after their contributions have been maximized.

Product Houses and Changing Markets

Product houses thrive when recessions end because surplus inventory is plentiful, in part because shakeouts have often driven many conventional firms into bankruptcy. Increasing employment and rising economic expectations increase the utility of premiums, prizes, and bribes in the eyes of buyers—the target of a product house. Product houses also benefit from pulses of sectoral growth. When an industry is growing in general, its buyers have more latitude to make purchases. When profits grow, the discretionary spending of purchasing agents is less monitored than during hard times.

Technological innovation, however, is almost always accompanied by an information lag. When new products are introduced it takes time for knowledge of their attributes to diffuse into the consciousness of all members of the user community. The skills of a pitchman work best when buyers are uncertain about a product's attributes. Demographic trends are also important in this regard. If an industry is characterized as having many "old-timers" or inexperienced newcomers in positions of purchasing authority, that fact can be artfully manipulated by a skilled pitchman.

Fear, on the part of a customer, of not being in tune with the times or of lacking what are seen as industry experiences is easily met with creative embellishments. For example, a new buyer who may not be experienced enough to have attended the regional trade show in his field can be led to believe all manner of imaginary happenings at such events.[9] An old hand in a given industry can, in like manner, be convinced of imaginary technological breakthroughs.[10]

Those firms that withstand the fluctuations of the business cycle may emerge stronger in the aftermath of an economic contraction by firing the cold floor, reducing the number of regulars, eliminating a manager, and shaking up the back rooms, which contain the pros. A leaner company (now composed of only the best salesmen who work only the company's "choice paper") is well poised for an expansion period. The two techno-cultural changes most instrumental in the phenomenal growth of product houses during the 1980s—the historically increasing "economies of dialing" (the availability of inexpensive, efficient, long-distance, rapid dialing capability) and the birth and vast expansion of the list brokerage business—have reached the point of diminishing returns. That is part of the explanation for the decline in both the number and general prosperity of product houses.

A business sales call has become a contemporary annoyance. In some industries even a relatively inexperienced receptionist can discern the true nature of the call. That has driven up the cost of finding the buyer. Good leads are expensive and hard to find. The result is that the closing ratio (of sales to calls) takes on lower and lower values. At some point, especially in smaller shops, the size of the telephone bill has driven many companies out of business.

Since the end of the 1980s a shakeout has occurred in product houses. The majority of mid-range companies (those employing more than ten but less than thirty) have vanished. Another trend is that, without regard to size, there are fewer managers and almost no trainees. Newspaper advertisements have all but dried up. That means that a small cadre of pros and regulars are working the better accounts, and no one is doing a great deal of hiring. Product houses, to use a commonly heard term, are downsizing.

The final displacement wave of the late 1980s—which hit the industry during a down cycle—contained a disproportionate number of college graduates. Many people were well positioned to learn some of the skills of pitchmen. Many were distressed that their employment prospects are so poor, and, for the first time in the history of boiler rooms, a new cohort of boilers carries substantial debt from student loans that must be repaid.

It will take some time for the impact of this to work its way through the sales floors of product houses, but few pro boilers have been college graduates historically. If just a small percentage of those on the sales floors in the late 1980s remain on the telephones there will no doubt be a transformation in the industry.

Most economics textbooks focus extensively and intently on what are taken to be factors of production (labor productivity, capitalization, resource

allocation, working conditions, and motivational factors) yet ignore the social organization of predation. Thus, the fact that the second variety of boiler
rooms, service operations, is becoming stronger, more vibrant, and more ingenious will not likely appear in their pages.

Service Shops as Speculative Ventures

Scams target the discretionary funds available from investors, tourists, gamblers, and the unsuspecting. Service shops are risky ventures, and some scamsters make enemies over and above the numbers of their clients and customers. The profit motive, however, thrives only under certain circumstances and
requires certain social preconditions before the personnel with the requisite
skills can be assembled into a working service operation.

Greed, telephones, start-up funds, and sales skill are insufficient. Want-
ing to participate in what appears to be extremely rewarding schemes that
provide instant financial success and being willing to take some risk to achieve
this end does not define the attributes of a pitchman in a scam operation,
however, it defines those of his marks.

The entrepreneurs who set up the scams and the pro boilers who work the
telephones are some of the hardest-working, most innovative people in the
sales field, and they must perform their feats daily. Winners literally "pack
their bags": first the fronters and then the owners. Losers are unemployed.
Moreover, there are few coaches, only associates. These are not the kind of
skills that can be communicated by management, hence management is irrelevant. Service shops are driven by operatives; all norms are emergent,
shared, contingent, and transitory.

The social sources of the personnel in service shops stem from strategic
displacements in parent industries. First, an industry collapses, then some of
its displaced talent takes to the telephones. Being an unemployed salesman,
however, does not a boiler make. Unemployed salesmen are as old as the field
of sales itself, and some may have great-grandfathers who were once unemployed salesmen. Few have a great-grandfather who was a boiler, however.

A displaced salesman may start his own company, but it only becomes a
one-man shop when deception of some kind is used. This transforms a dialer
into a boiler, and his small operation becomes the first boiler room in whatever industry is to be worked. The effort may fail, however. Boilers face the
same contingencies as do all small businessmen.

Clients initially come from the industry that the entrepreneur is most
familiar with. In certain scams, these clients are investors. No boiler room,
however, typically has the skill, capital, or credibility to win over conventional
investors because conventional investments already trade in highly compet-

itive, sometimes tightly regulated, markets. Boilers seek a special type of investor—speculators—who are willing to take risks in hope of high returns.

The effort still may fail. Speculators are not known for their ignorance, and speculation requires even more specialized knowledge than does general investing. A boiler thus seeks a special kind of speculator, one willing to absorb extremely high levels of risk for a promise alone. That is not any easy task, but it is not an impossible one. It represents the basic problem faced by all con men throughout the ages.[11]

When a telephone room is established for this purpose, a service shop is formed. Dialers (Postulate 4), now defined as boilers, must be hired. Some of these men will not be recruited from the industry served. This cadre forms the nucleus for other boiler rooms as may develop, but there is no assurance that these ventures will prove successful. That largely depends on market conditions. There is no available data on the number of proto-boiler rooms that fail, on the number that are reabsorbed into conventional industries, or on the number that mutate. Only newspaper advertisements provide a crude first approximation, and smart shops keep publicity of this kind to a minimum. The general outline of development, however, follows the business cycle.

Riding Investment Waves

If displacements correspond with an inflationary cycle where the value of real assets is depreciating, creating what economists call "money illusion" (wherein a unit of currency buys increasingly less real goods), this can create a business climate where it appears that windfall wealth may be generally possible and also widespread. Such periods facilitate the vast expansion of scams. A pro explains the logic:

> There is always heavy action after an *investment wave*. . . . Here's how it works: first, the [precious] metals go crazy; that gets everyone's attention. Then, one market takes off. Then you start to see the ads for numismatics, and the gold bugs come out of hibernation. This stuff happens in waves. So what? Well, when the waves crash, you've got brokers looking for work. They start the *phone rooms* [emphasis added]. Mooches come out of the woodwork when it looks like anyone can make a buck. That's how this stuff works. Then what happens? Well, the deal folds. Even dreams don't last forever; you have to wake up. So what do you sell? Well, you look in the papers. . . . Look here [shows newspaper advertisements]. Look at all *the words*: Art [investment lithographs]. Coins. Franchises. Distributorships. Biotechnology. Oil and gas. Commodities. Life insurance. They are all phone rooms. . . . In one year, maybe less, none of these companies will be in business. This [newspaper want ads] page will be blank. Well, not really blank, it will have other phone deals that

none of us have heard of yet. Why? Because this stuff is being created now, while we eat our lunch. When you see all the [want] ads, explaining all of this stuff, you know that all the heavy money has already been made. That's the third or fourth string [of boilers] puttin' out the ads. . . . *Action* doesn't explain itself. Action uses two-liners [two-line advertisements]. The guys who tell the world are looking for workers to fill the cold floor.

A major investment wave ended in the late 1980s. Although there was a brief burst of telephone action after the crash of 1987, it was short-lived. That suggests that the market for conventional investment skills widened significantly to absorb those who were displaced and that the telephone sales marketplace became much more extensive and diversified following the heyday of the investment ruses in the early 1980s, when many then "on the phones" had to have direct investment experience to be so situated.

The industry has mutated since the 1980s. Telephone rooms set up to service the original scams have long since vanished, but they produced many generations of boilers.[12] The skills required to vend imaginary investments are the most abstract in a boiler's repertoire and are thus the most flexible in adapting to changing markets. Moreover, many scams thrive on the downside of an investment wave. School house operations are an example. Their social sources stem from public policy failures coupled with the profit motive. Three master patterns converge with the smooth lines of pitchmen: suburbanization, tight urban budgets, and property-based school taxes. All have spawned school house boilers to prey upon the aspirations of the vulnerable for their children's futures.

Suburbanization, whatever else may be its impact, drains inner cities of their middle classes. Faced with increasing fiscal austerity, public schools in these settings have suffered notable declines.[13] As middle classes flee to the suburbs, they bring their property tax potential with them.[14] One result, outside of the rhetoric that lauds the coming "information age" as the economic analogue to spiritual salvation, is that educational opportunities for the children of working people have declined.[15] A school house offers a cosmetic solution: debt and useless vocational training.

School houses are growing and will likely continue to do so until a good education is defined as a basic right that ought to be made available to all children without regard to social class. The patterns of growth are, however, regional and sectoral. There are few school houses in the suburbs, in high-income areas, in rural areas, in areas served by high-quality public schools, in areas where public school teachers are paid adequately, or in areas where private schools are the norm. The upper class is resolute in its hatred of educational fraud, and pitchmen from quasi-boiler rooms do not waste telephone time on them. Router maps assure that few calls will ever be made from a school house to disturb the routines of the privileged.

Sports betting is an activity that thrives when the economy is either expanding or contracting, but experiences lull when the economy is not moving rapidly in either direction. Many sports rooms shut down in the 1990s. A pro offers an explanation:

> Man, these are bad times. Plays are off. I used to get lots of action when the business deals were hot in the late 1980s. Most guys follow sports. Hell, I used to have whole *offices* subscribe [to the service]. Some did it for the laugh. You know, to listen to me pitch. What does [his telephone name] predict? . . . Now, I can't tell who will come on board anymore. Poor people, yeah, they come on board because they believe in magic. They do it because they need the bucks they think that they will win. . . . I had a lot of this in [certain cities] a few years ago when they were hit by all the plant shutdowns. I even got some action from the hurricane a few years ago. Sort of blew me away [laughs]. You know, they reconnect the phone lines and my phone starts ringin'. But it's been very slow.

To somewhat the same degree, and for the same reasons, travel scams are sensitive to extreme fluctuations in the economy. In prosperous times, most people can afford the loss when their dream vacation turns out to be just that. In tight times, a "dream vacation" can represent an escape from pressing circumstances or serves as a spiritual sign that is, to some, evidence that Lady Luck or some higher power is on their side.[16] When the economy is flat, however, discretionary funds are monitored more closely. For many, a vacation itself is not a realistic possibility, and thus even the idea of a "free" one loses its appeal.

Changes in the competitiveness and availability of inexpensive air transportation, notably the growth of frequent flyer and discount programs, have also cut deeply into the revenues of travel scams. Two cultural factors also drove many travel scams out of business in the 1990s: saturation mailing densities and greater societal familiarity with air travel. Many people are extremely suspicious of the bulk mail they receive announcing that a telephone call to the 800 number will bestow free gifts "if they qualify." Moreover, many more Americans are air travelers and more familiar with being tourists. Hence, the "magic holiday" is less of a novelty than it once was.

Travel scams still have some regional appeal, however, and many operations target those who live in smaller towns and who are not likely to know about boiler rooms. Cert operations consolidated in the 1990s. Road boilers spend less time in distant places, and all the calls are made from a handful of locations. Sophisticated telephone systems and bulk mailing rates provide economies of scale in this regard. More important, the flatness of the economy and the popularity of other types of promotions have drained the appeal of free trips to the Bahamas as an incentive to move big-ticket items.

In a tight retail market it is hard to buy back the heat when a customer fails to receive a promised free trip. That creates bad will among merchants, and much of the appeal of this approach has been undercut by deals available through legitimate travel agents and the use of manufacturers' discounts by automobile dealers. Public awareness has destroyed much of the lure that these operations once offered to the gullible. Thus, many more questions are being asked over the telephone on the boiler room's time. That alone has driven many operations out of business, because the con is designed to pitch people who believe that they have won something. When that belief is questioned, it takes too much telephone skill and time to overcome the objections.

Cert operations, however, rarely disappear entirely; they mutate. One operation met the shifting market by hiring ethnic speakers and having material printed in languages other than English. Because the pitch and the concept of 800 numbers are virtually unknown to those who are foreign-born, and there is, to the best of my knowledge, not yet a foreign-language term for "boiler room," these populations represent entirely new markets. However this turns out for the owners of these shops, one thing is certain: The next generation of boilers will be bilingual.

Contract Telemarketing: The Bid as a Confidence Game

A bid is one of the most elementary forms of business transactions in a market economy. It involves the verbal request for the asking price of goods or services that are customarily delivered at a later date. Thus, the bid is the single most important act that aligns supply and demand. All known markets are reducible to bid structures. A buyer of goods or services, upon questioning a seller, ascertains a price (the quote).

Quotes differ in their deliverability, however, because a quote is only as good as the reputation of the vendor making it. It is beyond the scope of this book to evaluate all the possible risk configurations that emerge from these types of cultural understandings, but the single act of requesting a bid links all telephone rooms to the conventional marketplace because that establishes the basis upon which markups are based (for products) and the base cost of doing business (for services).

Even an imaginary service—say, providing telephone conversations informed by the spirit of your late Uncle Charlie that supposedly operates through the vibes discernible to the psychic on the other end of the telephone—requires overhead that must be met within the confines of a knowable bid structure. Contract telemarketing firms work the available bid structures in a given market at a point in time and amplify accordingly. This permits a glimpse of what may be possible in the future, based on whatever combination of pitches moves whichever program being touted.

Contract telemarketing (TM) is the mechanism that ensures the evolutionary survival of a boiler room as it moves freely in the world of products and services to perform its screening function in a ruthless, cost-effective manner. It procures the initial contracts to promote wares and services that fail to move in traditional markets, thriving in good economic times and during downturns as well. Because only those firms with telephone-promotable goods and services survive, "flat markets" make for a concentration of the victorious into a few industries.

A contract TM operation provides telephone talent for hire. In its smallest, simplest form, a lone telephoner dials from his "company of one." He is his own dialer and is transformed into a boiler if deception is used. On the other end of the continuum, based on size and function, lies the conventional TM industry. If deception is not used, dialers become phoners. Three examples demonstrate the key principles: one is a product and two are services. All were processed by a contract TM operation and illustrate the close interaction among cultural norms, technology, entrepreneurs, and telephone rooms.

The Curious Case of the Battery Brothers

Tim and Fred, the "Battery Brothers," are involved in the auto parts business. Tim is the entrepreneur, and Fred is the parts maven, a mechanic with an accountant's mentality, his friends say. Tim noted that a recent change in technology (the advent of the sealed-case battery) coincided with the slow displacement of conventional batteries and an upswing in the prevalence of new car purchases.[17] As the nation's auto stock ages, used cars are resold and eventually junked. As cars are kept longer, however, the likelihood of replacing their batteries increases.

Thus, whether an old car is kept, traded, or junked, the stream of old batteries increases. Tim saw his opportunity in the fact that old car batteries have salvage value because of the lead in their cells. By paying 25 cents over salvage, an almost unlimited stock of used batteries can be obtained. The Battery Brothers' reconditioning operation began by buying discarded batteries from anyone who would sell them. Assuming some discarded batteries can, with the addition of electrolyte and water, be brought up to operating standards, there is a variable chance that profit can be made. Those batteries truly dead still fetch the salvage price. Thus, the "net risk price" (the price of a complete failure) is 25 cents per battery and the cost of the time involved.

Their market was those who wished to sell their cars but were unable to do so with dead batteries and those unable to afford new batteries. As the business grew, they turned to a contract TM house to expand their market. The pros in the boiler room immediately saw that this was a specialized market and therefore not amendable to telephone presentation, but they took the deal anyway. The Battery Brothers were convinced that they would make a great deal of money, and their ambitions prevented them from undertaking a more realistic analysis. It cost them roughly $5,000 to discover that it was not the kind of deal that can be promoted over the telephone.

The contract TM house in effect screened the product out of the telephone marketplace. As a service, however, the Battery Brothers' operation could be touted as an investment opportunity. So, armed with data on the markup and the profits possible in reconditioning batteries—and another fee for their services—the contract TM shop was able to sell shares to interested parties, investors who knew nothing about batteries but were adept at profit projections.

It is this marketing flexibility that keeps the "phone boys"—as the Battery Brothers called them—on top of breaking opportunities. Technology, however, is not the only source of sustenance for contract TM shops; changes in cultural norms work equally well. Consider the case of the "gym phone" operators, where selling health club memberships spawned a new type of boiler room.

Gym Phone Operations

Fitness and dieting fads have been growth industries since World War II. Because advanced industrial societies contain sedentary people, businesses have evolved to rid fashion- and swimsuit-conscious individuals of unwanted pounds. What in the 1950s was the "local sweaty old gym" has mutated into a variety of upscale establishments catering to a number of interests. Regional variation has produced health clubs, swimming clubs, racquet clubs, dieting clubs, and martial arts centers. The fitness industry has grown to include saunas and spas and the marketing of exercise equipment, vitamins, and health foods, all of which fuel the growing demand for the requisite costuming needed to partake of these new public roles. One example concerns the huge trade in athletic clothing and shoes.

Members of the affluent society can be seen almost everywhere, jogging, bicycling, running, and power walking in what appears to be a cultural fetish against recognizing the fact that people naturally age and cannot perpetually maintain the physical appearance of twenty-one-year-olds. Contract TM houses thus gain clients with all manner of health, beauty, and fitness aids in need of promotion. That most of these wild schemes are doomed to failure does not prevent their entrepreneurial creators from being bilked for the requisite fee to discover this harsh fact of telephone promotion.

When a telephone room discovers a viable market, however, from among the many useless products, gadgets, and business dreams appearing daily before its outside closers, pros take notice.[18] One such market is composed of overweight women; to a much smaller but still important degree, another is based on the class-based fascination with martial arts programs. Gym phone operations are the result. That most boiler rooms are smoked-filled and few therein are health-conscious does not stop the pitchmen from using the language of health, fitness, martial prowess, and the illusions of popularity and well-being derived therefrom.

Gym telephone operations target two different populations. Health clubs target affluent women desirous of losing weight, whereas martial arts telephone operations target working-class families. The former has tapped a growing industry, whereas the latter cannot be promoted over the telephone. The pivot point is that health clubs make sizable sums by offering a service whose contract length far exceeds a typical patron's willingness to remain enrolled. This market imperfection attracts the interest of contract TM shops and some smaller, in-house operators.

Health cubs typically offer four membership classes: the "trial membership" for a few sessions, the "silver" (annual) membership, the "gold" (two-year) program, and the "platinum" (three years or longer) program. In this industry, most women who buy club memberships do so to lose weight, and many become interested in the social and recreational aspects of exercise programs. Most patrons, however, typically become active enrollees only for a few weeks, and the typical client loses interest after six months.

As all dieters know, serious exercise programs, with or without medical supervision, require discipline and commitment. Most who enroll lack both of these requisites, which is why they make such good marks. The cultural pressure on women, however, to do something to lose the excess pounds they have been socialized into believing makes them unattractive is what makes health clubs so appealing—peer support for the portly. To the number enticed by this possibility must be added those who must lose weight for health reasons. Gyms have been around for years, however; what is novel is the participation of affluent women.

Health clubs are an elegant con because they work on the premise of natural attrition. The "incoming class" always contains a few who are less overweight than most and a few exercise fanatics who are not overweight at all. That results in emergent comparative norms. Because obesity is stigmatized, those who are less proficient at losing the requisite pounds face additional stress for this shortcoming. Thus, a self-defeating possibility emerges: People are driven to health clubs to change their physical appearance. Failing to do so, however, brings ostracism from the very group from which they seek social support. Hence, active memberships typically nosedive before six months have passed.

Perhaps if these programs were less technique-driven (for example, daily weigh-ins, calorie counting, dress size comparisons, and careful measurements taken of thighs, bust, and hips), more fun and sociability might take place in less self-conscious environments. But it is precisely the comparative, evaluative assessments that make gyms profitable. For each unused membership, a new client can be entered into the program. Attrition is facilitated by the fact that many on the staffs of the clubs are salespeople who have a commissionable stake in high levels of clientele turnover.

Another natural advantage of the con is that given a normal distribution of overweight women, those in one tail of the distribution (the 5 percent who actually lose a great deal of weight) readily become spokespeople for the benefits of the program. The other tail of the distribution (the 5 percent who fail abysmally) are shown the door, another reason for the salespeople, a social control function. No one in the business of physique modification can permit highly visible losers to contaminate the aesthetics of the scene. For this reason, all sales personnel on-site are carefully screened for athletic ability and physical attractiveness (the hooks), two attributes irrelevant to pitchmen in boiler rooms, which are always segregated from the areas where exercise actually takes place.

Thus, health club memberships, promoted as a key to the active life, to popularity and health, to longevity, and to trimness and fitness, turn out, in all cases where a boiler room is used, to be sharp business operations that have a pecuniary interest in selling long-duration memberships that most clients will not use. Whether or not, and for how long, such membership sales remain brisk determines when a boiler room will be used to vend franchise expansion possibilities as investment opportunities. That typically happens when a health club has passed its maximum revenue-generating point and the ownership realizes that its past earnings are larger than its future growth possibilities. Specialized boiler rooms catering to this scenario are called "health venture operations."[19]

The case of the "martial arts phone" (contract TM operations selling martial arts club memberships) demonstrates how entrepreneurial immigrants get bilked, because these services cannot be sold successfully over the telephone. The reasons primarily concern American adolescent norms. First, martial arts programs are popular among working-class youths and gain clients primarily through referrals. Second, the business logic of promotion does not work on the parents in this target population, because the assumption that savings can be achieved on expensive memberships calls forth no sense of urgency. Third, the notion of having young boys develop martial arts skills is not the prime selling point and, in fact, is a negative with most parents.

The primary selling point is having potentially wayward youths under adult supervision, where they can supposedly be taught discipline. But that is not "pitchable" because parents are both unlikely and unwilling to cede that they may have shortcomings in this area. Thus, martial arts programs are sold by quasi-boiler room staffs to the owners of such establishments, who learn, after paying the initial program fees, that telephone promotion does not work. I know of no boiler room that has been successful in this area. For a boiler room to be successful it must influence the user of a service directly, that is, the buyer.

Affluent, overweight women, the group targeted for these marketing efforts, often have the funds, the time, and the ability to be persuaded by a pitchman skilled in health and fitness rhetoric, as do affluent, overweight men. Adolescents seeking the mystique of the martial arts, however, do not respond to telephone marketing but rather to peer groups, where they learn how to impute fantasies of power and prowess from the latest moves, punches, kicks, and exercise routines that they teach each other or mimic from the movies and television.

Gym phone operations thus serve to screen "in" those health and exercise clients who have the economic wherewithal to afford such services and to screen "out" those who do not. They also provide temporary training to boilers, who, although being able to add another line to their list of telephone skills, will soon be unemployed. No gym telephone operation, to the best of my knowledge, has lasted more than a year—the longest time it takes to establish a critical mass of patrons from which referral business is possible.[20]

Innovation

Innovations on the floors of contract TM shops that ultimately result in new scam operations are not common in flat markets because extremes heighten the sense of urgency and certain forms of conspicuous consumption. Losing weight is less central when people are losing their jobs. When few are making a killing in the speculative market venture of their choice there is little enthusiasm that can be contagiously communicated by a skilled pitchman. Many contract TM firms close their doors. They only thrive when other small businessmen—their prime clients—are interested in what they perceive to be opportune times for growth and expansion. There are some sectoral exceptions, however. These are located in those parts of the economy most sensitive to media manipulation and that elicit some kind of emotional response on the part of prospects that is subject to manipulation by pitchmen. Growth areas in contract TM operations are personal safety and fad medicines. There is also growth in targeted port and border cities, where pitches for new immigration-related scams are being worked out in distant back rooms.

One targeted market in the personal safety field is the urban and suburban near-poor, those individuals who are "house poor" or have recently amended bad credit records through years of hard work and thrift. These clients are sold fictional security systems that offer, for a fee chargeable to a credit card, a service contract for the installation, servicing, and maintenance of imaginary electronic surveillance and protective devices. One boiler room offers imaginary theft insurance at very reasonable prices to targeted customers who live in declining neighborhoods, where, in the words of a salesman, "The mopes have been screened to be able to afford it, and worried enough by the daily [news]papers to be concerned." The marketing strategy is to use router maps color coded by home value, police crime statistics, and data on recent real estate sales.

Some boiler rooms now run what are called "medicine shops," where a careful read of a neighborhood's demographics and other data provided by list brokers provides clues about the prevalence of self-medication among certain groups. A carefully worded pitch keeps the boiler rooms within the letter of the law, and they make all manner of quasi-medical products available. Medicine shops represent an entire industry of "gray area medicine" where common veterinary items, chemicals, salves, and ointments—not approved for human use—find a market. Many of these items have trade-name recognition and have been used for generations on livestock. Horse liniment is a typical product, and many folk cultures in rural areas offer preparations for other animals.

A sharp boiler can embellish as required, and the high prices of prescription medication and medical care and the shortage of physicians in many areas add the lure of cost-effectiveness to an already strained societal health care system. A Washington, D.C., pro offers his comments:

> Did you catch the coverage of the [health care] hearings on the Hill? . . . I mean, do you think that some guy with arthritis, *who is in pain*, gives a rat's ass about the politicians? Or the doctors? Or the insurance companies? Or the lawyers? Hell, no. He wants [name of horse liniment]! This stuff has worked for years on race horses. . . . The owner [of the boiler room] is making a pile

of dough because many people just can't afford to go to a doctor. . . . There's more money in this gig than in lots of other things I've sold [cites list]. And there's no heat. None. People want this stuff.

Immigration scams involve false documentation, work permits, and Social Security cards. The boiler room, however, only trades in the illusion of being able to provide these. In response to a 900 number strategically placed in the appropriate newspapers, "card shops" provide an English-speaking talker and solicit an application fee (credit card only) for whatever a customer may require. Because these protracted conversations typically involve non-English-speaking marks and are paid for by the caller, they are often costly. The customer is sent information on whatever the federal regulations may be concerning whatever subject area the caller requests. Most of this material is available, in most cases, free of charge from the appropriate governmental agencies.

A carefully worded disclaimer protects the boiler room from legal action, and it is unlikely that many complaints will be received by immigration authorities who, given their work loads and low levels of popularity among clients, have other pressing public relations problems. Moreover, anti-immigrant hysteria in certain parts of the country also works in the boiler room's favor in two regards. It generates interest among the relatives of illegals (who likely have credit cards) in obtaining documentation for their kin, and it makes it more likely that the champions of immigrants' legal rights will be otherwise too preoccupied to press their already thin resources to track down sharp pitchmen located out of state.

Although boiler rooms advertise in targeted port cities and border regions, none are actually located in those areas where immigration authorities and local police may wish to generate busts to clear their otherwise tarnished organizational images in response to possible politicization. Thus, New York boiler rooms work the California market and San Francisco rooms work New York; both work the Mexican border and Florida. Moreover, federal and local budget-tightening, coupled with the sensationalistic nature of crime news and generalized, widespread fears of drugs and violence, keep the pressures on social control resources highly localized. A boiler room thus has free reign to tout its fictional services from afar.

The Technological Crisis in Telemarketing

The TM industry since the early 1990s has, because of the increasing capitalization requirements of a state-of-the-art infrastructure, undergone substantial changes in social organization. When dialers are hired as telephoners they are increasingly likely to be subject to machine protocols. Shifts in consumer purchasing patterns, the increasing dominance of marketing, as opposed to sales, ideologies, and the division of labor, abetted by the absence of owners on the scene, have led managers to adopt strategies that ensure their own survival.

One irony of the success of conventional TM companies in transforming the ordering process into an almost continuous process of industrial production is that the basic cost of such services has become prohibitively high for many small- to medium-sized businesses. These business clients are effectively driven into the waiting rooms of smaller contract TM shops, which, being populated by boilers, can "talk a much better deal" than the high-priced telephone banks that at the largest operations can contain more than five hundred telephones linked to computer terminals and a small army of support staff.

Virtually all of this capital-intensive, high-tech gear is not used to sell— the forte of a boiler room—but rather to market products and services over the telephone to residential customers. Boiler rooms have abandoned this market. Except in contract TM shops, boilers and phoners live in different telephone worlds. They do different types of work, and they are not employed by the same companies. Marketing, unlike sales, involves the social organization of administrative procedures that are used in combination with an expanding advertising effort. That was not always the case. Conventional TM firms began expanding during the 1970s and predate the large-scale expansion of boiler rooms. In large part this represented a marketing response to the increased use of credit cards in retail transactions and the birth of the direct marketing industry, where customers could, for the first time, telephone in their orders. Telephoners did not evolve as salesmen but as order-takers. Boiler rooms could only thrive on a large scale after the cultural assumption of "phoning in an order" was first firmly established by conventional TM firms.

The logic of TM expansion is a marketing logic. As more accounts are brought on board, a telephone room experiences segmented growth and more lines are committed to the most active corporate clients. Marketing directors in conventional industries are typically paid to assemble creative talent (artists, advertising writers, and designers) to create income as a function of the organization of human capital in the development of advertising campaigns.

Assigning telephoners to cubicles does not, however, capture creative, but rather administrative, talent. As products and services become more standardized, telephoners increasingly concentrate not on selling but on writing up orders for the offer—the one item being advertised. When the level of skills required of telephoners drops to processing simple orders, it is just a matter of time before these workers are displaced by technology.

The TM industry responded by bifurcating into two types of telephone rooms: specialized operations set up within a given industry to handle the increased traffic brought about by the success of mail order catalogs and very large TM companies serving large corporate accounts. The former are product and service telephone rooms tied into the basic structure of their parent industries, whereas the latter are general-purpose telephone rooms.

Natural differentiation follows. Telephoners working the industry-based, in-house operations learn about other services and products the sponsoring company may provide (a stock brokerage firm may have many kinds of stocks, bonds, and funds, for example), whereas telephoners in large TM houses can only answer questions about filling out an order. The first group can use available technology to increase the market share of the host company. For example, the first stock brokerage firm to provide real-time quotations gains a comparative advantage over its competitors that do not. The second kind of telephoner is used by the technology. When orders can be more efficiently accomplished electronically than with human prompting, that telephoner is soon out of a job.

Useless telephoners, however, may seek other kinds of telephone work, and, in part, the rise of boiler rooms could not have occurred without this kind of displacement. By the 1990s, however, many of these people were unemployed because the boiler rooms that survived required more, not less, skills from practitioners. Neither the scams nor product houses are hiring many trainees; large TM houses have come to dominate the industry. That raises two questions concerning the future of conventional TM companies. First, why it is reasonable to equate their dominance with the increased use of boiler room techniques? And, second, why will these operations soon evolve out of existence? Partial answers to both questions lie in the role played by TM managers and evolving technology. Because both questions are related, it is useful to review the basic rules governing all telephone rooms.

A telephone room is a social construction organized as a business whose mission is a managerial decision. The role of mid-management in white-collar crime is well documented.[21] In conventional TM operations it is the mid-managers who are most vulnerable to having to justify their salaries compared with those of the telephoners in their charge. Following the notation of Reskin and Roos (1990), although the generalized cultural preference for male dialers is a gender queue (males are the preferable employee of choice), that preference becomes a job queue favoring women only when most of the money is out of the game. The reason is that managers in TM operations, unlike boiler rooms, are typically unskilled in operative sales techniques but can command high salaries for their supervisory abilities. Thus, a full-time manager can earn the weekly salary of perhaps eight of his part-time telephoners working twenty hours per week each (at \$5 an hour, $20 \times 8 \times 5 =$ \$800).

Class conflict in such settings requires no barricades, only control over the definition of work. In TM firms part-time workers regularly rotate, and managers prefer to hire the most docile and verbally skilled for the lowest pay. Women fill the bill because they are typically grateful for the work and are likely to be more conscientious than men at this level of wages, more punctual, more likely to take seriously what management says, less willing to complain, and more likely to treat the management in a courteous manner. At the extreme, a part-time female telephoner is not likely to threaten the management physically, is not likely to "ask to see the books," and is more likely to be totally innocent of boiler room techniques, when and if they are used. The purpose of a telephone room is a managerial decision, however.

There is no law of economics that requires, in the preceding example, that a company must be organized such that \$1,600 in wages should be allocated to one manager and eight part-time workers. That depends on the profitability horizons of the ownership, the type of telephone work being accomplished, the nature of the industry, and the kind of chemistry and tone sought in the telephone room. When all of these factors are assumed to be given, however, *and* managers are paid \$800, *and* a part-time job is offered at \$5 per hour, this configuration is likely to be defined as one that is the result of the prevailing market. Thus, the social decision to engage in such arrangements has its locus in an invisible back room and appears to be a normal market outcome.

Dialers become less necessary when a market is dominated by increasingly sophisticated advertising (mail order catalogs sent to regular subscribers); focused television spots that are demographically driven; the popularity of product and service tie-ins that promote a package of related items; cable programming that can tap specialty markets and interests; and infomercials and enhanced ordering technologies (automated credit card readers and direct-dialing-to-order accomplished electronically). Those who supervise such personnel ultimately become redundant as well, because the controls built into a machine-ordering process are often self-correcting and self-monitoring.

This permits some speculation about when, in the evolution of telemarketing enterprises, boiler room techniques are most likely to be used: at the point when mid-management is threatened with obsolescence. To protect its own interests, fraudulent techniques offer one way to increase profits dramatically, if only temporarily, and achieve the rewards associated with increased productivity. Although I have not gathered sufficient systemic data to forecast this trend decisively, careful analysis of critical sites suggests this possibility. Mid-management is already totally unnecessary, for example, in those operations where dialers already have the most autonomy: fronters in certain kinds of scams; sophisticated legitimate brokerage operations; pros in product shops; small shops (of the smart variety) in investment scams; and in some specialized parts operations. This observation is also consistent with current trends of conventional companies ridding themselves of excessive tiers of management.

Postulate 3 states that the mission of a telephone room is a managerial decision. If I am correct, when escalating technology renders most managers obsolete the world of telephone work will be composed of entrepreneurs running small boiler rooms and large electronic bureaucracies running huge customer service operations. In an ironic sense it is the illusion structure of the boiler room that sustains it. That is not true for telemarketing. TM operations offer only tasks: routine, endless, repetitive work and invariant procedures performed by part-time workers in cubicles. It is likely that the technological innovations that formed this industry (computer-assisted telephoning, direct dialing, electronic queuing of scripts, and real-time transmission of account data) will replace its workers for those multi-million-dollar firms that can afford the substitution of capital for labor.

After the last telemarketer has hung up her headset, "the service," however efficient, sophisticated, and complex, will still have to be sold. There will still be the requisite levels of investment needed to launch the new technology's delivery systems, and there will still be the possibility of turning such capabilities into profit-bearing schemes. In what follows, a boastful pro boiler describes some of the summary lines of a pitch used by a quasi-boiler room set up to bilk some of the clients and investors in one of the nation's leading growth sectors: information technologies and services delivery. He intersperses these with his comments on a recent deal. I have capitalized the points of cadence and inserted the proper pauses to show that the qualities of what is being vended are irrelevant to a skilled pitchman. Boilers can use technological images as readily as any other and will likely remain a few steps ahead of the technicians—if for no other reason than sales skill and technical expertise are two distinct capabilities.[22]

> It's a BEAUTIFUL product [names service; pause]. It provides real-time stock quotes and market data right into the modem of a personal computer. It's got all the CYBER-MAGIC [pause]: high baud transmission, band compatibilities, and liquid crystal or digital display [pause]. . . . Real-time DATA FEEDS. . . . Our buyers are MIS [management information systems] guys. Our talker is a techie. . . . Hey, sometimes I don't know what he's really talking about. . . . What I do is *sell the concept* [emphasis added]: a portable, affordable data transmission system that can compete with the news wires, the financial services, and the stock-quote analysts. . . . AND IT EVEN FEATURES ANALYTIC MODE [laughs]: a touch of the button and you get charts and graphs.

How does that sound? Sound good? Damn right! . . . Does it work? Hell, no. . . . All we had was a black box with lots of stuff we had produced through [names source]. . . . All we did was talk capabilities. That, my friend, will always be a *phone deal*.

Dialers as a Marginalized Labor Force

All telephone rooms generate unemployment, they simply differ with regard to the rate at which, and the circumstances under which, that will be accomplished. When dialers are set to work as boilers, their sales skills are pitted against each other, and they face gyrating markets and fleeting, although highly variable, expectations of economic reward. Goods and services are promoted using fraudulent techniques until it is no longer profitable to continue, then these operations mutate or go out of business. Each cycle of expansion and contraction produces a new generation of entrepreneurs who engage the available means of predation and modify it in accordance with personal inclinations, hopes, and dreams. That, in turn, creates the varying kinds of tone, style, and chemistry to be found in emerging and dying telephone rooms. When all is said and done, only the entrepreneur typically remains. He may start another operation, work part-time to hone his skills in another boiler room, or work as a fronter in an industry different from the one that provided his start.

When dialers are set to work as phoners, they are employed as adjuncts to an advertising effort of some kind, and they compete against alternative forms of advertising. Their employment is influenced by larger movements of the business cycle that determine the general availability of disposable income in different consumption-publics known as various "industries." Each sector of the economy produces a different likelihood for purchasing over the telephone. As products and services become more standardized, the ordering process becomes more amenable to technology using the latest, most capital-intensive information-gathering and storage systems, and fewer people are needed.

At the most sophisticated level, advertising, ironically, evolves to the point of being functionally unnecessary because product knowledge alone, without embellishment, is sufficient to generate orders. That has already happened in certain parts of the wholesale market (vitamins, lumber, steel, pencils, original equipment manufacture auto parts, milk, grains, and other commodities) where purchasing agents can order variations of some established industry standard by coded identifier. Computerized inventory systems are another example of a closed ordering system where competition occurs through price alone.

At this extreme, one set of bar codes communicates all of the necessary data for what used to take a small army of people a great deal of time to assemble (pricing), organize (accounting), and deliver (distribution). On the retail side of such markets looms the potential of the electronic sales station, where customers, after being presented with video or electronic descriptions of varied wares and services, simply punch or dial assigned code numbers directly into an encoder that has also been programmed to handle billing and shipping. Home television shopping is a relevant example. Telephoners thus face displacement from technological innovation.[23] The economies of scale that are possible from such arrangements are being seen in the huge telemarketing rooms, where what is said over the telephone (i.e., detailed attention to data collection) is already more important than how it is said (i.e., sales skill).

The result is a complex of industries composed of relatively few well-paid managers and thousands of expendable, part-time, mostly female workers. With the advent of the electronic sales station, these workers will become even less necessary. Their overseers will also soon join the ranks of the unemployed, but not before a final wave of fraud, via the use of boiler room techniques, is launched. Overseers will struggle for survival as they are overcome by the self-same technologies they have successfully promoted to increase the cost-effectiveness of the workers in their charge.[24]

The fate of telephone rooms will be largely sustained and defined by the degree to which the United States continues to produce expendable numbers of middle-class workers. This harsh reality fuels both entrepreneurs in boiler rooms and telephoners in the telemarketing industry. Dialers are a marginalized middle-class, one of the first to be so situated in postindustrial society. They are articulate to the extreme on the scam phone; literate, patient, and hardworking in most other industries; sometimes creative; and always office workers who are more comfortable with a cup of coffee and a tall tale than a lunch pail and a few quick beers.

Dialers are clearly one of the first expendable "products" of the information age, and that portends some grave concerns over the heralded movement into a service society as being an indicator of social progress. Unless one believes that disposable workers are a commercial asset, it is an upsetting social trend. Some dialers represent the most modern forms of white-collar crime, whereas others are lucky to work twenty hours a week at a few cents above the minimum wage.[25] Most, however, ultimately join the ranks of the unemployed when some combination of greed, entrepreneurial spirit, market configuration, and technology takes its due course. Ironically, it is only the degree to which some boiler rooms are able to mutate that permits something approaching stable, full-time work, at least for a while.

That combination is unavailable on either the scam phone, which shuts down in the wink of an eye, or in most conventional TM rooms because of the onslaught of rapid technological change. Thus, neither wholly deviant nor wholly conventional solutions to the displacement problem have proven viable. In light of that state of affairs, it may be wise to carefully scrutinize the plethora of remediative schemes championed by those who seek to address the contemporary world of work.

Virtually the entire field of labor economics, to the degree that it almost religiously assumes an easy transferability between labor and capital and between managerial imperatives and imagined productivity, may require serious revision. In fact, neither dialers nor their managers have actually experienced long-term material benefits from quality circles, positive thinking, or the empowerment rhetoric that dominates many management circles. Nor do (or did) rising educational qualifications portend a solution to the problem of exploited labor. Indeed, before the crash in the telemarketing field in the early 1990s most managers of these operations had extensive business experience, and many had business degrees that proved useless.[26] Marginalized middle-class workers, to the degree that they may represent a new vanguard reacting to common postindustrial realities, portend even more serious problems for those below them in the stratification system: the underclass, the vast army of social workers who serve them, and the keepers of the social institutions that have evolved to produce them.[27]

It is totally inconceivable that the "old disenfranchised" (the poor, ethnic minorities, immigrants, and the functionally illiterate) will somehow benefit from a global economy where all the purported advantages said to result from traditional industrial solutions to the labor productivity problem (training, education, high-spiritedness, well wishes, therapy, encouragement, and genuflections toward the power of technology and the legitimacy of authority) have failed to provide full-time jobs and benefits to those who *already have* the requisite social qualifications.

The educational and interpersonal qualifications of currently unemployed telephoners is already much higher than that which characterizes the underclass, and, considering that most of the population of telephoners are women, that does not bode well for the future. Indeed, the feminization of telephone rooms has produced exploited women. Few, however, are deficient in job skills, aptitude, work-related talents, education, or training, and all have successfully been screened for pleasantness of voice, reading ability, personality, and elementary social and office skills.

Nor will equality of opportunity before oppressive conditions solve the apparently intractable problem of markets that create a surplus population. Witness the fate of boilers, most of whom are white, healthy men who have ample exposure to formal education, familiarity with technology, team spirit, and, for some, uncommonly high levels of interpersonal skill. The structural problems of a service economy—represented, in part, by those who work in telephone rooms—cannot be fine-tuned through the logic of cost-effective-ness and by arguments that favor the "development of human capital." Indeed, it is such reasoning that permits the predation in telephone rooms to proceed methodically. It is always cost-effective to exploit labor. In fact, it is only in the "irrational" small companies—more guided by the idiosyncratic whims of the ownership—where creative approaches to telephone work prevail. Dialers only get a fair shake in the dens of con men, at the hands of petty entrepreneurs, or when they are lucky enough to stumble onto a sales floor run by an ownership that has intentionally decided not to replicate the industry norms of the telephone room.

The realities in boiler rooms and in telephone rooms using boiler room techniques will only change if there is a massive labor shortage in the United States, because that would virtually dry up the supply of talent to the cold floors in most telephone operations. It would not eliminate the social form, however, because a few sharp pitchmen would be expected to survive, as they have always done throughout the ages.

What would change would be that most incentives that permit products and services to be touted actively would vanish, because no boiler room offers an alternative to a stable, well-paying job. Indeed, it is the absence of decent jobs that drives many to read the classifieds in the first place. It may or may not be true that "you can't con an honest man," as the folk adage has it, but it is clearly more difficult to sell something to a buyer not animated by financial insecurity, boredom, or contemporary fears that call forth fantasy escapes into the world of instant wealth, glamour, physical safety, popularity, or having the physique of a twenty-one-year-old.

Meaningful well-paid work, of course, will not eliminate the quest for fantasy, but it would make predation in this area more difficult to achieve via the telephone. Labor scarcity would also eliminate school house operations, which can only exist because the educational system produces failure for the very categories of labor most vulnerable to being unemployed as markets tighten. That useful skills are not for sale in the marketplace is common knowledge among school house boilers. None of those I've met are foolish enough to believe their own pitches or the claims touted in the corporate literature.

It is likely true that labor shortages are inherently inflationary to the degree that labor is organized, there are no readily available capital intensive substitutes for labor, and the distribution of profits remains unchanged. Historical evidence suggests, however, that labor is less organized than ever before, that technologies that displace labor are being routinely generated, and that the issue of redistributing profits is rarely mentioned in debates of this kind.[28]

In societies characterized by labor surpluses, the market mechanism will always call forth ingenious and innovative accommodations to the desires of those seeking income to survive. The drug scene is a case in point. Unlike the social pressures put on pushers, the use of deceptive techniques has the advantage for those who run boiler rooms of never having to deliver on promises. As advanced technology continues to displace many in the middle class, those boiler rooms that remain will no doubt accommodate quite well.

On the demand side of the boiler room equation, all that is needed as a cultural prerequisite is an imperfect market of some kind where information, goods, or services do not flow freely. That encourages belief in the idea that perhaps a nonconventional remedy may be realistic. Imperfect markets and the idea of readily available quick-fix solutions to whatever problem can be imagined form the basis of a pitch: the unique area of comparative advantage available to a boiler room.

In the 1950s it was probably inconceivable to the residential users of rotary telephones that the commercialization of this novel means of personal communication would spawn industries of dialers to prey upon countless numbers of marks, customers, operatives, and clients.[29] Even more bizarre is the fact that most of these operations are ultimately cannibalistic. They consume themselves along with hundreds of workers for each entrepreneur who sets out on the great telephonic quest.

In the future, the form will no doubt undergo many mutations. If, for example, "picture phones" gain widespread public acceptance, it does not take too much imagination to speculate that boilers will invest heavily in the requisite props and scenic backgrounds from which to present their spiels. In the mid-1990s, an operation in Florida—before being banned from the airwaves—was broadcasting infomercials touting imaginary investments in the "wireless communications" field, and a similar con, working out of New York, was offering a "sure way to profit from the price fluctuations in fuel oil." The novelty of these scams was that they were presented in the format of "special news reports" for investors, complete with simulated call-in questions from shills and a professional job of film editing to create the illusions of urgency and spontaneity.

Boilers in cyberspace will have an easier job in obtaining qualified leads than do the conventional variety of present-day telephone pitchmen. The Internet already features defined categories of users and areas of interest. Moreover, it represents a vast untapped territory shrouded in technological mystique.[30] Even the most rudimentary of list brokers can provide telephone numbers and zip codes for any commercial purpose. It is only a matter of time before some cyber-boiler figures out that people who spend large amounts of time engaged in digitized interaction may prefer that, in part because they lack the interpersonal skills for live human exchange.

The best fish, for boilers, are the invisible kind where only symbols and credit card information need be exchanged. Illusions are not limited by the constraints of the physical. Boilers have, in fact, been living in a kind of virtual reality for some time, and they will no doubt continue to evolve—well behind the horizons of technology, slightly in front of conventional marketing efforts, and always a few steps ahead of the law.

I am not aware of any cross-cultural work being done on the evolution of boiler rooms, but I suspect that the volatile mixture of entrepreneurial spirit, free-market ideologies, and displaced middle-class labor will soon add another little-noticed cultural artifact to the portfolios of emerging markets in India, China, parts of the former Soviet Union, and Latin America: the drone of a telephone pitchman working the newly installed telephone lines in those recently established businesses and newly affluent communities that cast a hopeful eye to the United States and have yet to come to understand the many meanings and purposes of unrequested telephone sales calls. However these varied economies fare in other regards, it is certain that economic development will generate social tensions. Tensions resulting from the gyrations of the business cycle make people ripe for promises. Delivering promises in lieu of what is really needed or desired is one of the few areas of business life in which a telephone pitchman faces little real competition—at least for a while.

Epilogue: The Ethics and Choices of Field Research in Natural Settings

The world of telephone promotion has changed substantially since the early 1980s when I first stumbled upon a small operation selling agricultural chemicals to farmers. Yet it has attracted scant attention in the social science community. Worse still, the list of cop-outs that social scientists use to avoid the study of active deviants in natural settings has lengthened.[1] If unchallenged, this pattern will come to influence the methodological canon, and future generations of scholars will know even less than is now known about the interactive qualities of firms, scenes, and perceptions that facilitate varied kinds of rule-breaking.

The problem of boiler rooms involves issues in the social organization of work. To understand how these operations function, a researcher must gain access to them. Seeking employment therein is the most straightforward choice. After that is accomplished, it is possible to learn from those in the industry, but four immediate difficulties must be overcome. First, there is no research literature in this subject area; second, there are no established guidelines for covert research in the social sciences; third, it cannot be assumed or known in advance which boiler room techniques will be used on a given site or, especially when beginning to collect data, what these may be or how they will present themselves; and, finally, informants must be protected from the necessarily dangerous knowledge that a researcher will acquire by spending protracted amounts of time on a deviant business scene.

All of these obstacles can be overcome with some thought and care before entering and becoming active in the field; fortunately, there is a substantial body of literature on conducting field research. That little of this addresses issues related to the assumption of an occupational role for the purpose of conducting research, however, is largely due to the historical fact that most social science research is done under the sponsorship of formal organizations. That fact may in part explain the popularity in criminology of studying captive, that is, "caught," populations (jail-house research); of surveying the general population; of teasing out data from court records and judicial proceedings (court house research); of relying almost exclusively on official statistics;

and of interviewing varied school populations for their perceptions of victim-hood or crime potential.

However creative in managing the tools of a survey researcher's art—or the state's data archives—most criminologists continue to avoid settings in which white-collar crime is actively being done. There is high irony in that and a self-fulfilling component as well. "Safe" research, like an investment without risk, produces meager results: the line of argument is typically mea-sured by the degree of consensus already existing in a typically narrowly defined academic field; the artful manipulation of data sets becomes the stan-dard upon which a claim to more funds (called "support" in research circles) is typically entertained; and the cries for "more research" are taken to mean more of the same kind of studies with, of course, larger (more costly), "more representative" samples and "more sophisticated analysis." More sophisticated analysis that has big bucks and small, incremental refinements added to the basic research design yields two results. First, most criminologists will con-tinue to know little about flesh-and-blood people, and many students will still be bewildered that their professors know more about the white-collar crimi-nals studied by Sutherland, and the languages of the con described by Mau-rer (a linguist) in 1949 than about what is going on today.[2]

I suspect that the reason that more is known about the petty thefts con-ducted by college students (typically shoplifting) than about the social struc-tures that produce systemic fraud is due to a curious lack of sociological in-terest in how businesses work in the planet's premiere business culture.[3] It is also convenient to assume, like a fish in water, that the prevailing norms of a specific culture can be taken as given, and it is much easier to administer ques-tionnaires than to leave the comforts of an office or raise uncomfortable ques-tions about what is going on in business schools—those ever-popular, enroll-ment-driven centers of education fraud closer to academic home.[4]

One problem with official research (bureaucratically sponsored studies conducted by organizationally aligned technicians) concerns the etiology of support and practice. An individual first becomes a researcher and then hires on with an agency, organization, or institute to do their bidding by promul-gating a conceptual status quo. Only independent academic researchers, how-ever, who have full control of the research agenda can, if necessary or required, withdraw from a scene. That critical possibility of withdrawal distinguishes scholarly research from the applied variety.

A scholar can say no. He or she can withdraw from a site, can choose to delay or not immediately publish findings, can postpone a project, can change the research design, or can terminate a project of his or her own design. Ap-plied researchers are not free to do that and must follow an organizationally approved agenda. It is not surprising that few pieces of sponsored research are on record for having their principal investigator turn down hard-won grant dollars once the project has begun.

It is beyond the scope of this book to ascertain whether or not it is true that "he who pays the piper calls the tune." That issue—once hotly and now "warmly" debated—remains unresolved.[5] If true, however, it may suggest why most official research is often as methodologically sophisticated as it is substantively trivial. Careful review will often reveal that this unfortunate finding frequently holds because of the popularity of an intriguing con common in research circles. In spite of the title of the research project (usually very broadly defined), what is delivered in the majority of cases of interest to criminologists and students of social deviance is typically not insight gained into the behavior of those actively involved in norm violation—or even the trilogy of violence, abuse, and racism—but data on the tabulation of reactions (arrest rates, anecdotal outrage, newspaper column-inches, and lawsuits) to these subjects, or opinions (questionnaire responses) on them held by members of various populations.

Thus, to name a classic, sadly relevant example, virtually all criminology textbooks can cite the most recent statistics on national or regional arrest rates for prostitution, but few criminologists have met a hooker in other than police settings or medical facilities. They assiduously assemble a great deal of information on the correlates of vice arrests but do not have a clue about what the behavior may mean to the participants or how that meaning may come to change. Moreover, when more successful practitioners are not caught (as is usually the case with those who have some skill and resources) and their johns—and payoffs to police—are not studied, academics learn little about the realities of prostitution. Those realities were not included in the research design to begin with. In part, the omission occurs because such information may prove disquieting, embarrassing, or uncomfortable to funding agencies or, more important, to those charged with suppression, rehabilitation, or expansion of the varied missions of agents of social control or claims of interested parties.

That does not mean, however, that institutional actors will soon change. Entire research industries feed off the fact that large numbers of people are vulnerable and powerless, two qualities that make them the subject of much research in the first place. Consider the con called "psychiatric epidemiology," in which the medical establishment and its research arm seek to carefully document the obvious distress suffered by the underclass. "At-risk" populations could as easily be located from a boiler room router map.

Not a dime of this "heavy grant action" goes to assist poor people, however, and no one has yet to dispatch any of these contemporary magicians who conjure up "symptom protocols" to the State Department, the Pentagon,

Capitol Hill, Wall Street, or Madison Avenue, where the social forces that
generate much of the strain in society acquire the patina of public policy and
come to define contemporary consumption expectations. And so the story goes
for many social problems (illicit drugs, juvenile crime, the plight of the elderly, educational decay, teenage difficulties, and unemployment), all products
of the operation of a system of markets and conveniently studied at the clinical level so as to merely identify victims.

It is a curious "research universe" indeed where there are typically no
pushers above the street level and none who live in foreign lands; no buyers,
fences, or other intermediaries for pilfered goods ripped off by inner-city
young men and sold in the suburbs; no beneficiaries available for interview
who profit from the geriatric trade, such as nursing homes, hospitals, medical establishments, and other recipients of the bulk of all societal medical
dollars spent during the final five years of a citizen's life; and no comments
from the real estate industry in southern climes or those in the personal protection trade (security services, devices, and related hardware). Nor is there a
clue that many rotten public schools continue to support an invisible army
of useless administrators and ancillary personnel who have nothing to do with
directly teaching young people and who are being overpaid for work that does
not exist in the private sector, or that young girls (in the news of late for having
their promiscuity result in out-of-wedlock births) might have a better chance
in life if young men in their communities had better, and more, economic
opportunities before becoming fathers.

As long as the lack of jobs and meaningful work remains a social reality,
there will always be an entrepreneurial response. Some will hustle to keep
society as it is, and others will hustle to get their piece of the resulting action—
bureaucratic, institutional, or professional. To the degree that the young thief,
the traffickers in discredited substances, the educational administrator, the
physician with a small army of part-time workers in accounts receivable, and
the thousands of businesses and organizations that prey upon the economically displaced and the vulnerable are unseen, researchers as "enterprisers"
fail to understand the full meaning of that term. In research, however, as in
most other areas of life, there is no free lunch.

To understand how people actually come to do many of the kinds of
things in which social scientists are interested, at least some of that knowledge must be informed by direct observation. The coin of the realm in organizational circles, however, is typically conventionality. That involves the
tacit acceptance of a sponsoring organization's agenda and the inevitable
crises of legitimacy that may follow if the research proves unpopular or
critical. There are, for example, those who seriously debate the public funding of the arts by holding a funding agency responsible for the output of

artists, but the clash of interest is actually over social control activities rather than artistic dialogue. The same is true concerning much of the research on crime and deviance.

The decision to engage in unsponsored research frees researchers from a number of organizational roles endemic to all projects not of their choosing, where research protocols are not of their design, and where deadlines, committee meetings, and related aspects (grant procurement or administration) of conducting research are irrelevant. Conducting truly independent covert field research is very much like the best parts of scholarly writing. Researchers must pursue their hunches wherever they may lead. Sometimes the hunches lead nowhere. Sometimes an idea proceeds in fits and starts. It may also take a handful of years before someone is well enough positioned in the field to make any kind of systematic sense out of what is being observed.

Such work requires patience, but no more than that required in amateur astronomy, archival research, history, or exploratory studies in any of the descriptive sciences where it is impossible to manipulate artificially the independent variables under study. Geology, archaeology, and the field studies of anthropologists and biologists come to mind.

Those who enter an occupational role to conduct covert research, however, are exposed to the full brunt of whatever life offers their subjects, a problem not faced by researchers who do not have to interact with their subject matter. Covert research, of course, entails a certain amount of risk, some creativity, and some discomfort. Although it is not illegal to become a salesman for a marginal company, it often requires the observation of unethical behavior and, in certain cases, subjection to tough choices.

The most difficult obstacle to overcome is psychological, because research minus the benefit of an acknowledged research role affords few of the protections and comforts afforded conventional researchers (an organizational identity, a salary, a position in a research group, and a set of defined tasks) yet is as vulnerable as those with whom one works with regard to the contingencies of the environment. I was fired, for example, more frequently than I quit; I worked for a number of companies that went out of business (most of them); and I saw entire organizations (save for the owners) turn over during one season.

Social scientists should spend much more time contemplating how modern societies create such vulnerabilities rather than merely taking care to avoid them. Once a research problem is framed it is much easier to anticipate possible ethical dilemmas and maintain a balance between the research project and other academic interests and responsibilities. The latter provide an insulating barrier as well as a psychological shield and an alternate identity removed from the erratic nature of the studied scene.

This is one set of resources and experiences—based in part upon past training, prior fieldwork exposure, and academic discipline—that distinguishes a researcher from those who cannot leave the scene to write up fieldnotes. If the research is conducted properly, that task should be the only marker that separates a researcher's social space from that of the subjects, because when the workday ends the researcher moves into academic worlds not shared with fellow workers. In that the researcher then takes up cognitive residence in some of these worlds, reflection can take place, and the research is accomplished. The "rules of the field" for negotiating such arrangements, however, typically emerge over time and cannot be logically derived beforehand. Each setting (and the degree to which a researcher can or should participate in all of the available work roles and after-work activities presented) will be, of necessity, different, mutable, and problematic because the sites and actors change frequently. One procedure, however, has proven invaluable in all the scenes and settings that I have observed: sequential observation.

A Rule of the Field: Sequential Observation

I have found that the first rule of field study, to protect the confidentiality of informants at all costs, was most easily done by conceptually segregating the site wherein I was currently employed from all others. Thus, I would learn as much as I could about a given setting but would limit my conversations during working hours to other sites. Doing so produced three kinds of data subject to analysis: present site contingencies (the array of procedures and technical knowledge needed to work as a salesman in a given company, drawn from direct observation); perceptions of other companies (drawn from conversations with salesmen who had relevant experience); and perceptions of the industry (information gleaned from informants and others). Such information was supplemented with data from the classified advertisements that was, at times, interpreted by informants until I learned enough to do so myself.

This always produces three informant pools (fellow employees, those who work in other companies or have acquaintances who do, and those in the researcher's telephone informant network) and a regionally based source of data (an unobtrusive indicator of boiler room action taken from newspapers). Over time, this proved critical for assessing the validity of any account coming from only one of the previous four sources. Readily available computer technology permitted masking the identities of all informants.[6] The covert nature of the research also assured me that my research role was never an issue.[7]

Sequential observation requires assuming the role of a salesman and accommodating as best as possible to the norms of a given operation. That is somewhat easier to do in the initial stages of the research because boiler rooms are universally secretive concerning their true purposes. It is possible to work for a boiler room for some time and know nothing of the facility's more deviant aspects.[8] Such an exercise in humility may be difficult for many researchers to sustain, however, because being a subservient or subordinate employee is a discordant status when compared to the kinds of professional personas that researchers and scholars often acquire by dint of experience and training or to which they aspire through anticipatory socialization.

Simply being in a position where professional knowledge is neither sought nor relevant nor required nor germane can be disquieting at best and frustrating at worst. Making such knowledge public, however, immediately sours and hopelessly contaminates a work setting. Covert methods must be used. No corporation, all of which have established authority structures, can be expected to share its operating procedures and sensitive issues with an outsider. All work settings are contentious in this regard, and aligning with any faction in a firm (owners, managers, staff, or workers) by virtue of engaging in a professional conversation will make others uncomfortable or might result in being promptly shown the door.

Making people uncomfortable is obviously detrimental to good work relations, and being fired is detrimental to having access to a scene. Those who may feel that becoming any kind of salesman is an affront to their ethical sensitivities should avoid this type of field study entirely. They would best serve social science in other capacities, because they will likely never be granted protracted access to a sales floor to be able to begin a study for at least three reasons. First, it is necessary to pass screening calls to secure employment; second, no firm will tolerate internal critics for long; and third, public alignment with values alien to the context of the job makes it impossible to establish rapport with those with whom it is necessary to interact in order to gain insight into their activities and reasoning. Failing that, without regard to the inevitable bias it would introduce into the research, a researcher will quickly be shown the door.

Sequential observation involves somewhat of an existential posture that may be difficult for some to acquire. For example, there is the likelihood of being part of a scene for a period of time not of the observer's choosing. Boiler rooms turn over personnel rapidly, go out of business (announced and unannounced), change managers, modify their terms of employment, and shift their lines of products and/or services in unpredictable ways. Any of these events may result in unemployment and the termination of access to a site. The up side is soon having access to a number of informants who are rapidly dispersed into varied social spaces. The down side is facing some of the disruption that could have been studied in a more abstract manner. Although that is experientially rich, it is not likely to be pleasant. With increased exposure and experience it is possible to manage most of these contingencies, but sequential observation also requires being able to terminate the observer's employment as circumstances warrant.

Self-termination must be determined by a researcher's own ethical system. Some individuals are distasteful at best and despicable at worst, and there are tasks that an observer will no doubt refuse to do and certain kinds of operations best learned about through informants alone. The hallmark of all field studies in natural settings is that researchers can expect to learn at least as much about themselves and their societies as they do about their subjects, but none of it can be rehearsed beforehand and the insights gleaned may require a great deal of time to sort out.

It must be stressed that these are not research choices in the strict sense but personal ones that affect the research. Although it is necessary to learn as much as possible from a particular scene, it is not necessary to be wholly informed by direct participation in all imaginable scenarios of the field. Drawing the line is partly a matter of personality, partly a matter of not doing intentional harm to people, and partly a matter of deciding if there are no alternative ways of gathering the information sought. Stated otherwise, a researcher is morally bound not to amplify destructive norms that may be part of the occupational role being assumed and not to make a scene any more deviant than it already is. That might mean having to stop the research, shift emphases, do something else for a few months, engage in other roles, make a few telephones calls, and find another job.

I have found that I benefited least by posing a common question that is often phrased in terms of taking sides. Although the article to which the phrase "taking sides" usually refers in sociology—Howard Becker's seminal "Whose Side Are We On?" (1967)—raises many important points, the fluidity of the actors and roles in a boiler room makes it difficult to prejudge allies or antagonists. Sometimes the actors change, and sometimes the roles change as well. Moreover, wearing a white hat, although no doubt gratifying, is likely to be less so when the cattle rustlers are the objects of study. It is difficult to enter a morally contested social terrain and expect the audience to cheer; only in a fantasy world is that possible. If a researcher sides with workers on a particular issue, for example, managers will become less willing to share certain kinds of information, or the ownership may view an alignment with either side of an issue as a sign that the researcher is not capable of offering truthful opinions but only those that serve a vested interest.

Thus, trying to be loyal to informants often means remaining silent, because key informants may be found on all sides of an issue. A childhood rule comes to mind: Be seen and not heard. Keeping the trust of informants at all costs, however, is critical because of the shifting characteristics of a given scene and the fact that observation sites may change frequently. Sometimes earning the trust of informants makes it possible to learn about a scene long after leaving it or to gain access to knowledge about entire industries that had been unfamiliar although practitioners may be only a few blocks away. What results is more like having access to the privilege of visiting those who live in a number of castles, each containing many rooms, than a "snowball sample." Many types of telephone rooms do not hire the same kinds of people, and it is possible to work in settings that are hundreds of miles apart. Thus, work will likely involve segments of an informant pool rather than a contiguously intact group.

The decision to continue on in these many sites and settings and write this book, as opposed to writing a small number of articles in academic journals, came about when a trusted informant, Bob Miller, died an anonymous death in a rented flat. This once-prosperous small businessman had spent his final years chasing the dreams of the boiler room to no avail. His death forced me to see that all that happens in telephone rooms is not as simple as it first seems and that the resulting social isolation can be devastating. Those findings mandate a wider audience than that typically available to academic specialists.

The commitment to write was also precipitated by exposure to another aspect of occupational life in the United States that exists as a dark secret in the academic world: the institutional position of the adjunct professor. Adjunct professors are the academy's expendable people: a reserve army of part-time workers from many disciplines who assume all of the professional responsibilities of a higher calling without any of the benefits, such as decent pay, health care, retirement provisions, sick leave, vacations, or stable employment. I have found that, as a group, most of these people are truly in love with teaching and research, but many are, sadly, struggling way out of proportion to either their qualifications or their contributions. Few can support their families, many must work odd jobs, and their dedication is typically ignored. Their numbers are increasing, and, despite all manner of redeeming social qualities, adjuncts are sometimes as marginalized as people in boiler rooms.[9] When the difference between them and traditional academics revealed itself in a flash of structural insight, there was no recourse but to write.

It was while "adjuncting" that I gathered most of my data on the telemarketing industry and some material on badge shops, investment scams, and coin houses. I would often go on job interviews at nearby operations with which I had been unfamiliar and meet potential hires and sales managers. The former would become part of my informant network, and the latter sometimes proved useful in securing employment at a later date when, as was always the case, the telephone room where I worked shut down or I quit or was fired.

Sometimes it is easier to quit or be fired from a scene that violates one's ethical sense than to explain to overseers why that may be the case. This attitude, and strategy, comes with the territory. When I was engaged in academic and other research projects that consumed all of my time, I dropped out of the telephone world to return at a later date, when living in a different state, or, when academic employment was not forthcoming, to collect more data.

Research of this kind will always likely generate tensions, anxieties, and dilemmas for a researcher to face, resolve, and overcome, because these are integral to field research on deviance in natural settings. The more conventional world of work, however, may contain some aspects of the boiler room scene yet to be recognized as such. That may yield unexpected surprises of another sort. I have found, for example, that it can sometimes be relatively easier to "work the phones" in an environment that I fully expect to be predatory than to teach classes in the company of exploited adjuncts and witness the collective indifference of colleagues who benefit from their oppression and should be expected to know better. Con men in boiler rooms, convincing as they can be, rarely believe their own lines.

The serious study of any occupational scene would make an excellent research project for those who may have a working knowledge of a wide variety of fields gained from employment therein. A fuller knowledge of how the business world operates would be one obvious result. It is also possible that business ideologies may be much more widespread—and thus extremely effective in the socialization of Americans—than is now suspected in many areas of life. But that cannot be known for sure until more researchers are willing to step outside the confines and comforts of conventionally sponsored research protocols.

After the next sanitized government study is conducted; after the bland results of the latest corporate opinion survey are tabulated; after the next tired research grant is issued to study captive and/or powerless populations to tentatively report the last weak surface correlation between an apparently endless stream of "variables of interest" and the latest ad hoc hunch that passes for theory in criminology (a condition now putting an entire generation of students to sleep), social scientists will, sooner or later, be drawn back to the more basic questions concerning the social organization of work as rich sources of hypotheses about how normative and criminal orders function. Attention directed at numerous curious hybrids like boiler rooms will no doubt continue to emerge. Some may actually venture out, or send their students, to explore these worlds, and some may take some of the findings from this book and apply them to other occupational contexts—perhaps their own.

⌗ Notes

Acknowledgments

1. No tacit or explicit research bargain (Douglas 1972, 5–15) was negotiated with informants, who served as such only to the degree that they would share conversation with a fellow salesman.

Introduction

1. Becker (1966, 20). Moreover, Reiss's study (1987)—one of the few on "secret deviance"—of adolescent male prostitutes engaged in homosexual acts showed that practitioners saw themselves as neither homosexuals nor prostitutes. That suggests that it takes less cognitive work to non-define deviant behavior than to provide alternate value systems.

2. All corporate names are fictional, and salesmen's names are fictional or telephone sales names. The salesmen's own words are used when possible. I have created composite statements when necessary.

3. Miller and Moe had just left the employ of another boiler room and work together at Moe's newly formed company.

4. I felt a sense of pride in having survived my first year "on the phones," because turnover was high, and the firm appeared to be stabilizing and expanding its product line. Miller convinced me that it would soon fold. He was correct. That I was totally unable to see this and that the operation was, in fact, a boiler room (a term I had yet to hear) were revelations.

A boiler room functions as a business, and deviance therein differs from other varieties, where there is typically a greater degree of consensus among actors, who may come to self-define as norm-breakers after having failed to-counter contesting claims (as in certain kinds of juvenile crime), due to conflict (as in most kinds of adult crime), and among audiences where the sense of norm-violating is clearly felt or stated or proscriptions are solidly in place.

5. Through these informants I was able to learn about the sports telephone (betting advice) and about commodities fraud, real estate scams, cemetery plot "investment" programs, telemarketing operations, secured collateral credit card schemes, franchise and multilevel pyramid programs, the "porn phone" (fantasy sex operations), foreign research tax write-off schemes, currency speculation scams, beauty products operations, travel and promotion scams (called "cert operations" after the certificates

that they offer), and a number of schoolhouse (bogus training) operations—one of which I was able to briefly observe. Data on the operation of the telemarketing room at a nationally recognized media company were obtained through in-depth conversations with former managers.

Conversations with new hires provided current impressions of the telephone operations that previously employed them. I have collected data from workers, managers, and owners in a given room—to the degree that this was possible. Conflicting accounts were resolved, over time, by gathering data from many sites and from different industries.

Because salesmen often keep in telephone touch with others in the industry, I had inadvertently stumbled upon access to an ad hoc focus group that could be used to discuss almost any issue that popped into mind or just to pass the time. That proved invaluable, not only for testing hypotheses about the world of telephone sales and keeping abreast of industry trends but also in locating alternative employment if the shop where I worked was about to go out of business or if there were layoffs (quite common) or firings (even more common).

Chapter 1: The Boiler Room

1. The historical origin of the term *boiler room* lies in the fraudulent stock and commodities schemes common during the 1920s, that is, bucket shops where customers' money was invested against price movements in the market in lieu of actually purchasing the agreed-upon shares. These brokers sold over the telephone and were located in the lowest-rent areas of business districts, physically close to the boiler rooms of the commercial buildings that housed them (Harris 1983).

2. Although this is a fictional characterization, it captures the idea that a salesman should be friendly and appropriately attired to present the proper image to sell the product (Miller 1949).

3. For a historical overview of the varieties of confidence games in the United States, see Maurer (1949).

4. Terms include the commissionable rate and commission rates for products sold and order of payment, as well as the draw schedule (chapter 3). Terms are subject to routine review and revision.

5. Polsky (1969a, 41–42) states that deception is necessary for pool hustling to take place. This distinguishes the con from mere differences in performance among players.

6. Scheff (1981, 62) uses this concept to refer to negative conceptions of others by which we can become known to ourselves. In a boiler room, the pivotal dichotomies concern sales expertise and mastery of techniques. After writing a deal, a salesman becomes "sharp"—in the eyes of other salesmen—and his customer is defined as one who has submitted to superior skill. Prospects are "fish" until caught by the artful lure: a well-honed pitch.

7. The clientele are primarily male. Female phoners are used because male customers feel more comfortable when women process their applications. Further evidence that telephone presence is gender-scripted is provided by the rejection of a prospective client who wanted a contract TM house to try to collect credit card factors (in-

voices purchased for pennies on the dollar) generated when their male clients refused to pay their debts. The reason, according to the resident pro: "Look, the phone works when both parties, the buyer and the salesman, can come to Disneyland. . . . You want men to own up to or acknowledge their bad habits over the phone to another man? It will *never* happen. No one is going to own up to having blown the family budget on porn. We turned down the deal."

Gender-scripting is embedded in the larger culture and thus subject to change and modification. A major cosmetics company, for example, uses telemarketing to move its wares: Women sell to other women.

8. All stereotypes greatly simplify reality, thus permitting the labeling of individuals (Scheff 1978, 172–75). Observation, however, suggests an economic rationale. Thus, interests, not linquistic structures, appear dominant in this case.

9. Boilers are always "on" (performing) for their customers and associates. Sales language thus comes to dominate even leisurely conversations, which become laced with inauthenticity. An informant explains: "This [working on the telephone] is really neat. I don't think that anyone will ever *sell* me anything again. I'm learning all the tricks. . . . A funny thing happened though, last week my wife and I went to church, and the pastor was trying to raise money for a new addition. . . . Bong! It's like a bell in my head went off. *He was into the pitch and going for the close.* It's a weird feeling. I mean I could almost see Jack [the training manager] in the back of my mind saying to the pastor, 'Go for it! Ask for the money. Close 'em.'"

10. A working ideology is composed of varied sales techniques and one-liner sales axioms, inspirational messages, punchlines from commercial advertisements, and quotations from popular self-help sales books. This provides both legitimacy and a rationale for everyday tasks. Pitches are also used to manage economic and emotional uncertainties that might otherwise be destabilizing. They permit the sales persona to separate from the self, a phenomenon Lifton (1986, 418–29) calls "doubling." One result is that both the insularity and ruthlessness of boiler rooms remain invisible to those therein. One pitch fires a worker, another is used to bilk customers, a third manages the spouse, a fourth "buys back the heat," and yet another builds morale.

11. This is the "money pause," the most critical in the presentation. If successfully negotiated, there are usually few objections that follow, and a sale results.

12. Two exceptions prove the general rule. One informant, a veteran of many chemical boiler rooms, is a bright, attractive, single, female college student in her early twenties. For her, the boiler room is temporary play. She is highly skilled and has a personality that virtually commands even the sharpest of hardnosed boilers to be protective of her—a classic sexist response (her moniker: "Princess Beverly"). She is well liked and out-sells most men. Her personal identity and social life, however, are artfully shielded from the boiler room, which, for her, involves obstacles similar to those encountered in a drama class: learning techniques, getting into a role, and drawing social support from the audience. Thus, she uses sexism to her advantage.

Those aspects of sexism that are less manipulable are revealed in an "art house" (arts telemarketing room), another extreme case. Here a typical telephoner has a college education, many have advanced degrees, and about half of the workers are women.

That scene proved transitory, however, because a boiler room emerged when a new manager took charge. The new agenda involved the introduction of boiler room techniques: an ethos that permitted the extraction of sexual favors from some of the women, the diversion of accounts to a newly formed back room, and the purging of those intolerant of the new norms ("a sweep"). The room, originally composed of sixteen people, lost thirteen telephoners in about seven weeks. In most cases, however, sexism is part of the chemistry of a room and not imported from elsewhere.

13. The skilled are those who survive the cold floor to become regulars. The social similarities across boiler rooms are more important than differences among them in defining the skill of the salesman. All learn to use a pitch; what is being sold is less important. In the scams it is totally unimportant. It is necessary, however, to survive long enough on the sales floor to learn the techniques.

14. "Parent" refers to the site where salesmen receive their initial training and experience. The term is unknown to trainees and to those whose experiences are limited to only one telephone room.

15. For a discussion of larceny sense, see Clinard and Quinney (1973).

16. The salesman telephones the next digits—higher or lower—closest to the disconnected number until someone knowing the disconnected party responds. These discoveries on a sales floor are initially the tacit knowledge of a small number of people, but they eventually become boiler room folkways.

17. "Truck driver" is a telephone room pejorative for a man with few office skills and no knack, inclination, or temperament for the art of telephone sales. Others include "fumble fingers" (those whose hands, callused from manual work, make dialing difficult); "greasers" (mechanics of varied sorts, usually of the automotive variety, not known for their verbal skills); and "block men" (urban men, usually black, whose use of street language disqualifies them for telephone work during the initial job interview).

18. Managers reluctantly fire salesmen unless more productive replacements are available. A firing wave results, however, when total revenue levels out. To preserve a given level of profit the room turns over, freeing accounts for the pros. If total revenue should decline, experienced salesmen must be fired. Over time, however, total revenue always declines, hence the dilemma management faces.

19. That many boilers continue on in the boiler room world is largely due to the perceived lack of other opportunities. The only source of structural change, that is, in the opportunity structure, lies in the marketplace itself. Thus, the application of therapeutic techniques, retraining, schooling, or other misguided remedies to the small army of the displaced, based on the assumption that the worker is deficient in some regard, are likely to prove fruitless.

As is true for drug-traffickers (Adler 1992), the social meaning of the income received through understandable and somewhat controllable means offers a compelling reason to "stick to one's line." Ultimately, no program has a chance of changing this reality unless the economy is able to provide decent jobs to workers. Thus, an irony results. Throwing money at the problem of displaced workers is not irrelevant; it is likely the only possible solution, an alternative frequently ignored by those who already have a sufficient supply.

20. Important concerns are the ability to select, train, and retain a suitable sales force. The nonavailability of pros, however, is a more serious problem, because these skills can only be acquired in boiler rooms. Thus, a firing wave is always two-pronged. The distribution of the accounts of fired salesmen to the pros rewards them and also signals to all that labor is expendable. Pros come to realize that their account base is the only source of economic security that they have.

21. The criminogenic character of the automobile industry has been identified by Faberman (1975). Boiler rooms work dozens of other industries, however, and democratize the fraud process because it is workers, not owners, who receive premiums when they make over-the-telephone purchases.

Chapter 2: The Product Houses

1. It is never known when seemingly useless information may have future value. One pro, for example, kept what he called a "pissed-off list" of irritated prospects. When he ultimately started his own sports betting operation, his insight proved to be right on the money. Many on his list were having gambling problems, and the list proved to be an invaluable source of leads that were otherwise unobtainable.

2. This "economy of boiling," to coin a phrase, explains why boiler rooms tend to locate only in those areas where they can tap into workers who have had previous experience in other shops. It may take months to discover a new product line, but a new hire with experience can immediately implement proven procedures.

3. Although a given salesman's longevity, in part, depends upon the personality of the owner or manager, a boiler room often distinguishes itself by the sheer level of cruelty involved in terminating workers. Of that there is no shortage of evidence, ranging from the "burnout" (the boiler room shuts down, unannounced) to "house cleaning" (a manager decides to fire a handful of people). Trainee attrition is taken for granted, and at some larger shops a manager and the salesman with whom he is most closely associated will be fired at the same time ("tier cleaning"). That technique brings in a new manager and ensures the rapid salvage of the house accounts previously worked by the terminated men.

4. The salesman found it useful to feign that he was calling from Kansas City, Kansas. After some ribbing from the owner and manager (for sounding "corny"), he persisted. A Kansas City location was awkward (and unconventional) enough to generate some believability among the farmers he was pitching. A boiler room usually adopts whatever stance that works. In this case, claiming to be located in Kansas City, Kansas, did the job.

To a skilled boiler, even music and recorded information given when a call is placed on hold prove useful because they are often feeds from the local radio station, which is full of regional economic news, weather, and sport—all grist for a well-developed pitch. Dialect is carefully noted and mimicked, first few words at a time and then whole phrases. This is especially useful in discovering which varieties of weed, for example, the boiler room's product "has been especially designed to destroy" (a line from a pitch), and it establishes the "working credibility" needed for a sale.

A pitchman carrying on for a few seconds about the "gawd-danged leafy spurge that's been a-sproutin' up aside my grain bin" need never have seen a weed or a grain bin, nor does he ever have to have been on a farm. Nor does leafy spurge have to grow, or be capable of growing, near grain bins. After such conversation, however, the pitchman is not likely to be pictured in the customer's mind as calling from a smoke-filled room. Other embellishments depend upon the personality of the pitchman. For example, one salesman mimics a distant storm as it might sound over a telephone; another, by speaking into a coffee can, duplicates the sound of the paging system used in airports. Both create the illusion of being on the road.

5. The German economist August Losch (1967) wrote his classic on locational economics in the early 1940s, well before product boiler rooms were on the scene. He has captured the logic of the classical school: "the partial equilibrium approach means that *other things which have to be assumed as given* are demand, the location of raw materials, and the *location of markets*" (ix, emphasis added).

6. Gift certificates from popular retail stores are sometimes used, and name-brand premiums are shipped to the home of the customer. Cash is never sent. Common premiums include clock radios, portable television sets, hunting and fishing gear, steak knives, cheese packages, carving sets, subscriptions to magazines, small kitchen appliances, power and hand tools, gauges, electronic testers, fruit baskets, smoked meat packages, pocket calculators, computer games, and "store deals" (whatever an owner, manager, or pro may pick up at a discount house, flea market, or liquidation sale). Such purchases boost sales for all of these items available from the retail and wholesale sectors of the economy.

7. All telephone numbers end in four digits. By pausing and then answering, "Extension 1234," it appears that there are multiple extensions from which Extension 1234 has been selected. Another variation of this technique is to have a pro present an incoming caller with a number of fictional choices until the proper "division" has been correctly located. The pro gains some sense of the nature of the calls, and the customers gain the impression of dealing with a very large company.

8. This is a major source of tension between pros and managers. The pro is a craftsman skilled in promotions and is most put off by management edicts because he is on commission. Any time spent off the telephone is money lost. When a boiler room reaches a certain size, pros are driven out because it is more profitable to manipulate regulars and trainees than to change or reeducate a pro. Their skills ultimately benefit other companies, sometimes their own.

9. For a succinct review of the classical economics of pricing, see Rima (1967, 148–57); a discussion of Say's Law appears on page 152. In the long run, overproduction is impossible. Any product will ultimately sell, even if at a price lower than the cost of production, with the lower limit being the salvage value. Say's Law takes account of the fact that some products sell at a loss.

10. LeFebvre (1968, 111). Marx did not anticipate a contemporary form of false consciousness: greedy consumers looking for sure deals over the telephone.

11. "Urgency" is readily understood by examining the content of any advertisement promoting a sale and is found in those areas of technical financial analysis featured regularly in the business press. In the former, the illusion of urgency is orchestrated. In the latter, any fluctuations in stock, bond, or commodity prices can appear substantial if a small enough time frame is selected. It is important to act promptly to

reap gains or avoid losses. A salesman has the advantage most times but not always. The exception (when a salesman comes out of his role and experiences the call) proves the emotional power of telephone exchanges, because sometimes a traumatic event can totally disrupt the sales persona of the pitchman. A "death call," as an example, can render a salesman unable to work for a period of time. One owner was so touched by the sudden death of one of his regular customers that he sent a premium the man had always wanted to the widow, who had answered the telephone. He then took an early lunch break and was unable to continue to make calls for a few hours.

12. For a discussion, see Prus and Sharper (1981).

13. Because it is highly unusual to meet such a person, his presentation warrants careful attention. This is probably one of the most concise statements of "first principles" available in print. The informant began his long career on the telephones during the Korean War after being fired as a young stockbroker. He opened his first boiler room with a co-worker and sold a financial product related to currency speculation. Now in his early sixties, his last scam involved a Florida-based, multilevel partnership deal vending franchises promoted as business opportunities. In his career as a boiler he has sold investment art (lithographs), futures contracts, put-and-call "limited partnerships," time-share arrangements, and is said to have started one of the first chemical houses.

14. The concept of a social form is Simmelian (Simmel 1964). By conceptualizing a boiler room as a social form, product houses become a type of stylized response to economic opportunities that are afforded by a technology that creates surplus and allows for its distribution under varied pretexts. The form is a twentieth-century artifact. Boilers move through social space configured by elements of drama, the quest for sales, and an electronic connection to fragments of a market. Individual salesmen are manipulated and set against each other in search of a solution to the economic problem that proves elusive.

15. No product house has laboratories, technicians, test apparatus, or any kind of quality control in spite of the fact that many of these operations are artfully named so as to suggest otherwise. A boiler room's expertise is limited to sticking its own name labels on shipments of industrial chemicals—and sometimes diluting them by adding water—or reboxing a part, assembly, or component.

The combination of unsold inventories and cash-flow problems can create circumstances where virtually any liquid will be sold as whatever is in demand. One shop keeps a spillage drum filled with liquids and waste collected from broken containers that is tapped and sold as a product "guaranteed to kill weeds and vegetation," which, in all likelihood, it will. The shipment of inferior product also occurs in a "last shot," where it is deemed unlikely that a customer will ever place another order with the company, and in a "wild card" shipment, where unordered product is shipped in hope of receiving payment. When the fraud is detected, an account will sour (be in a state unlikely to result in a future sale). This is called "souring the paper" or "burning the industry." Such sales often represent the final wave of profits before shutdown. Because many checks come in the mail rapidly, this phenomenon is called the "last cash crash" and may include credit card fraud (false billing).

16. One boiler room sells 2-4-D and 2-4-5-T dilutions (the components of Agent

Orange) as "stump and root killer." These products are effective but banned in certain states because of adverse ecological impacts. In one chemical house it turned out that the "protective coating" being sold was corrosive to metal.

17. One reflective salesman who is running a scam in the field of investments raised a number of harrowing possibilities. His monologue frames the problem of substandard materials from a point of view that can only be developed after having spent many years in various boiler rooms: "I've been reading in the papers where every once in a while there is some spectacular accident. You know, an airplane crashes, there's unexplained ice on the wings; some train's brakes fail; some car goes over a bridge; the space shuttle has a problem with 'tiles.' All of this stuff happens for no apparent reason. Yeah, right. Everyone is quick to cover their own ass. Everyone's lawyer has all the answers. It's driver error, pilot error, drunkenness, sleeplessness, it's unexplained mechanical failure. . . . My first question is, *Where is the mooch?* My second is, *Where is the five-gallon bucket?* Why don't they ever ask that? You wanna know why? 'Cause they *don't know* to ask that. Look, you name it, I've sold it [runs through a list]. One of our guys sold deicer to airports. Yeah? You call rubbing alcohol and water mixed up in some guy's bathtub deicer? Gimme a break. How could that happen? I'll tell you. There's a mooch got a [premium] to make the deal go down. . . . Somewhere out there there's the box for CHEAPO parts. . . . Me, I'd only ask *one* question: 'Show me the invoices.' . . . What I do now brings in the bucks. . . . Ain't no women and children get fried 'cause some greedster mechanic cheated his company out of good product for a god-damned pocket calculator. Suckers get burned, that's all."

18. Liquidators buy military surpluses. For every specific piece of apparatus, a handful of related products (chemicals, greases, jellies, lubricants, and hardware) also appears on the surplus market. A boiler room sells these materials through repackaging and promotion, targeting commercial buyers and builders. One specific type of boiler, an "ambulance trader," sells safety specialties. First-aid kits, their contents, and a white metal container (typically with a caduceus) are sold, along with other kinds of medical ware (splints, stretchers, crutches, and antiseptic), on a contract basis to companies that because of insurance requirements or state laws must have such material near work sites. The kits must be assembled from component parts—a signal well received and anxiously sought by pros ("medical men"). Boiler rooms are thus linked to markets created by well-intended health and safety legislation.

19. There is a black market of unknown size in banned goods. The degree to which suppliers make such information available is unknown, but some suppliers do identify "prime buys" and ask a low price for "the prime" (sometimes called "the beef"). Others secretly provide banned product (called a "spike" when discovered) mixed with their regular line. Most boiler rooms seek to avoid banned goods because of the attention they attract from the authorities. There must be a sufficient number of "beef traders" on the scene, however, because most boiler room owners are concerned with this issue. One of the reasons for their concern is the somewhat underhanded manner by which authorities plan and execute sting operations. According to informants, a boiler room's competitors can arrange to have a chosen supplier plant beef in the inventory going to a weaker room. Word then gets out that "beef is in the neighbor-

hood." Given the proper political climate, authorities may seek to intervene. Knowing little or nothing about suppliers and less about boiler rooms, they will need cooperation, which is secured from the supplier (at the behest of the stronger boiler room), who agrees to "keep his eyes open for beef traders."

Typically, a small-time trader is located who sells to the supplier. The supplier then, responding to the request of a plant (a representative of the authorities), sells to the weaker boiler room. That is, the weaker boiler room is set up by the plant and served by the supplier. The small-time trader, having cooperated with the authorities, is not charged, but the weaker boiler room is.

During the bust, authorities "discover" the previously spiked inventory. A bust has six outcomes. It puts the supplier on good terms with authorities; it drives one of the boiler room's competitors out of business; it gives authorities a source in the form of the small-time trader, who, having cooperated, is free to earn extra money as an informer or to carry on his previous dealings; it strengthens the relationship between the stronger boiler room and the supplier; it makes it appear as if authorities control the black market; and it allows the stronger boiler room to be a good citizen by finding a supplier who will cooperate with authorities. A boiler room owner must, ultimately, trust his suppliers. Sometimes this trust is misplaced, however.

Chapter 3: The Boiler Room as a Deviant Scene

1. For a discussion of the concept of deviance disavowal, see Davis (1964); an application appears in McCaghy (1968).

2. An exhaustive classification of social deviance as either a process or an outcome is provided by Rubington and Weinberg (1987, 2–3).

3. Because marital status and age are revealed on a job application, different "lines" (odds) can be offered for a given case. One manager gave his "list of ladies"—as it is called—to the salesmen in his back room so that they could entertain themselves.

4. Readers of *The Grundrisse* will recognize the contradictory alienative and self-realization elements of capital in this example. See Marx (1971, 96–102, 124–27).

5. The conceptualization of a master status is from Hughes (1945). A master status is the most central, or important, status that one occupies when viewed from the value orientation of a specific group. A salesman projects many statuses to a potential customer, and his role performances require that he see himself as occupying many statuses, but his real position as a pitchman is never revealed. Thus, all of his projections and some of his self-images are based on illusions.

6. Douglas (1972, 30–31) refers to the tension a researcher experiences by simultaneously living his or her research role as well as participating in the life-world of subjects. Those without the training, background, or inclination to assume a research role are likely to experience psychological anxiety, frustration, stress, and bewilderment in such instances, as often occurs when illusions are seen for what they are.

7. Hochschild (1983) argues persuasively that in certain types of work the emotions are manipulated for corporate ends.

8. The psychological impact of complaints are minimized through the classic use of cooling-out strategies. These refer to the redefinition of expectations that have not

been fulfilled and where lines of action have failed to deliver the promised outcome (Clark 1990). For a review of the use of these techniques in confidence games, see Maurer (1949).

In deviance disavowal, discrediting aspects of a salesman's persona are underplayed by aligning his reference group and perceptions in such a manner as to result in a favorable self-image. Deals made are rewarded with commission income and praise, whereas the techniques used are seen merely as a manner of routinely conducting business. See McCaghy (1968) and Davis (1964) for discussions involving bodily stigmata and proscribed behaviors.

Techniques of neutralization redefine customers' complaints by offering alternative interpretations valid in the context of a boiler room. Thus, customers' apparent greed and implied stupidity are seen to override their concern with the quality of the product offered. See Sykes and Matza (1981, 430–33) for applications in the area of gang and juvenile delinquency.

9. See Humphreys (1975a, 54); the concept applies to face-to-face interaction. If Humphreys is correct in his assertion that an interaction membrane necessarily evokes a moral exchange between actors (i.e., a set of mutual responsibilities and obligations), its absence in telephone interaction may suggest why manipulation is so easily facilitated.

10. The direct observation of how telephones are actually used yields methodological insights applicable to telephone survey research. For example, a random-digit calling device ("the dialer") presents a prerecorded sales message. By selecting telephone numbers randomly, the device demonstrates that the market for goods and services is not randomly distributed. These devices fail miserably enough to be promoted by certain boiler rooms seeking a fast buck in certain markets. Yet by insisting on the use of mechanistic rules of random selection and proper technique, that is, invariant presentation of the script (Lavrakas 1987), pollsters ignore what in a boiler room is called "qualification." There are three lessons for telephone survey researchers:

1. Information gathered from a random sample of telephone users is useless unless the research design concerns telephone use. Interested publics (or market segments) are never distributed randomly.

2. The telephone style of a speaker influences a listener. Without accounting for that fact, results will be seriously compromised in terms of validity. A telephone call is never neutral, and responses vary in different populations. Moreover, it is not possible to use a telephone successfully without interpretive work, as is obvious when someone who is not a native speaker of the language is encountered.

3. Because a telephone transaction is social interaction, the social characteristics of the caller, the timing of the call, and the interests coded by the interaction cannot be assumed to be either constant or irrelevant to the quality of the information gathered.

Other problems surround telephone survey research as well. A pro made the following statement after having sold some telephone time to one of the larger survey houses: "How can these guys conduct research using part-time broads? . . . I saw their operation firsthand: the screens, the scripts, the prompters, the headsets and gadgets, the whole deal. Did you ever get a look at the people they hire? Minimum wage. No benefits. Irregular, part-time work. Mostly housewives. It's a sewing circle. I wouldn't have any of 'em in my shop."

Telephone survey research permits boiler room techniques such as deception and underemployment to thrive in the name of science and victimize expendable female telephoners by promising them a chance to "contribute to knowledge" or "participate in the world of public opinion surveys" (pitch lines used by researchers) while simultaneously lining the pockets of grant hustlers and sharp marketeers who provide the illusion of credible research. If the methods for data-gathering by telephone go unchallenged, this quick fix to the vexing problems of social research will triumph. Ephemerality is the classic mark of all con games.

11. The Meadian "generalized other" refers to societal values that young children internalize in play (Mead 1934). I take this to refer also to the real, or imagined, values of other groups as well. Because the socialization process continues until death and the vast bulk of social interaction occurs well beyond the early formative years, much of this is occupational.

12. The list is created to suit the needs of the moment and is entirely fictional. As tension grows, a salesman gets a chance to work on his skills—for him, a gamelike challenge. The proficient may actually get another sale, those less skilled get practice, and others in the telephone room may have a chance to take a break and be entertained by the fireworks. Because the call is incoming, the customer pays for it.

13. The problematic circumstances surrounding all the variables that constitute a correct application under proper circumstances virtually ensures that this will be the case.

14. A rare exception to this general rule occurs when an extremely powerful or articulate customer is stung, threatens to publicize the activities of the boiler room, and the threat is seen as credible.

15. This occurred the day before payday. The return serves the legitimizing function of formally placing the salesman's job at risk at the hands of management while also serving as a control on sales managers. Can they be trusted to act in the company's best interest, and do they have sufficient authority on the sales floor? Gender differences are critical in this regard. Women, because they can disrupt the allegiance structure in a boiler room, are usually screened out quickly or they must risk social affiliation with sales managers to keep their jobs.

A combination of business, sales, and sexist ideologies, however, makes it, ironically, easier to apply boiler room techniques to men because their anger, resentment, and reactions to firing are more predictable and thus controllable. Men can more easily be defined as having impersonal shortcomings that make them unsuitable for "this line of work" or "sales" (lines from firing pitches). As a pro advised, "Never hire a broad unless you *are* crazy, need a shack-job, or want to *go* crazy. First, you'll catch heat from the old lady [your spouse], if she [the hired woman] is a looker [attractive]. Then, sooner or later, you are going to have to fire her anyway 'cause that's the way this business works. Do you want to do that? She's got kids. She tries hard. She wants the job. . . . It never ends. Then, you've got the problem of everyone trying to get into her pants. If you are protective, she takes a liking to you. If you could care less, the guys see you as a cold sonofabitch. You can't win. Let's say she's a dog [unattractive], or a bimbo [stupid]. Then somebody's got to train her. Not me. Only telemarketing and the telephone company hire broads. That's fine with me. I have enough headaches. It takes a special kind of guy to do this work. Women bring in too many problems. I've never seen a broad who can do this kind of work."

16. The salesman was never informed that his return was a complete fabrication. He was fired because of this, and his accounts given to the pro in the back room. The house netted $175, which was taken out of the salesman's pay. Pros in back rooms earn a share of such action by way of a spiff (bonus) for buying back the heat from victimized salesmen.

17. Boiler rooms never issue a price list for their products; price is always negotiable.

18. If an industry uses a yellow wholesale price list, the salesman creates a blue sheet. Whatever marketing gimmick or fad that happens to be popular, gains the attention of the customer, and is consonant with the personality and verbal style of the salesman will be used.

19. Salesmen have a record of all previous purchases and a range of possible prices given the commission structure. The procedure for determining a specific price is called "closing by line" or "line closing." Trainees who have not yet mastered the technique are said to have been "clotheslined" (left out to dry in the sun) by a customer. Such wordplay is common in telephone rooms with skilled practitioners and is virtually absent in telemarketing operations.

20. A customer is never given the opportunity to purchase only the discounted item. For customers who insist otherwise, the product is sent at the retail price. A certain percent of orders so shipped are paid for, and some are refused—to be absorbed by the sales force as returns. Outstanding accounts receivable are sent to the back rooms, where the pros work collections. "Hard asses" (categories of customer who are not easily burned off the telephone or who call back after a terminated telephone conversation) may be shipped and billed anyway, because some salesmen like the challenge of buying back the heat and some training managers seek to offer realistic training to their charges by using actual displeased customers in lieu of inventing hypothetical cases.

21. Boiler rooms rarely receive emergency shipments of anything, reveal sources of supply to salesmen, or vend current, nationally recognized products in new, unspoiled, original condition in manufacturer-provided packaging. The term *shortage* is used if it will help sell the product. When a number of quickly spoken phrases contain the words *original* and *equipment*, the connotation is usually clear enough to make a sale.

22. Trainee lunch hours are scheduled together. For a regular salesman to dine at the trainee hour excludes him from lunchroom interaction with his peers.

23. Jones lasted three months after this conversation was recorded.

24. In a pitch, form is more important than content. A rare field observation of a salesman caught in the act of writing wood illustrates: A manager secretly disconnected the telephone jack from a suspected salesman's telephone when the latter took a work

break. When the salesman returned to his desk, he proceeded to pitch a fictional customer, write up the order, and annotate his commission sheet for the amount of the sale. He was fired on the spot. The salesman had so successfully internalized the correct form for a sales call that he could attempt to create a fabrication for his own purposes.

25. The criminal justice system is episodic, in that a crime is usually seen as having taken place in a given place and at a given time and is documented using certain objects from a site, which are brought forth using evidentiary rules. This is a carryover from an earlier age, when "time, space, and place" implied unitary qualities. In the electronic age, these distinctions are less meaningful. On a Tuesday afternoon, for example, a telephone room in New York can vend a product out of a Michigan warehouse, and the product is drop-shipped on Thursday morning for delivery to an Arkansas farmer the following Friday night. Moreover, the order can be paid with a credit card that clears through a California bank on Wednesday. The envelope of classical logic weakens substantially when transactions become increasingly complex. As a practical matter, it becomes extremely difficult to produce evidence of boiler room fraud and even harder to achieve redress.

Chapter 4: The Illusion of Services

1. A close may last more than thirty minutes, and a few may last as long as an hour.

2. Those boiler rooms promoting mineral rights are called "rock houses."

3. We had both seen the same advertisement in the newspaper and were intrigued by the idea of such an operation.

4. Once the imputation of value is accepted, all the comparatives of economics follow logically. A pitchman manipulates the mark's store of factual information to achieve a sale. One pro, after having successfully pitched an engineering professor, commented, "This guy is some kind of a math nut. . . . He burned my ear with all kinds of talk about parameters and stuff like that. . . . He really just wanted to give me a lecture. So he did. Then he signed up. He's a mooch. Brainy, but a mooch. He talked *himself* into the deal. He quoted all the probabilities and then he came on board." That con's work is consistent with cognitive dissonance theory, which posits that people need to view their operative worlds in an internally consistent manner (Abelson et al. 1968).

5. The same contract will sell for different prices, depending on what, to a pitchman's ear, sounds workable.

6. Most boiler rooms promote coins. Those that contain silver or gold have "melt" (bullion) value derived from their precious metal content. Thus, a 1964 U.S. dime containing 90 percent silver has three commonly recognized values: a face value (10 cents), a bullion value, and collector (numismatic) value equal to the amount, over and above face value, that a collector would be willing to pay for the coin.

7. The numismatic condition, called "grade," of a coin concerns its state of preservation. A number of numerical and descriptive schemes are commonly used. Ascertaining the degree of wear is of critical importance in the numismatic marketplace.

8. Numismatic overgrading inflates the value of a coin. The price difference is created by the pitchman and can be validated. If insured coins are destroyed by fire or

stolen, an imaginary value becomes real. The ontological standing of the coins themselves, in this instance, is irrelevant.

9. This is called the "buy-in" (finding a supplier). Two specialized forms of baiting are called the "roper deal" and the "big buy-in." In the former, a boiler room owner "ropes in" (entices) a coin dealer to make progressively larger consignments. In the latter, the dealer "buys in" to ownership of the boiler room via an investment offer. When a boiler room folds, a dealer is left with a number of dreams but without the merchandise and/or cash he advanced for a chance to "cash in on a ground-floor opportunity" (a line from a pitch).

10. The longer pitchmen ("talkers") spend qualifying prospects on a 900 line, the greater the profit. A prime talker in a coin room can earn a small base salary, "talkie time commish" (a percentage of the revenue generated by his telephone), "lit spiffs" (small bonuses for each piece of qualifying literature he sends out), "riders" (a percentage on sales made from his "lits"), "deal spiffs" (a bonus from the closer), and, in some companies, a small percentage of all net company business written ("red eye"). Like pros in product houses, their skills are much sought-after.

11. A percentage of clients are also burned; less valuable coins are sent instead of those ordered. Some customers are never sent coins for which they have paid. Closing a boiler room down is a relatively simple matter. Coin cases are packed, telephones disconnected, and cubicles broken down; an empty office can be achieved in a few hours. Because coins are typically shipped from another location or hidden in back rooms, coin houses are among the most spartan of boiler rooms. Only their doubly locked doors and the bulletproof glass in their front offices make them visually distinctive.

12. As long as it remains easier, and more career-enhancing, to point a camera at a street corner in a high-crime neighborhood or stake out a hospital emergency room than to venture into the many labyrinths of criminal activity, the entertainment value of such accounts will dominate the reportage. The few accounts I have read on telephone rooms have their origins in the business press and share an amazing similarity with the format of the evening television news. The news is not that the reported event is somehow related to the systemic conditions of work and enterprise but rather that marks are gullible and such scenes are something that we (the readers) should avoid if at all possible.

Many social institutions (academic, professional, and political) also evolve favored cop-outs for avoiding uncomfortable truths. These preserve a perceptual status quo. In the social sciences, for example, it is much easier to train graduate students to manipulate statistical procedures or collect clinical data than have them venture out into the social worlds these data are taken to represent. In like manner, some physicians practice administrative medicine rather than attempt cures. Corporate law likewise provides more comforts and career continuity than the quest for justice, and often politicians seek popularity over fairness or truthfulness regarding a particular issue.

There is a pattern: The greater the social distance between those who experience a phenomenon and those who account for it to some interested public, the greater the distortion, bias, and possible corruption. As a classic example, the state sends an army of social workers, therapists, health professionals, and social control agents out to regulate the poor (Piven and Cloward 1971) instead of generating opportunities for them.

13. Locating a target city is done by considering population density and the presence of public transportation (so urban boilers can easily get to work) and locating a suitably sized business core critical for the first (selling commercial accounts) and third (selling franchise opportunities) stages of the operation. List brokers provide the relevant data. Prime sites are those in high-vacancy commercial areas where owners will be most willing to negotiate terms. Important in this regard is the "build to suit" option, because a boiler room (telephone banks, doors, switching equipment, cubicles, and acoustical padding) must be custom-made.

14. A potential franchisee sees people working and telephones ringing, and elementary computations reveal substantial money being made. Franchisees are sold a percentage of the action and the rights to expand (called an "expansion package") into fixed territories. The HBR's lawyers write the contracts. The marks make a substantial, two-pronged, up-front, good-faith, cash payment: one part for the rights to ownership and one part for the territory rights.

15. The nature of the work involves living for a year in a distant metropolitan area. Road boilers spend most of their time running the operation and managing the administrative staff—all of whom are locals and none of whom has any idea of the fraudulent nature of what is going on—and setting up the training programs. Because this requires total monitoring by at least one of the road boilers, during working hours—which can be from 9 A.M. to 9 P.M., six days a week—they typically split the task. This geographically mobile, protracted, unstable form of work is not conducive to having a family life. Because everyone on the scene will ultimately be defrauded, secrecy replaces the camaraderie between pros and salesmen in product houses or pros and owners in other types of boiler rooms.

16. These include coupons assembled from the offerings of regional hotels, restaurants, and recreational facilities. The dollar value is the sum of all discounts. Virtually all of the coupons have some kind of limitation, however. These are called "tie-ins" in the travel business, because they are honored only if some other purchase is "tied in" to their contingent use.

17. Everything in the "procrastination pitch" is true, but the most important omission is that there is a comeback for every request for an itinerary. Herein lies the con.

18. Technology permits call-routing, the principle behind call-forwarding services. This is useful for working smaller cities and rural areas because the local number given in the pitch—and used in conjunction with a local address to a business box—is forwarded. A variation on this idea is called a "hard line": A pro answers a designated telephone line (the "credibility number") in a very curt manner as, say, "Hartford Police, Main Desk Operations." That puts the caller into an embarrassingly defensive posture because it appears that he has called a police department. If the caller wishes to make a complaint he is put on hold, and the call is transferred to the "Public Affairs Department" manned by one of the many available telephone personas of a pitchman.

19. Most customers forget the specifics of the initial telephone solicitation, but boilers keep notes that are passed on to the technicians.

20. A few months after I left the franchise operation there was some regional hysteria over the quality of the water supply, and the owner bought some radio air-time to advertise "free water tests." He is apparently prospering.

21. The salesman is describing a delousing powder used on incoming prisoners, which is sold to jailers through the use of premiums. It is not known whether the name-brand product is being vended or if the name-brand company in fact produces such a product.

22. Those who "leave the phones" permanently quickly abandon these contacts. For those who remain, the "boiler network" is a constant source of information—and sometimes gossip—on opportunities in different shops. Because the network works in real time, it is possible to know of events before they are advertised (in the case of job openings) or reported in the newspapers (in the case of busts). The network can also provide ideas to the entrepreneurially inclined. One pro, for example, was able to set up his own retail operation as the result of an idea he picked up from the boiler network. He became a former boiler and a conventional businessman because of the tip.

23. To become clear, experiencing a scam often requires interpretation long after the fact. First, and perhaps most obvious, is the fact that scams are never presented as such. Thus, the operation is typically very successful before the fronter leaves. Second, all boilers are familiar with turnover. When the room begins to "shrink," most assume that is natural. Third, there are extremely high autonomy norms. When a boiler leaves, the matter is typically not pursued further. Fourth, there is a certain amount of collective ignorance on the sales floor. Most salesmen assume that the ownership will be providing whatever it is they are touting. It never occurs to most that an operation will shut down, much less that they will not be paid.

24. Fronters do not internalize the illusion structure of the scams and do not have the knowledge acquisition goal of the rippers, but they acquire substantial knowledge nonetheless. Upon examining the "out ratio" (the ratio of calls made to leads generated); the "closing ratio" (the ratio of deals to leads generated); the "payout ratio" (the ratio of his total payments to leads generated); the "coverage" (the geographic distribution of leads); and, most important, the spread (the time it takes, in days, from the date of mailing the literature to closing a deal), a fronter has an accurate picture of the difficulty of his job, its income potential, and the projected duration of the operation. It is tacitly understood that the fronter must never "spook the room" (reveal this strategic information to others). For his silence, he typically receives a goodwill payment ("tap") before leaving the scene.

25. See Simon and Eitzen (1986) for a description of elite deviance.

26. There is little political awareness in boiler rooms. Scams provide a type of fantasy that finds a home in affluent, advanced, postindustrial societies where the many roles that people fill are often tentative, fragmented, and subject to change. If this line of argument is correct (Simon and Gagnon 1976), modern societies may need scams to siphon off and redirect social energies that would otherwise seek political redress.

27. The Mertonian "goal paradigm" (Merton 1991) does not treat deceptive operations that are presented as conventional firms. The scams, for example, are highly innovative, but only for the owners. Most workers wind up cheated and unemployed. A boiler room is not a conventional businesss, but neither is it part of the underworld.

Boilers do not follow a retreatist arc because, although unemployed men do move from scene to scene, they do so in quest of the next big deal, so conventional income aspirations are never relinquished. Nor is a ritualistic response descriptively accurate because most do not stay on the scene long enough. For boilers who leave the telephones entirely, the boiler room provides neither legitimate nor illegitimate means to any goal. Finally, the case where a boiler room evolves into a conventional business is a case of conformity arrived at unconventionally. Nor is a boiler room conventional by a deviant standard or a form of rebellion. Few forms of deviance are so self-predatory. Most con men, for example, do not con themselves, nor do organized criminals violate their own turf and victimize their own kind. According to many of the PBS nature programs, apparently even a hungry pride of lionesses will not eat one of their own who may have been wounded. Boiler rooms represent an anomic social institution, a possibility not considered under the goal paradigm.

28. Lemert's remarkable finding (Lemert 1981) concerns a loss of identity that forced his forgers to make stupid mistakes and thus get caught, under the assumption that some identity, even that of a caught criminal, is better than none at all. Boilers have an occupational identity, however, which temporarily counteracts the negative aspects of a scene. Livingston (1984, 192–98) shows that compulsive gamblers become isolated because they are ashamed of their failure and debt—outcomes that presumably would not trouble successful players. Thus, it is failure more than the gaming itself that is sought to be concealed. Cressey (1971) notes that social isolation results from possessing "unsharable knowledge." Professional track gamblers are isolated from conventional social circles due to the stigma surrounding their activities (Scott 1968), but they have subcultural support from fellow players. Humphreys (1975b) found that men who perform homosexual acts without having the support of a like-minded community suffer great psychological pressures that force them to overcompensate in other areas of their lives by adopting extreme views. This is less of a problem for gays who have an occupational identity that encourages and supports homosexuality. For two supportive arguments see Humphreys and Miller (1980) and Perkins and Skipper (1981).

29. For an understanding of this role in organized crime, see Ianni (1972, 1974, 1976, 1980).

Chapter 5: Variations on a Theme

1. To avoid this very possibility, nonprofit organizations and foundations rely on volunteers, alumni, patrons, and those whose social standing will presumably reduce the temptation to apply boiler room techniques. No one, to the best of my knowledge, is currently studying the extent of cooptation, however, so the success of such attempts is unknown.

2. The sports telephone (betting advisory service), unlike the bookmaker, is perfectly legal although disreputable. These operations work on what one informant calls the "addiction principle," which he describes as follows: "Look, there are guys out there who need to play. . . . So I give them *the line* [a favored pick]. I pick the winners. Some of my customers will really hit it big once in a while. When that happens, I have a believer. . . . The typical customer, however, plays for about six months, loses all his money, catches hell from his old lady, and quits playing. But there is always new blood

in this business. It is my problem to try to find it. . . . What is strange is that they need to believe. They are hooked."

The method of selection varies. When all of the possible outcomes in a sporting event are given as "best bets" to different gamblers, however, a certain percentage of winners is assured. The operation stays in business by turning over the client pool, not by providing a consistent string of winners to individual bettors. The informant is searching for what might be termed a "grift cohort": age-specific proclivities for gambling that are present in each generation. This is sought through trial and error.

3. Trainees are not permitted to sell other than to new accounts. These are then given to the house pro, who works them from a back room.

4. Informants who have sold insurance, real estate, encyclopedias, and automobiles note a common practice called "rounding." Newcomers are intentionally hired to use their own families and friends as contacts. After the newcomers exhaust their networks, they are fired. Such accounts are said to have been "rounded out."

5. The school house offers a scholarship as a covert sales tool. The procedure is to waive some of the tuition after ascertaining a student's ability to pay. "School house scholars" are the sole product of a pitchman's creativity. A counselor explains the power of the illusion generated: "Look, you take some stupid kid and give him a scholarship. Hey, he loves it. His parents love it. It's the perfect pitch. Everyone believes it, no one argues about it, and it always lands the deal. I mean, who is going to say, 'Not me, I don't deserve a scholarship.' What parent is going to question a scholarship? We give some kid who flunked out of high school a 'scholarship.' It's sure-fire."

6. The school house is a predatory business that uses sharp marketing techniques. That its instructors spend countless hours correcting and grading the performances of the marks enhances the illusion of a school. Fueled by market instabilities in the very trades in which it offers instruction, the school house offers teachers a chance to moonlight in the classroom of a business enterprise which, even if the training is competently performed, is functionally useless. I leave it to others to validate this interpretation. A cursory glance at the student loan default statistics (U.S. Department of Education 1989), however, suggests that the techniques used by school houses are effective in creating mountains of unpaid debt.

7. See Harris (1983) and Alexander (1983). Both of these accounts are accurate but treat boiler rooms as exceptions to, rather than as products of, business logic. A few pitchmen have discovered a national audience for their contrition tales, because many cable stations that cover business issues now feature taped "news" interviews with them. That boilers can make these appearances is a mark of both their high levels of sales skill and their shrewdness in reading a market. It also shows that many television business-news reporters have little training in critical thinking.

8. I did not take a sample of students but quickly scanned the information sheets provided on new prospects and consulted informants.

9. City grid maps are coded by income and property values. The operation seeks out those who come from poorer neighborhoods. Potential marks are made to feel embarrassed when a salesman discusses income and assets—for an understanding of the mechanisms involved see Sennett and Cobb (1973)—then they are given a "big break" and told that they will be considered for a scholarship.

10. Limiting work hours to less than that of full-time employees excludes workers from unemployment benefits, corporate medical benefits, vacation time, sick leave, retirement programs, and overtime pay.

11. Conventional TM companies charge between $50 and $75 a telephone hour, with a minimum of five hundred to a thousand hours for the basic contract. A quasi-boiler room's minimum offering is a hundred-hour program at between $35 and $45 an hour, a sum more affordable to a small company. Pro boilers are skilled. Thus, the lower the asking price for their talent, the more the program appears to be too good to be true. Of course, it is—and therein lies the con.

12. Two physicians (vending a line of medical products and devices carefully selected to be eligible for coverage under the provisions of government programs) contracted a hundred-hour program to offer free physical examinations to elderly people. The program failed for four reasons. First, the leads were selected out of the telephone book, thus assuring a virtual random selection. Second, the elderly tend to be isolated and lonely, thus the telephone conversations were uncommonly long—and costly. Third, the sense of urgency weakens when most of a pitch is spent explaining a complex offering. And, finally, the pros thought it was a sour deal. One said, "Thank God we get paid up front. . . . Well, I guess that shows you that a mooch is a mooch. So, we'll take *them*. What the hell, they want to take a bunch of money off of sick old people."

13. The quasi-boiler room secures a tie-in with third-rate banks and marginal insurance companies. Interviews take place in rooms segregated from the telephone room. Marks fill out many forms; make a number of deposits (security, retainer, and administrative fee) amounting to about $65 ($35 or so up front, the remainder in monthly installments); and are given the choice of securing their account with cash (minimum of $200) or enrolling in a term insurance/annuity scam that requires a $50 initiation fee and a charge—proportional to the size of the credit line they wish to secure—added monthly to their credit card balance. This typically revolves at high interest rates. Over time, it costs each mark roughly $650 for a secured bank card.

14. The scam works because many companies use collection services to cut administrative costs. This represents one of the few cases where the inexperience of the telephoner enhances the credibility of the operation. Because no collection service can typically pay for prime telephone talent, the cultural expectation that mindless, routine, administrative work is being accomplished by a lowly paid clerical worker is not violated.

15. A press report documents the profitability of this market: "Ten companies have agreed to pay the Federal Trade Commission a total of $292,000 to settle allegations that they illegally used confidential credit card information to charge about one million consumers for services they never agreed to buy. . . . Companies that produced the confidential credit card information sold their customer's names, addresses, and credit card information to list 'brokers' who, in turn, sold them to telemarketing firms. . . . The TM firms offered consumers a trial period so that they could use the product or device without paying a fee in advance, but billed the customers anyway for a fee—according to the FTC, an average of $49.95—without obtaining authorization from the customers and telling the customers that they had the credit card infor-

mation" (Glater 1994). In this case, roughly $50 million in revenue ($49.95 × 1,000,000) cost the TM firms $292,000 in fines, or about half of 1 percent (0.58) of their take.

16. Sending the bill before a shipment can often result in getting paid. When the actual shipment is sent, it can then be rebilled, as if by administrative mistake.

17. This informant provided the story of the origins of his company over a number of months, via telephone and during a business trip. The quote is extracted from these accounts.

18. Three months after this conversation took place, the pro was fired and the owner began to invest heavily in a multilevel networking scheme. The company went out of business eight months later.

19. It is estimated that the U.S. telemarketing industry generates two hundred unsolicited calls each second (Harper's Index 1991). Lead acquisition (acquiring prospects' names and telephone numbers and other data about them) alone is an enormous industry using state-of-the-art technology. Data can be delivered in any format: cards, magnetic tape, sheets, labels, disks, and CD-ROM.

20. Many of these companies locate in the Midwest, where land, construction costs, telephone installation charges, and wages are lower than on the coasts. Women who work the telephones are likely to speak unaccented English and be grateful for a part-time job in a modern, high-tech office, and they are unlikely to have any knowledge of boiler rooms.

21. A pro who is the director of marketing for a quasi-boiler room explains, "Look, it basically amounts to dollars. Can the company that hires us make a profit? It's that simple. A client figures out his present advertising cost and what it costs him to use his outside sales force. If we come in cheaper, we have a winner."

22. Those who have an interest in labor economics or gender-based issues may wish to verify this statement. I base it on asking questions of virtually every unrequested caller who telephones me at home. I have yet to find one TM company that offers workers full-time employment and company benefits, much less a chance at promotion out of that kind of work.

23. The worldwide demand for new telephone installations would suggest as much. I do not know how "Euro-boilers" got their start, but I suspect that this reflects a latent impact of American technology that would have been impossible before the mid-1980s.

Conclusion

1. The idea of a strategic research site belongs to the methodologist Paul Lazarsfeld (1967). The late Hanan C. Selvin, in personal conversations, however, has suggested that there is no reason that this notion could not be logically extended by trying to find an actual field setting that would meet the Lazarsfeld criteria. TSC is such a site in the sense of Selvin's elaboration.

2. This is not to say that managerial ideologies are unimportant but only that they do not generate wealth—they distribute it. At the extreme, some managers need not know how to "work the phones" at all but only how to oversee those who do.

3. Andy worked for Power Parts, a brutal environment even by boiler room standards. It uses virtually every possible ruse to exploit workers, including making everyone work an unpaid extra half-hour each day. When payday finally arrives, the company is notorious for withholding, delaying, garnishing, or otherwise reducing a salesman's pay. Andy had to be extremely motivated to survive in this company for as long as he did—a tribute to his hard work and persistence.

4. All boiler rooms foster a certain amount of paranoia in this regard, and rumors add to the putative power of the management. No one is especially eager to find out if, for example, a telephone call can really result in one's car being reported stolen, credit rating destroyed, wife insulted, heat, electric, and telephone services being turned off, or bank being told that one is moving. The frequency and magnitude of such dirty tricks is, however, both unknown and unknowable.

5. Andy invested a great deal of time, expense, and attention to detail in making the site a comfortable place in which to work. Even the location was selected with an eye to how it would "feel" to drive to work each day. He also had a decorator tastefully cover half the height of selected walls with a rug that matched the color of the room to soften the light and mute the sounds that would soon be coming from the gab of his soon-to-be-hired sales force. The company reflects Andy's tastes, style, and business aspirations. His corporate business cards feature a logo that he designed himself. Printed in two colors, they fit smartly into a conspicuous brass holder located to the left of his main desk. They carry his true name (not a telephone name) and identify him as president and CEO.

6. This was not conveyed with a sense of irony or prophesy. In the "Star Trek" episode to which he refers, the renegade device becomes troublesome when changing circumstances render it obsolete. The device was ultimately destroyed by the starship *Enterprise*. When TSC transformed into the Silver Telemarketing Group, the salesman was fired because his specialized skills were no longer needed. This notion of enterprise ultimately drove the TM group, along with the franchise operation into which it had mutated, out of business. It became, indeed, a figurative doomsday machine.

7. Another indicator is that none of the parties in this conversation, when contacted randomly throughout the day, knew the exact time. In most telephone rooms, workers watch the clock religiously.

8. Some of his analysis is offered in friendship, some includes a cautionary tale. He wanted me to see that although I had discovered an honest telephone room, "this was not in the nature of things."

9. Knowledge of a target industry's information-gathering routines is sought. If the "Nashville show" is important, that is worked into a pitch. Over time, a salesman can create a number of believable tales based on conversations with show attendees. Thus, lines like, "Our amazing product was introduced next to the [industry leader's] booth at the Nashville show," and, "What did you think of the babes in the [competitor's] booth?" are easy to produce. Most industrial trade shows feature booths sponsored by industry leaders, and I have not heard of one that does not somehow incorporate scantily clad women into product demonstrations, the general ambience, or the

local hotels. That this attracts attention among attendees is what permits an illusion of a shared reality. Having attended the Nashville show thus becomes a qualifying question. Being willing to talk about it is another that establishes the salesman's credibility as a "man of the industry." This impression is powerful because long after a business convention ends its image will thrive and pay off in a boiler room. With practice and experience gained talking about the Nashville show, it is possible to readily talk about the "Dallas show" or the "Las Vegas convention."

10. A product has as many possible uses as a salesman is willing to invent, but he must first be given a reference point, from which embellishment follows. "Old hands" are a rich source of lore in this regard. A salesman willing to listen reaps "tales from the experienced," which are used to promote products.

11. Some of the more interesting works produced in the first third of this century (Hambly 1932; Irwin 1909; James 1914; Johnston 1906) describe the cons popular at the time. The grand master of this tradition is Maurer (1949). These catalogs of scams, however, never suggest that practitioners themselves might be victimized by the logic of the schemes they create. Early con men were well integrated into supportive underworld networks, and systems of deception had yet to evolve beyond direct, face-to-face interaction. Modern telephone scamsters face a much harsher fate.

12. A "generation of boilers," in a given shop, is equal to the number of founders and ground-floor hires. When boiler rooms expand, they acquire and train newcomers. A cohort of boilers is composed of all boilers working the telephones at a given point in time. High turnover ensures cohort expansion at a rate faster than new boiler rooms can be created, thus some workers find their way into sectors of the economy where boiler rooms are presently unknown and a natural skill hierarchy develops. The talents of those in a cohort ultimately determine the number of mutations possible for a given firm and the likelihood that new types of scams will emerge.

13. This is brilliantly demonstrated by Kozol (1992).

14. Urban traffic patterns at the close of the workday, for example, all radiate away from the central city. That patterns of school decay follow declining property values was noted by an informant with experience in the real estate business.

15. It is beyond the scope of this book to address the ideologies of technological ascendancy. I only note that the uncritical acceptance of technology always generates very creative scams. This is so because data must ultimately be interpreted, and that requires analysis and expertise—two qualities notably absent in most marks.

16. The case for attributing gambling luck to magical, or supernatural, forces was classically treated by Veblen (1963, 182–91). Other studies include the work of McCall (1964) and Henslin (1967).

17. Sealed-case or maintenance-free automotive batteries do not require the addition of water or electrolyte. They are now the industry standard. The Battery Brothers took advantage of the window of opportunity existing before this technological change was widely adopted.

18. A partial list of such products includes "power stones" (quartz crystals); diet programs (health profile services and vitamin distributorships); elastic pants (for weight reduction); brass balls and bracelets (for channeling psychic energies and summoning "curative" ones); plastic-coated magnets (for arthritis); a cigarette-punctur-

ing device (for smoking cessation); vibrating devices (nonerotic); foam pillows and bed cushions; space blankets (plasticized aluminum foil) for "celestial energy alignment"; "work-at-home opportunities" (envelope stuffing, writing medical histories, starting an import or wholesale jewelry business, and typing); diet coffee and nasal and sinus decongestant distributorships; herbal teas; craft supplies; immune system enhancers; debt consolidation services; government auction "hot tips" and newsletter services; lawn fertilizers; stun guns; laundry detergent distributorships; and invention-patenting programs. Entrepreneurs hope that telephone rooms will tap into lucrative and stable sources of income. The fee for discovering that these schemes do not work over the telephone, however, is an ironic contribution of the quasi-boiler room. It fleeces the fleecers, after being paid up front for its services.

19. "Health ventures" include, but are not limited to, health clubs. Other related telephone-promotable schemes include franchises for diet programs, cosmetics, vitamins, health foods, and the marketing of tapes and seminars involving hypnosis, smoking cessation, and investment opportunities. Over time, many of the same people gravitate to ownership positions, and they change the array of services or opportunities being vended.

When hypnosis seminars lose their appeal for, say, smoking cessation, they can be modified to produce sales-training programs. These, in turn, can be used to promote certain types of real estate acquisition schemes or multilevel franchise opportunities. Boilers make excellent workers in these fields because they have been trained to deliver a pitch and know the virtues of persistence. A number who master health and fitness rhetoric and have a streak of showmanship do well working the mall circuit, touting cookware, hair creams, beauty preparations, and small kitchen appliances from temporary kiosks set up for this purpose. Boilers who are skillful at the microphone and costumed in medical gowns, smocks, or lab coats attract considerable attention in department stores and at fairs and shows popular in rural areas.

20. Telephone rooms are instrumental in starting a health operation because a pitch communicates a sense of urgency. Once a customer base is established, however, it is cheaper to advertise in local newspapers, so telephone rooms are shut down.

21. For a general overview, see Clinard (1983). Middle managers are best situated within a firm to have a working knowledge (Harper 1987) of a given industry and be most aware of illicit opportunities (Browne 1973, 1990). This "locational focus" is also noted by Clinard and Yeager (1984). Another approach, reaching the same conclusion, is to examine the natural economics of the labor process itself (Gibbs and Short 1974). Intra-corporate manipulations are, of course, invisible to outsiders (Stone 1975) and inversely follow the class structure (Hagan and Parker 1985). The higher a person is located in the corporate order, the less likely are serious punishments for fraud. Thus, it is ironic that worker controls (against theft) are implemented by the very mid-mangers most likely to gain from the illicit use of such knowledge (Zeitlin 1971).

22. At least one electronic pre-filing tax scam—occurring before the IRS verified Social Security numbers—had its origins in a California boiler room, and a boiler room in New York has pulled off a scam on the Internet. It offers inexpensive, high-quality pornography in what is presented as a trial offer. When customers receive roughly $70 worth of "top-of-the-line" videos (the hook) for only $9.95 (credit card only), they

anxiously await the next "hot offer," to tentatively arrive thirty days after they return a "customer preference questionnaire." Before then, their credit card accounts
are drained using fraudulent billing techniques. The high quality of the product delivered buys time for the scam to work. Technicians working in largely male environments make especially easy marks in what are called "C-P [cyber-porn] operations"
on the boiler room gossip circuit.

23. Ellul (1969) has argued that technologies generate outcomes that are necessarily evil because they are arrived at through the use of amoral means. This line of inquiry merits further research. The ideology of cost-effectiveness may latently make
white-collar criminals more efficient at what they do.

24. In TM rooms, salaried managers are rewarded by lowering unit costs (the cost
per telephoner) or by increasing the return per telephone hour on the wages paid to
telephoners. The easiest way to do this is to eliminate full-time workers. At first, this
brings "fresher" personnel to the telephones because four hours of work is less tiring
than eight. It also creates a career incentive to invest in any device that increases the
rapidity with which telephone calls can be placed and pitches uniformly delivered.

By the mid-1980s most larger TM shops had computerized call-merging. The next
innovation was computer-assisted dialing and routing via specially designed software.
In this stage of development telephones are replaced with headsets and monitors. Thus,
the first irony of the age: a telephone room without telephones: headsets, computer
terminals, and cubicles replace desks and telephones—and virtually all social interaction among dialers. Profits soared, in general, as markets expanded.

In the late 1980s, the linkage between high technology and telephone rooms was
forged in the public mind and was no doubt reflected in the bottom lines of electronics
firms and computer companies. Newspaper employment advertisements for telephone
salesmen virtually disappeared, and contract TM shops began to cash in on the TM craze.
High technology, however, was oversold. TM managers scrambled to justify the very
large capital expenditures by inventing all manner of control uses for the new devices
that could easily record, display, and print hard copies of data related to telephone use—
state-of-the-art tools to assess the yield per telephone hour per telephoner.

When the technology evolved to the next stage, however, that of computer-con-
trolled, interactive ordering, the TM industry imploded; vast numbers of managers
were no longer necessary. Advertising and electronics have clearly triumphed. By the
early 1990s, TM managers existed only at the very large companies that serve national
markets and at a few multinational firms that export U.S. innovations.

Thus, a second irony of the age: TM managers promoted their own technological
obsolescence. The information age forced a mutation in the industry. Many telephoners, and their once highly paid, redundant overseers, now both share the status of being
unemployed and their fond memories of the golden age of the 1980s.

25. To the degree that female telephoners are indirectly involved in the deceptive
practices used by TM operations—and directly involved in a few boiler room contract
TM shops—they constitute one of the hottest growth sectors in white-collar criminality. The work of Adler (1976, 1979a, 1979b), however, offers a strong corrective to
exaggerating the meaning of this trend. Female participation in the work force has in-

creased regularly since World War II. Thus, even small numbers of women, where there had previously been none, will appear more significant than is actually the case. As is true for female participation in crime, in general women are more often the victims than the victimizers.

26. While increasing deindustrialization corresponds with the rise of the boiler rooms, it also corresponds with the vast expansion of the telemarketing industry and the increasing popularity of business degrees awarded by the nation's colleges, many graduates of which become managers in the telemarketing field. A glance at a report of the National Center for Education Statistics (1993, 334, table 41-3) reveals that in 1990, of all bachelor's degrees conferred, 41.4 percent were in the field of business.

27. The most concise treatment of the concept of the underclass can be found in Wilson (1989).

28. A good overview of the process of deindustrialization is available in the work of Bluestone and Harrison (1982, 1986). That most fears, however, focus on the underclass is perhaps because the images of minority youths with guns and drugs are easiest to capture on videotape. For a realistic corrective, see Hagedorn (1988).

29. One researcher in this field missed this point entirely regarding women and telephones. Gender is a social construction, not a biological given. To say that a talent, preference, or human capability is gender-linked, as Fischer (1988) does, implies a stability and permanence that are purely rhetorical. Five minutes spent in the company of a (male) pro boiler "working the phones" clearly demonstrates that the pitchman's art—like that of a master chef—has nothing whatsoever to do with gender. Worse still, Fischer (1988, 211) reifies a concept from chemistry by imputing an "affinity" of women for the telephone. Such affinity assignment merely derives from the observation that women use residential telephones. Presumably, peasants who tend the soil, without complex machinery, and may have acquired a fondness for both the land and animals can then be said to have an affinity for the hand-held hoe and for oxen and rural settings.

30. The wave of "fax fraud" that swept the United States in the late 1980s had its origins in boiler rooms in New York, California, and Florida. This was not a singleton event but a case of simultaneous discovery. Although members of the investment community were in the vanguard of incorporating fax machines into their offices, they were also being pitched by boilers unfamiliar with fax technology. It did not take them long to become astute students.

The Internet offers a richer potential source of clients, customers, and marks waiting for cyber-boilers to explore. The pivot point is that it is already stratified by income and education. One of the few joys of telephone scam artistry lies in "taking down" those who have genuine expertise of some kind. The Internet will likely prove an interesting challenge for years to come as cyber-boilers develop novel ways of finding those who qualify for whatever is being touted.

Epilogue

1. This issue is treated in depth by Polsky (1969b, 109–43). New concerns, however, have strengthened his critique: the increased federal funding of police science programs where the emphasis is on law enforcement rather than criminology, and the

growth of advanced degree programs in police administration, which offer public relations and management skills rather than criminology. In such a climate, a small,
important study documenting the elementary forms of common retail fraud had to
be published anonymously (Anonymous 1984), quietly breaking ground in an important area ignored by the powerful and complacent criminology establishment.

2. Sutherland's article on white-collar crime appeared in 1940, and Maurer's study
was published in 1949. Why these classics have not generated a flurry of fieldwork is
due to the fact that there are not now, nor have there ever been, criminology programs
in the United States that encourage the field study of active, uncaught criminals. Likewise, fewer doctoral programs in sociology offer such training than was the case in
the 1980s. The muting of scholarly work in this area does not require formal censor-
ship but merely the gradual aging of scholars in the field. They compete with the gravy train of state funds funneled into police science, corrections, and applied research
and become comparatively less able to attract graduate students and thus to pass on
the tradition of free-ranging field study to the next generation.

3. Until sociology and anthropology become as commonplace in the curriculum of
elementary and secondary schools as mathematics and English, most citizens will remain innocent of what it may mean to organize work exclusively around the pursuit
of profit. There is no general theory of work (legitimate or illicit) in sociology, and
few studies are informed by the lived experience of workers. Moreover, we know little about the impact of different kinds of displacements in the economic order on crime:
white-collar, blue-collar, or khaki-collar. For example, I would expect that some of the
dischargees from the volunteer military are capable of any task as may be imagined
in the black market for terrorism, a possibility unthinkable just a generation ago before a social construction called the "military obligation" was replaced by marketing
logic to draw people into uniform. That possibility has not been considered, however,
by a generation of academic hustlers more interested in the available grant action to
study safe issues relevant to the official views of the armed forces.

4. I refer to the public relations–centered practice of pandering for head count, of
relinquishing academic heritage for a nod from the administration, and of dumbing
down an academic program by not taking prerequisites seriously and by watering down
reading lists, assignments, and examinations—in short, of conning students out of a
higher education. That even sociology departments can be enthralled with such market logic is suggested in Stevenson (1992).

That boiler rooms profit from this is clear. For example, one green house intentionally located next to a college with a large business program after having conned some
business professors into believing that time spent boiling would be good work-study
experience for students in applied marketing. Thus, one of three divisions of a large
multistate boiler room was able to actively recruit business students as part-time
workers. That permitted a sharp road boiler to achieve high sales figures for the year
and a half before the operation shut down. At first, the boiler was reluctant to approach
professors—for obvious reasons—but confided that the business school was a laydown
because its administration was desperate to increase enrollments.

5. I believe that the folk adage is, for the most part, true. The classic warning is stated by Blumer (1967) and has been validated by Thomas (1980) in the area of police science studies. Some balanced accounts of the fieldwork process are found in Emerson (1981), Jackson (1987), and Wax (1971, 1983). The problem for sociologists is well stated by Becker and Friedson (1964) and Galliher (1980). Sociologists, however, are not of one mind on this issue. The classic Weberian (Weber 1949) goal of social research is understanding, no more (changing the scene) and no less (advocacy of the views of a particular group or interest). Some, however, feel that intervention is required (Bodemann 1978), and others are cautious regarding the use of covert methods (Erikson 1970). Moreover, Sagarin (1973) has argued that some scenes are best left unstudied. The relationship of values to sociological research is raised by Gouldner (1976).

6. I used telephone sales names or fictional names to identify informants and companies. With each iteration of fieldnotes, and when I changed sites, I created new names. After nearly twenty months in the field, I developed a workable system of codes for keeping notes. A similar procedure was used for site descriptions and pitches. Pitches were transcribed verbatim and coded so as to conceal the identities of firms. All handwritten notes were destroyed after transcription onto magnetic tape. After nearly five years in the field I created thematic accounts of each type of boiler room, updated files, and worked these into transcripts, with all references to sites, firms, and informants deleted.

7. None of the people on a given site, while I worked there, was aware of my research interest.

8. What is presented is a sales job, not an invitation to become a white-collar criminal. Stated otherwise, there are no readily available indexical reference points from which to assess or evaluate much of the fraud that regularly takes place (Bar-Hillel 1954).

9. The reasons for the academic reserve army are, in part, due to the declining number of scholars who serve as university administrators, the collective ignorance of the professoriat, the overproduction of those with doctoral degrees, and the dumbing down of the curricula. The first condition permits faculty to be treated as abstract labor. The second depends on the academic prestige of a particular discipline, the degree to which faculties are unionized, and the degree to which the discipline involves itself with contested issues. Rhetoric is irrelevant in this regard, however, because the English departments of many schools (well known for deconstructing all manner of texts except the college catalog) typically have the largest numbers of adjuncts. The third condition permits aspiring academics to undersell their own labor, and the fourth offers an administrative rationale. All of these factors interact to produce patterns of exploitation. I have sketched the fate of sociologists (Stevenson 1994) elsewhere. The increase in the size of the reserve army can be measured by the increase in the numbers of part-time faculty since the mid-1980s.

References

Abelson, R. P., et al., eds. 1968. *Theories of cognitive consistency: A sourcebook.* Chicago: Rand McNally.

Adler, F. 1976. *Sisters in crime: The rise of the new female criminal.* New York: McGraw Hill.

———. 1979a. Changing patterns. In *The criminology of deviant women,* edited by F. Adler and R. J. Simon, 91–94. Boston: Houghton Mifflin.

———. 1979b. The interaction between women's emancipation and female criminality. In *The criminology of deviant women,* edited by F. Adler and R. J. Simon, 407–18. Boston: Houghton Mifflin.

Adler, P. A. 1992. The "post" phase of deviant careers: Reintegrating drug traffickers. *Deviant Behavior* 13(2): 103–26.

Alexander, C. P. 1983. Reach out and bilk someone. *Time,* Oct. 24, 75.

Anonymous. 1984. Criminal deviancy in a small business: Superior TV. In *The sociology of deviance,* edited by J. D. Douglas, 226–31. Newton: Allyn and Bacon.

Bar-Hillel, J. 1954. Indexical expressions. *Mind* 63(3): 359–79.

Becker, H. S. 1964. In *The other side,* edited by H. S. Becker, 119–37. New York: Free Press.

———. 1966. *Outsiders: Studies in the sociology of deviance.* New York: Free Press.

———. 1967. Whose side are we on? *Social Problems* 14 (Winter): 239–47.

Becker, H. S., and E. Friedson. 1964. Against the code of ethics. *American Sociological Review* 29(3): 409–10.

Bluestone, B., and B. Harrison. 1982. *The deindustrialization of America: Plant closings, community abandonment, and the dismantling of basic industry.* New York: Basic Books.

———. 1986. *The great American job machine: The proliferation of low-wage employment in the U.S. economy.* The Joint Economic Committee of the U.S. Congress. Washington: USGPO.

Blumer, H. 1967. Threats from agency-determined research: The case of Camelot. In *The rise and fall of project Camelot,* edited by I. L. Horowitz, 153–74. Cambridge: M.I.T. Press.

Bodemann, Y. M. 1978. A problem of sociological praxis: The case for interventive observation in field work. *Theory and Society* 5(3): 387–420.

Browne, J. 1973. *The used-car game: A sociology of the bargain.* Lexington: D. C. Heath.

———. 1990. *Corporate corruption: The abuse of power.* New York: Praeger Publishers.

Clark, B. R. 1990. The "cooling-out" function in higher education. In *Social problems today: Coping with the challenges of a changing society*, edited by J. M. Henslin, 309–16. Englewood Cliffs: Prentice-Hall.

Clinard, M. B. 1983. *Corporate ethics and crime: The role of middle managers.* Beverly Hills: Sage Publications.

Clinard, M. B., and R. Quinney. 1973. *Criminal behavior systems: A typology.* New York: Holt, Rinehart and Winston.

Clinard, M. B., and P. C. Yeager. 1984. Corporate organization and criminal behavior. In *Deviant behavior: A text-reader in the sociology of deviance*, edited by D. H. Kelly, 643–55. New York: St. Martin's Press.

Cressey, D. R. 1971. *Other people's money: A study in the social psychology of embezzlement.* Belmont: Wadsworth Publishers.

Davis, F. 1964. Deviance disavowal: The management of strained interaction by the visibly handicapped. In *The other side*, edited by H. S. Becker, 119–37. New York: Free Press.

Douglas, J. D. 1972. Observing deviance. In *Research on deviance*, edited by J. D. Douglas, 5–31. New York: Random House.

Ellul, J. 1969. Technological morality. In *To will and to do*, translated by C. E. Hopkin, 185–98. Philadelphia: United Church Press.

Emerson, R. M. 1981. Observational field work. *Annual Review of Sociology* 7:351–78.

Erikson, K. T. 1970. Social settings and covert participation observation. In *Criminal behavior and social systems: Contributions of American sociology*, edited by A. L. Guenther, 149–57. Chicago: Rand McNally.

Farberman, H. A. 1975. A criminogenic market structure: The automobile industry. *Sociological Quarterly* 16 (Autumn): 438–57.

Fischer, C. S. 1988. Gender and the residential telephone, 1890–1940. *Sociological Forum* 3 (Nov.): 211–33.

Galliher, J. F. 1980. Social scientists' ethical responsibilities to superordinates: Looking upward meekly. *Social Problems* 27(3): 298–308.

Gibbs, J. P., and J. F. Short, Jr. 1974. Criminal differentiation and occupational differentiation. *Journal of Research on Crime and Delinquency* 11(1): 89–100.

Glater, J. D. 1994. FTC settles suit over card misuse: Agency cracks down on telemarketers. *Washington Post*, Dec. 29, D11, D14.

Gouldner, A. W. 1976. Anti-minotaur: The myth of a value-free sociology. In *Sociology full circle: Contemporary readings in society*, 2d ed., edited by W. Feigelman, 14–21. New York: Praeger Publishers.

Hagan, J., and P. Parker. 1985. White-collar crime and punishment: The class structure and legal sanctioning of securities violations. *American Sociological Review* 50 (June): 302–16.

Hagedorn, J. M., with P. Macon. 1988. *People and folks: Gangs, crime and the underclass in a rustbelt city.* Chicago: Lake View Press.

Hambly, C. R. 1932. *Hold your money: A sucker's handbook—con games exposed.* Los Angeles: Monitor Publishing.

Harper, D. 1987. *Working knowledge: Skill and community in a small shop.* Chicago: University of Chicago Press.

Harper's Index. 1991. *Harper's Magazine* 283 (Sept.): 15.

Harris, M. 1983. America's capital of fraud. *Money* 12 (Nov.): 225–37.

Henslin, J. M. 1967. Craps and magic. *American Journal of Sociology* 73(2): 316–30.

Hochschild, A. R. 1983. *The managed heart: Commercialization of human feeling.* Berkeley: University of California Press.

Hughes, E. C. 1945. Dilemmas and contradictions of status. *American Journal of Sociology* 50 (March): 353–59.

Humphreys, R. A. L. 1975a. *Tearoom trade: Impersonal sex in public places,* enlarged ed. New York: Aldine Publishing.

———. 1975b. The breastplate of righteousness. In *Tearoom trade: Impersonal sex in public places,* 131–48. New York: Aldine Publishing.

Humphreys, R. A. L., and B. Miller. 1980. Identities in the emerging gay culture. In *Homosexual behavior: A modern reappraisal,* edited by J. Marmor, 142–56. New York: Basic Books.

Ianni, F. A. J. 1972. *A family business: Kinship and social control in organized crime.* New York: Russell Sage Foundation.

———. 1974. *Black Mafia: Ethnic succession in organized crime.* New York: Simon and Schuster.

———. 1976. New Mafia: Black, Hispanic and Italian styles. In *The crime society: Organized crime and corruption in America,* edited by F. A. J. Ianni and E. Ruess-Ianni, 127–48. New York: New American Library.

———. 1980. Organized crime: A social and economic perspective. In *Crime and deviance: A comparative perspective,* edited by G. D. Newman, 294–312. Beverly Hills: Sage Publications.

Irwin, J. 1909. *Confessions of a con man.* New York: Huebsch.

Jackson, B. 1987. *Fieldwork.* Urbana: University of Illinois Press.

James, H. K. 1914. *The destruction of Mephisto's greatest web; or, All grafts laid bare.* Salt Lake City: Raleigh Publishing.

Johnston, J. P. 1906. *Grafters I have met: The author's personal experiences with sharpers, gamblers, agents, and their many schemes.* Chicago: Thompson and Thomas.

Kaku, M. 1994. *Hyperspace: A scientific odyssey through parallel universes, time warps, and the tenth dimension.* New York: Oxford University Press.

Kozol, J. 1992. *Savage inequalities.* New York: Harper.

Lavrakas, P. J. 1987. *Telephone survey methods: Sampling, selection, and supervision.* Volume 7, Sage Series in Applied Social Research Methods. Beverly Hills: Sage Publications.

Lazarsfeld, P. F. 1967. Concept formation and measurement in the behavioral sciences: Some historical observations. In *Concepts, theory, and explanation in the behavioral sciences,* edited by G. J. Direnzo, 155–202. New York: Random House.

LeFebvre, H. 1968. *The sociology of Marx.* New York: Pantheon.

Lemert, E. M. 1981. The check forger and his identity. In *Deviance: The interactionist perspective,* 4th ed., edited by E. Rubington and M. S. Weinberg, 453–59. New York: Macmillan Publishing.

Lifton, R. J. 1986. Doubling: The Faustian bargain. In *The Nazi doctors: Medical killing and the psychology of genocide,* 418–29. New York: Basic Books.

Livingston, J. 1984. From adventurous to compulsive gambling. In *The sociology of deviance*, edited by J. D. Douglas, 192–98. Boston: Allyn and Bacon.

Losch, A. 1967. *The economics of location*. New York: John Wiley and Sons.

Marx, Karl. 1971. *The grundrisse*, edited and translated by D. McLellan. New York: Harper and Row.

Maurer, D. W. 1949. *The big con: The story of the confidence man and the confidence game*. New York: Pocket Books.

McCaghy, C. H. 1968. Drinking and deviance disavowal: The case of child molesters. *Social Problems* 16 (Summer): 43–49.

McCall, G. J. 1964. Symbiosis: The case of hoodoo and the numbers racket. In *The other side: Perspectives on deviance*, edited by H. S. Becker, 51–66. New York: Free Press.

Mead, G. H. 1934. *Mind, self and society*. Chicago: University of Chicago Press.

Merton, R. K. 1991. Social structure and anomie. In *Juvenile delinquency: Classic and contemporary readings*, edited by W. E. Thompson and J. E. Bynum, 156–65. Boston: Allyn and Bacon.

Miller, Arthur. 1949. *Death of a salesman*. New York: Viking Press.

National Center for Education Statistics. 1993. *The condition of education*. U.S. Department of Education, Office of Educational Research and Improvement (NCES 93–290). Washington, D.C.: USGPO.

Perkins, K. B., and J. K. Skipper, Jr. 1981. Gay pornographic and sex paraphernalia shops: An ethnography of expressive work settings. *Deviant Behavior* 2 (Jan.–March): 187–99.

Piven, F. F., and R. A. Cloward. 1971. *Regulating the poor: The functions of public welfare*. New York: Pantheon Books.

Polsky, N. 1969a. *Hustlers, beats, and others*. New York: Aldine Publishing.

———. 1969b. Research method, morality, and criminology. In *Hustlers, beats, and others*, 109–43. New York: Aldine Publishing.

Prus, R. C., and C. R. D. Sharper. 1981. Road hustlers. In *Deviance: The interactionist perspective*, 4th ed., edited by E. Rubington and M. S. Weinberg, 327–35. New York: Macmillan Publishing.

Reiss, A. J., Jr., 1987. The social integration of peers and queers. In *Deviance: The interactionist perspective*, 5th ed., edited by E. Rubington and M. S. Weinberg, 353–60. New York: Macmillan Publishing.

Reskin, B. F., and P. A. Roos. 1990. *Job queues, gender queues*. Philadelphia: Temple University Press.

Rima, I. H. 1967. *Development of economic analysis*. Homewood: Richard D. Irwin.

Rubington, E., and M. S. Weinberg. 1987. Introduction. In *Deviance: The interactionist perspective*, 5th ed., edited by E. Rubington and M. S. Weinberg, 2–3. New York: Macmillan Publishing.

Sagarin, E. 1973. The research setting and the right not to be researched. *Social Problems* 21(1): 52–77.

Scheff, T. J. 1978. Typification in rehabilitation agencies. In *Deviance: The interactionist perspective*, 3d ed., edited by E. Rubington and M. S. Weinberg, 172–75. New York: Macmillan Publishing.

————. 1981. *Being mentally ill: A sociological theory.* New York: Aldine Publishing.

Scott, M. B. 1968. *The racing game.* Chicago: Aldine Publishing.

Sennett, R., and J. Cobb. 1973. *The hidden injuries of class.* New York: Vintage.

Simmel, G. 1964. Sociability. In *The sociology of Georg Simmel,* edited by K. H. Wolf, 40–57. New York: Free Press.

Simon, D. R., and D. S. Eitzen. 1986. *Elite deviance,* 2d ed. Newton: Allyn and Bacon.

Simon, W., and J. H. Gagnon. 1976. The anomie of affluence: A post-Mertonian conception. *American Journal of Sociology* 82(2): 356–78.

Stevenson, R. J. 1992. Open forum: When promotion goes too far. *A.S.A. Footnotes* 20(5): 13.

————. 1994. Open forum: The academic demand for sociologists. *A.S.A. Footnotes* 22(4): 8.

Stone, C. D. 1975. *Where the law ends: The social control of corporate behavior.* New York: Harper and Row.

Sutherland, E. H. 1940. White collar criminality. *American Sociological Review* 5 (Feb.): 1–21.

Sykes, G. M., and D. Matza. 1981. On neutralizing delinquent self-images. In *Deviance: The interactionist perspective,* 4th ed., edited by E. Rubington and M. S. Weinberg, 430–33. New York: Macmillan Publishing.

Thomas, J. 1980. The relationship of federal sponsorship of criminology and policing research in the social sciences. Ph.D. diss., Michigan State University.

U.S. Department of Education. 1989. FY 1986 cohort rates by instutition: Stafford Loan program. [Stapled data sheets, dated May 25.] Washington, D.C.: Office of Public Affairs, OPBE/PES.

Veblen, T. 1963. The belief in luck. In *The theory of the leisure Class: An economic study of institutions.* New York: Mentor Books.

Wax, R. H. 1971. *Doing fieldwork: Warnings and advice.* Chicago: University of Chicago Press.

————. 1983. The ambiguities of fieldwork. In *Contemporary field research: A collection of readings,* edited by R. M. Emerson, 191–202. Boston: Little, Brown.

Weber, M. 1949. *The methodology of the social sciences,* edited and translated by E. A. Shills and H. A. Finch. New York: Free Press.

Wilson, W. J. 1989. The underclass: Issues, perspectives, and public policy. *Annals of the American Academy of Political and Social Science* 501 (Jan.): 182–92.

Zeitlin, L. R. 1971. A little larceny can do a lot for employee morale. *Psychology Today* 5 (June): 22–26, 64.

Index

Robert J. Stevenson is a former assistant professor of sociology at Davis and Elkins College in West Virginia. He has taught at the George Washington University in Washington, D.C., the University of Maryland at College Park, and the State University of New York at Stony Brook.

University of Illinois Press
1325 South Oak Street
Champaign, Illinois 61820-6903
www.press.uillinois.edu